Academic Callings

Academic Callings

The University We Have Had, Now Have, and Could Have

EDITED BY

JANICE NEWSON AND CLAIRE POLSTER

Canadian Scholars' Press Inc.

Toronto

Academic Callings
First published in 2010 by
Canadian Scholars' Press Inc.
180 Bloor Street West, Suite 801
Toronto, Ontario
M5S 2V6

www.cspi.org

Canadian Scholars' Press Inc. gratefully acknowledges financial support for our publishing
activities from the Government of Canada through the Book Publishing Industry Development
Program (BPIDP), and the Government of Ontario through the Ontario Book Publishing Tax
Credit Program.

Library and Archives Canada Cataloguing in Publication

    Academic callings: the university we have had, now have, and could have / edited by Janice
Newson and Claire Polster.

Includes bibliographical references.
ISBN 978-1-55130-369-7

    1. Education, Higher—Canada. 2. College teachers—Canada—Attitudes.
3. College teaching—Canada. 4. Education, Higher—Research—Canada.
I. Newson, Janice, 1941– II. Polster, Claire, 1963–

10 11 12 13 14   5 4 3 2 1

Book design and layout: Susan MacGregor/Digital Zone

Printed and bound in Canada by Marquis Book Printing, Inc.

Table of Contents

PART 5: RE/GENERATING PUBLICS: CALLS TO COLLECTIVITY

Preface

We conceived this collection of essays in 2006 during phone conversations with each other about the state of the university in Canada. We were concerned that public policy discourses on the university had become starkly one-dimensional and almost exclusively focused on the university's role in the economy. We were concerned as well that these discourses rarely recognize, much less give a central place to, the university's role in advancing critical thought or educating citizens so that they can meaningfully contribute to democratic life. But living inside the university as we do, we were aware that many academics have been, and still are, animated by interests and concerns that are neither received nor understood within the narrow focus of these discourses, nor within the entrepreneurial and commercializing pressures that currently pervade contemporary university campuses. This book is a vehicle for putting forward their perspectives. Rather than providing a definitive account of what is taking place today in Canadian universities, these essays serve as a platform from which the contributors call out to Canadians in order to generate discussion and debate about issues that should concern everyone, whether as members of academic communities or as citizens.

Because this is not a typical academic book, we want to acknowledge up front some distinctive aspects of this collection. First, we solicited the essays from colleagues in English Canadian universities who have spoken or written about the condition of the contemporary university, not necessarily in their scholarly research but because they had things to say about the current state of the university. They come from two generations of academics—those who are nearing retirement or already retired and those who are in the middle of their careers. Although we tried to secure contributors with diverse disciplinary perspectives, areas such as economics, fine arts, and the natural and physical sciences are not represented equally to those of sociology and related disciplines such as cultural studies, women's studies, and equity studies. Perhaps this reflects the limits of our networks, but perhaps also academics in these disciplines are more inclined to comment on the social and cultural condition of the institutions in which they work. Interestingly, the majority of our contributors are female even though we invited about equal numbers of men and women. As one reviewer noted, however, it is perhaps a strength to find a collection in which women academics are overrepresented given that, until the most recent decades that these essays cover, women were decidedly absent from academic life and their views on it were rarely heard.

Second, the collection as a whole does not provide a comprehensive analysis of various aspects of university functioning, although several essays individually offer exactly that. Numerous books and articles contain such analyses, some of which have been written or cited as references by contributors to this collection. Instead, we asked each contributor to personally reflect on their sense of calling to academic life, on the vision (or visions) of the university that has (or have) guided their work, and about the changes that have affected their vision and the ways in which they pursue it.

We hope that you will critically engage with the material in this book, but not in the standard mode of academic criticism where the reader stands back from the work and assesses the adequacy of methodologies, the completeness of coverage, or the consistency of theories. Instead, we invite you to enter into dialogue with these writers, to critically reflect on the way they have expressed their vision and acted upon their academic calling, and to respond to what they have put forward by considering your own perspective on the purposes that public universities should serve.

Finally, please note that we asked our writers to experiment with the style in which they presented their contributions. As a result, the essays' styles range from the more analytical to the more autobiographical with many in between, including two that are based on interviews with one of the editors, two that are in the form of letters, and one that is modelled after a hockey game. Very Canadian.

Since the book doesn't have a homogeneous style or approach, you may find that you will resonate with, or connect to, some pieces and be provoked by, or not interested in, others. This is how it should be: Not everything in the collection will, or is intended to, please everyone. We encourage you to take what is useful and interesting to you and, after giving it a fair reading, set aside the rest.

We wish to thank our contributors not only for what they have written here but also for their ongoing dedication to the university as a public-serving institution. We also thank the editorial and production staff at CSPI who were a pleasure to work with. We are grateful to the York University Faculty Association Sabbatical Leave Program for funding for this project. And finally, we gratefully acknowledge the contribution of both of our families—each other's as well as our own—who gave generously of their practical as well as emotional support throughout this undertaking. So thank you to Susan Weinstein, Caleb and Baron, and Farida and Fulleh; and to Patrick and Zachary Maidorn and "Q."

Academic Callings and the Past, Present, and Future of the Canadian University

Janice Newson and Claire Polster

A freshly minted academic joining the university today will receive all kinds of advice and instruction about how to survive and thrive in the academy. Much emphasis is placed on building a successful career and finding funding partners. Scores of books tell them how to publish effectively; administrators offer workshops to help them acquire research grants; technicians support them in using instructional technologies; and colleagues advise them on how to maximize their performance outcomes by minimizing less valued and more onerous collegial work. But little emphasis is placed on how to shape their research, teaching, and service according to their sense of being called to academic life.

In this book, we attempt to recover talk about academic callings and their importance to the development of the university over the past 50 years. This talk is contained in thoughtful and often provocative essays from academics who have worked in Canadian universities during various periods over the last five decades—some of whom are about to retire or are already retired and others of whom are in the middle of their careers. We offer their reflections on academic life and the universities in which they have laboured as a rich resource and source of inspiration to anyone concerned about intellectual life and the future of the university, and especially to the younger generation of academics who will soon assume leadership in these important cultural institutions.

"Academic callings" takes on at least three meanings in these essays. Probably the most familiar is the sense of someone *being called* to do what academics do—pursue scholarship and research, educate citizens, and serve the public good by contributing to the university and to the needs of communities, organizations, and projects that have value for society as a whole. This notion of academic callings implies that the motivations for entering and continuing in academic life are not primarily or solely instrumental, such as financial rewards or social recognition, but rather are centred on the intrinsic value of intellectual work. *Being called* does not mean that a mystical jolt has settled once and for all what a person should do with his or her energies and talents. Instead, as our contributors reveal, the changing conditions and context of academic life have required them to continually refine what they are called to do, to be open and responsive to new callings, and even to *re-call* their commitment to purposes they have set aside or abandoned.

The second meaning of academic callings is *calling out* to others—contemporary colleagues, new generations of academics, and concerned members of the public—to preserve the university as a space for, and a symbol of, engaging in critical reflection and serving the interests of all segments of Canadian society. *Calling out* implies that something valuable about the university and academic life is under threat. On the other hand, *calling out* is also an invitation, often an urgent one, to build on the work that others have done or are doing, and on the progress that others have made or are making.

The third meaning of academic callings draws on the idea of the *calling card*. Calling cards were used in the Victorian era to accomplish what today we might call networking. Calling cards enabled people to identify themselves by making themselves, their interests, and their concerns known to relevant others. Setting aside their role in social ranking, we have employed the calling card concept to acknowledge our contributors' presence in, and influence on, the university that has been, now is, and could be. Their essays are their calling cards, which reveal to readers something of what their lives in the academy have been, and continue to be, about.

Why a Book about Academic Callings Now?

Over the last decade, universities in Canada have been replacing substantial numbers of their faculty as the generations who helped to build universities during the 1960s expansion period have either retired or are approaching retirement. This substantial turnover of staff can be welcomed as an exciting occasion for renewal. Newly trained graduates who are ready to begin their careers are emissaries of recent developments in their fields and may bring fresh energy and new ways of thinking into academic life. One reason for this book now is that this is a timely moment for this new generation of faculty members to think about the purposes that their careers will serve and how they can build upon and revitalize important developments that have preceded them.

Another reason is that the accelerated pace of faculty replacement imposes heavy burdens on academic units. Some departments have been filling three or four new positions annually, replacing anywhere from a half to two thirds of their faculty complement over the course of a few years. In addition to finding and hiring qualified faculty members, replacement also importantly involves mentoring and integrating new faculty members into the academic institution. However, as senior faculty members leave academic life, they take with them the institutional memory of the past 40 to 50 years. Institutional memory contains, among other things, the tacit knowledge and skill that faculty members employ in the day-to-day functioning of their universities. More than this, institutional memory contains a sense of the history out of which these taken-for-granted processes and practices have developed. Some might argue that this is for the best: that the practices and commitments of the now retiring generation are historical hangovers that stifle new ways of thinking and acting and since we are entering a new era with new problems and possibilities, that new solutions must be sought and new paths pursued.

However, we believe that the loss of this extensive institutional memory and five decades of experience should not be taken lightly. Links with the past do not have to smother creativity and enthusiasm. On the contrary, they are often needed to ground new energy and guide new efforts. We therefore intend this book to pass on institutional memory and the experiences, accomplishments, and disappointments of members of the retiring generation as well as of mid-career faculty members whose conceptions of academic life were shaped by the university of the 1960s and 1970s, but whose careers unfolded in the changes of the 1980s and 1990s. Neither our contributors nor we offer these essays in order to instruct a less experienced generation. We especially do not wish to impose our own generations' history on the imaginings and aspirations of a new cohort of faculty members who must face the challenges of their own times. Rather, these essays are offered as food for thought and inspiration to those who *will be* shaping the contemporary university and its future, and to members of the public who are concerned about the university's emerging role in Canadian society.

The third reason for this book now is that faculty replacement has been taking place at the same time that universities have been embracing commercially oriented approaches to knowledge production and dissemination. For example, universities across the country are restructuring their teaching and research programs and infrastructures so that they can better offer private-sector businesses—their potential funders and donors—the knowledge, products, and/or training that meet their commercial needs and interests. We are concerned that this convergence of faculty replacement and commercialization may fundamentally transform the Canadian university in ways that pose a serious threat to the public interest, yet we are mindful that the work of the university is accomplished through its faculty. Therein lies the potential for recovering and reinforcing a sense of purpose for academic life that is based on the intrinsic value of scholarship and teaching, and is oriented toward serving the diverse interests of the Canadian public.

Situating the Essays

The essays in this volume are written by seasoned academics from a variety of disciplines in English language universities across the country. All of them have contributed to scholarship in their fields, and many of them are internationally recognized for their work. They were invited to join this project because they hold strong visions of, and commitments to, a public-serving university and because, by contributing to institution-building and program development, they have carried the responsibility for the well-being and intellectual vitality of the university as an important cultural institution.

Each essay bears the marks of the writer's time in the academy, stretching from the late 1950s for some to the first decade of the 21st century. However, many if not all of the essays are written from the vantage point of two major transformations in Canadian universities that have taken place in the postwar period. These set the context in which our essayists have attempted to realize, revitalize, and sometimes revise their calling to academic life.

The first transformation is the expansion of higher education in Canada beginning in the late 1950s through to the early 1970s. During this time, universities not only increased in size and number, but also were qualitatively changed from elite institutions attended by a small and relatively homogeneous population of young adults—primarily male and of Anglo-Saxon heritage—to institutions more accessible to a wider range of the population. This transformation did not happen easily: Advocates had to struggle hard and long to open up space for less affluent citizens, women, visible minorities, different age groups, people with disabilities, etc. These struggles are still underway. Nevertheless, they have successfully altered the institutional landscape so that obstacles to their advancement are contestable, and their continued advancement is perceived as legitimate within higher education as well as in the wider society. A number of our contributors were and are active participants in these struggles.

The second significant transformation—from the late 1970s onward—is the growing corporatization of Canadian universities. Rather than as public-serving institutions dedicated to meeting a wide range of citizens' needs in a plurality of ways, our universities are operating more and more as businesses that are dedicated to generating income by meeting the needs of customers who pay for their services. This transformation is comprised of a number of specific changes that are still underway in the university.

One of these changes is the progressive centralization of power in the hands of university administrators and the marginalization of faculty as well as staff, students, and community members in shaping university affairs. In turn, the criteria that inform university decision making are narrowing, and bottom-line thinking is becoming the guide to university policy and action. These shifts are reflected in the growing pressures and rewards for engaging in profit-making initiatives, such as full cost-recovery boutique programs (including executive MBAs), spinoff companies, and other commercial forms of academic teaching and research. As well, academics are expected to meet intensified production demands that are increasingly enforced and monitored through a range of measures such as standardized performance indicators. Taken together, these developments encourage within our universities a more general emphasis on the utilitarian as opposed to intrinsic value of higher education and research—knowledge to make a living rather than to make a life.

The corporate turn in our universities is also changing academics' understanding of and relationship to their profession. As universities are run more as businesses, faculty members are being seen—and begin to see themselves—less as equal members of a self-governing community and more as employees of the institution or as individual members of their university's "team." In turn, solidarity and collegiality lessen while individualism and competitiveness increase. Growing careerism may heighten faculty members' sense of isolation, alienation, and vulnerability within the university and lead them to place their personal advancement over and above their public service mission.

One important role and function of Canadian higher education, from the 1960s until the present, has been to promote equity and social justice. Universities have done this not only by making their programs as accessible as possible to a wide range of citizens but also by engaging in research aimed at breaking down social inequalities. However, as corporatization proceeds, universities may either discourage or prevent members of the university community and others from engaging in these kinds of projects. Indeed, it is arguable that not only may our increasingly businesslike universities impede progress toward greater social equality, but they may actually help to re-establish inequities that had been partially overcome, such as by raising tuition fees to the point where only the wealthy can afford higher education. Canadian universities have also provided a safe and supportive space for critical and unorthodox thinking, writing, and invention that challenge convention and promote innovation in our society. However, closer ties with their corporate and other sponsors may be dulling our universities' critical edge as well as limiting the freedom and autonomy of academics to pursue inquiries that are crucial to the vitality of our citizenry and our society.

One final change is that a corporate vision of the university is increasingly being taken for granted and held above question. Consequently many who are now joining the professoriate have no memory or experience of other visions or models of the university from which they could draw to challenge the corporate vision. For instance, these faculty members have had little opportunity to participate in truly collegial processes, such as developing a university or faculty plan in ways that allow for wide-ranging debate and transparent decision making. Hence, they do not expect—much less feel entitled—to have meaningful input into institutional planning today. Likewise, they have little sense that 30 years ago, making profit off publicly funded research would have been disapproved of if not penalized by their colleagues and the public. Instead, sometimes grudgingly, often unreflectively, they accept that all commercial opportunities for their research must be pursued. That alternative visions of the university, and the requisite skills for realizing them, are disappearing has been a prime motivation for many of our contributors' participation in this book. They hope, through their essays, to help recover and reintroduce this knowledge and skill into the contemporary university, thereby opening up space to discuss, debate, imagine, and realize alternatives.

Thematic Organization

The essays in this book could have been organized in a variety of ways. We placed them in five sections, each organized around a particular theme and embodying a particular kind of call. Authors of the essays in the first section entitled "Against All Reason: Wake-up Calls" reflect on different visions of the university that have arisen in our country over the last five decades and critique the dominant vision that is shaping higher education in Canada today. They also address what recent developments mean for the future of our universities and the various publics that inhabit and/or are served by them. Part 2, "Taking Stock of Personal and Institutional Histories: Calls to Account," is comprised of accounts, from people who have lived through them, of significant transformations in Canadian universities since the late 1950s. The authors of these essays describe how these changes reshaped their own and others' calling to academic life and how the latter, in turn, affected both the particular institutions where they worked and the more general academic context. Part 3, "Between a Rock and a Hard Place: Calls to Administrative Leadership," includes essays written by and/or about academic administrators at various levels of the institution. They address the multiple challenges and contradictions faced by those charged with leading their universities and working with multiple constituencies in the changing academic climate.

The essays in Part 4, "Making Space: Calls to Open Paths," focus on the lack of opportunities for "different" individuals and groups to thrive in our universities. They describe various obstacles that these individuals and groups have and continue to face; celebrate some of the ways they have surmounted them; and/or advocate other ways of transforming or opening up the situation. The final section, Part 5, "Re/generating Publics: Calls to Collectivity," looks at forms of isolation and division within Canadian higher education. The essays here call for the creation and/or rejuvenation of collectivities of various kinds in order to strengthen our universities and their social contributions.

The order of these five sections parallels the subtitle of our book. The first section calls for reflection on the past, present, and future of Canadian universities. The second section is more focused on the university we have had. The third section and some of the fourth focus more on the university we now have. And some of the fourth section and all of the fifth focus on the university we could have. However, the reader may approach these essays in any number of ways, depending on his or her own needs and interests.

Uses of This Book

This book may be put to a number of uses. Academics, students, and citizens alike may use it to acquire a sense of the history of the Canadian university during a significant period of its development, based on the close-at-hand witness of over 30 active shapers of that history. This may help them to better understand and negotiate the context within which the university is currently embedded.

This book may also be used as a mentoring tool for newer academics. Through their experiences, reflections, and assessments, the contributors to this volume help pass on important academic values and traditions that are given little currency in the university today. Their accounts of how the work of the university has been practically accomplished also offer readers some of the tacit knowledge that is needed to preserve and protect these values and traditions and to create new ones.

Additionally, this book may serve as a catalyst for various forms of interaction among and between groups inside and outside the university. Among other things, it could be used as the text of a reading group comprised of academics, students, and/or citizens concerned about the current state of the university. It could be the basis of public events where one or several pieces are read and discussed. It could be the focus of a campus or community radio show looking at the transformation of public universities or public institutions more generally. And it could be used as a source of ideas and inspiration by various organizations and groups that are currently working to reform Canadian higher education.

Through these and other uses of the book, we hope to bring people together to generate enough energy and commitment to ensure that imaginings of "the university we could have" are drawn from all segments of Canadian society and are realized in the university of the future.

PART 1

Against All Reason:
Wake-up Calls

CHAPTER 1

Are We Losing Our Minds?
Unreason in Canadian Universities Today

CLAIRE POLSTER
Sociologist, University of Regina

Introduction

In the early 1980s, I gave up on a potentially lucrative legal career to become an academic. My experience as an undergraduate student encouraged me to question and challenge the inequalities and injustices upon which my society was built, and it called me to better understand, and to raise others' awareness of, these ills as a means of redressing them. At that time, the university seemed to be the ideal place from which to accomplish this mission. As a community of self-governing scholars, it supported free and unencumbered research, valued critical education, and, above all, was committed to public service.[1]

Since becoming an academic, I have watched my own and other Canadian universities become places where my values and goals are no longer accorded much priority, and indeed are often impeded. This deeply saddens me. It also perplexes me, as the university's transformation not only harms my personal aims but also academics' more general interests and those of the public whom we serve. This essay reflects my disappointment and frustration with what is happening and my attempt to make sense of why it is happening. It also includes a call to members of the university and the public to resist this process and reclaim our universities as autonomous, critical, and public-serving institutions.

Changes in the University

One of the most significant changes that troubles me is the transformation of academic governance. In the postwar period, Canadian university administrations were small and comprised mostly of academics who saw themselves as leaders of a democratic, self-governing collegium. Over the last three decades, however, these administrations have swelled in size, and they are increasingly staffed by executives from other public and private institutions, who see themselves as managers and the university as an institution like any other. These administrators, who are increasingly preoccupied with the university's bottom line, have centralized power and decision-making authority. As a result, academics are progressively less involved in developing university plans and policies. We are more often invited to rubber-stamp decisions made by others and to attend meetings where debate is supplanted by reports from administrators followed by limited opportunities to ask (preferably innocuous) questions.

This shift in governance deeply troubles me because it limits my ability to shape the context of my work, which has significant consequences for what I can and cannot do as a researcher, teacher, and public servant. It also restricts my ability to work collectively with my colleagues and thereby develop a shared vision for our work and solidarity among us. But this shift also perplexes me. It constitutes an enormous waste of the large pool of experience, insight, and creativity that resides within the collegium. It also squanders academics' time, for although we are less involved in setting university policies, we are still called on, perhaps more than ever, to consult and/or comment on them. Most significantly, this transformation provides little if any occasion for the next generation of professors to be socialized into, and gain experience with, a collegial academic culture. This harms the institution's interests. It also harms the public's interests, as it limits opportunities for the latter's needs to be heard and served.

Another troubling set of changes is in the area of university research. Although academics were always expected to engage in research, today there is great pressure to produce as much as possible as quickly as possible. There is even more intense pressure to bring in money by way of contracts and, preferably, grants. I struggle with these demands that threaten to compromise my research standards and commitments and to turn my work into a means rather than an end in itself. I find it difficult to maintain a balance in which I honour my own research rhythms, instincts, and ethics and simultaneously ensure a consistently high research performance rating, and it feels frustrating and demeaning that I must do this in the first place.

I am also bewildered by these changes as they seem to me to be profoundly irrational. Relentless production demands deprive academics of the time we need to let our ideas mature and to develop ourselves intellectually. They also contribute to an increase in the quantity, and arguably a decrease in the quality, of the literature we must master. The pressure to obtain grants increases the time, energy, and other resources that academics spend seeking funding, thereby reducing the resources we may devote to our core responsibilities of teaching, public service, and research itself. It is also leading many to modify, if not abandon, their preferred research topics, approaches, and collaborators for those that are more in line with the priorities of powerful research funders, which may compromise the integrity and utility of academic knowledge and undermine the quality, if not purpose, of our working lives. The importance of obtaining grants is also leading administrators to concentrate resources and rewards on those researchers and research areas most likely to attract external funding. This limits the ability of other academics and academic units to sustain their research quality and performance and produces various tensions and conflicts that poison relationships and erode morale.

Finally, I am concerned about changes in the area of university teaching. In the name of improving educational quality, universities are rationalizing teaching resources (expanding class sizes, reducing course offerings, etc.), investing in instructional technologies, and employing various performance measures, such as standardized teaching evaluations. Many of these changes make it difficult for me to sustain the kind of teaching practice to which I am committed. For example, large classes make it harder for me to assign essays, a task that helps students develop valuable skills. New practices around teaching technologies (such as providing online course notes or using clickers to hold students' attention) also produce expectations, even demands, in students that conflict with my sense of what is—and how it is—important for them to learn. While I am a strong proponent of student evaluations as a tool for improving one's teaching, the ways they may be used in formal review processes make me self-conscious and preoccupied with students' reactions to me, diminishing my energies for and joy in teaching.

These changes too seem senseless and harmful. I cannot see how diminished course offerings and larger classes improve education when they limit students' options and their opportunities to meaningfully interact with professors and peers. It also seems unwise to invest so heavily in instructional technologies when their pedagogical benefits have proved questionable at best. The use of standardized evaluations is perhaps the most irrational as they have been shown to be biased against certain kinds of classes and instructors and, in some cases, to lower teaching standards and promote "edutainment." Further, because these measures define educational quality entirely as the instructor's responsibility, they leave unaddressed many structural constraints on teaching quality, such as students' heavy debt loads and professors' heavy workloads.

There are many more troubling features of the contemporary university, but just those that I have mentioned have taken a huge toll on my hopes and goals for my academic career. While I have not been unsuccessful, my life in the academy has been much more difficult, stressful, isolated, and conflicted than I ever imagined it would be. I feel that I have invested far too much energy in battles that were needless and often fruitless. I have also had to work hard to sustain my morale when my efforts to defend certain academic values and traditions (such as keeping university research publicly available or preserving institutional democracy) have been ignored, ridiculed, or penalized. These energies should have been put to more important and productive uses. I feel angry and, to some extent, guilty that they were not.

I am not alone, however, in being disappointed and concerned about the contemporary university. Many colleagues around the country report finding academic life progressively demanding, harried, alienating, unhealthy, and unsatisfying and that this limits their contributions to their disciplines, students, and the broader community. Certainly not all academics are unhappy with today's university: However, there is an underlying and possibly growing malaise within the institution that stems from many of the new conditions I noted above. In light of this, two questions I continually grapple with are how to understand these changes that seem to be producing so much harm with so little payoff, and what can we do about them.

Explaining the Changes

One common explanation for these developments is that they are expressions and consequences of the privatization or corporatization process sweeping across Canadian universities and other public institutions. This process, championed by neo-liberal governments and industry and academic executives, involves running universities like private-sector institutions by having them work more for, with, and as corporations. (Hence, the increased managerialism, pressures to generate income, standardized measures to monitor and reward academic performance, etc.). It has been driven and justified by the belief that private-sector institutions are more efficient than public ones, and that rendering universities more like businesses enhances their performance and social contributions, a belief that I clearly dispute and that has been belied by much higher education research.

While this explanation is satisfactory on one level, it can be problematic by leading us to see corporatization as something that happened *to* those of us in the university, not *because* of us. Although much of the impetus for corporatization came from forces outside the university, it could not have been successful without the co-operation of faculty, nor can it be sustained without our continued co-operation. I say this not to blame academics for the developments addressed above, but to acknowledge and problematize our complicity in them. We need to understand why we have permitted these changes if we are to successfully resist them.

It is fair to say that in its early days, most academics were permissive toward corporatization for various personal reasons. Some were unaware of this emergent process. Others felt it would have little impact on them. Still others actively supported corporatization because they believed they could personally benefit. While some of these reasons still hold today, two other, more structural features of academic life reduce our willingness and ability to oppose corporatization and its attendant harms. These are the progressive normalization of a corporate ethos within Canadian universities and the new survivalism it is generating.

By normalization, I am referring to a process whereby a corporate ethos or sensibility is becoming mainstream, even taken for granted, within the university. A corporate approach is no longer seen as an inappropriate way to run the university, or even as one of many equally valid approaches, but as the only way to run it—period. Several factors have contributed to this. These include the growing marginalization of academics in university governance; the corporate university's many new demands, which sap the energies and morale that faculty need to assert and defend traditional academic values and practices; and administrators' aggressive efforts to re/socialize professors in accordance with corporate principles. Over time, the new common sense on campus has made it difficult—both conceptually and politically—to question, let alone challenge, the corporate model of the university, with the result that the latter has become even further entrenched. To be sure, there are still academics who are uncomfortable with aspects of our corporatized universities. For them, however, growing survivalism (i.e., concern with their status and security) raises another obstacle to resistance.

As Canadian universities have become more corporate in nature, academics' place within them has been redefined and the ways our performance is assessed has changed. Rather than as equal members of an autonomous community of scholars, we have been reconceived as university employees or as members of the university's "team." And rather than being evaluated on the basis of our contributions to our fields or the public good, we are increasingly assessed and rewarded in relation to our contributions to the institution's good (in terms of grants obtained, profits generated, inter/national honours awarded, etc.). In this new, more competitive context, academics have greater opportunity to advance or fall behind relative to our colleagues than we have had before. This makes us more aware of, and concerned about, our own institutional status and security, which constrains us to try to satisfy institutional expectations and demands rather than to critique or contest them.

Consider, for example, academics whose teaching and service loads have increased and whose access to resources has decreased due in part to the many perks bestowed on their "star" colleagues as reward for large grants or successful entrepreneurial initiatives. The former might consider protesting and resisting their declining working conditions; however, their diminished resources, influence, and support (from increasingly insecure or individualistic colleagues) make this a difficult—and risky—proposition. More likely is that they (as similarly positioned academics) will opt to try to join the ranks of their privileged colleagues and to work even harder within the system rather than to challenge it.

In short, I believe that two of the main reasons why many academics are acceding to harmful transformations in the university are because we have difficulty imagining alternative ways of running the institution and because, even when we can, the barriers and costs of attempting to implement them appear too high. From this it follows that if we wish to resist these transformations, we need to change conditions within the university so that these two impediments to resistance disappear.

What to Do?

Of the two tasks before us, it may be easier to shatter the corporate common sense that pervades our universities. One relatively simple but powerful measure is to increase interaction and dialogue between senior and junior faculty, and between faculty members and citizens, that focus on other visions of the university and on the institution's larger role and purposes as opposed to its immediate expectations and demands. This kind of dialogue can help problematize the prevailing corporate model and enable, even inspire, newer and older faculty alike to imagine and advocate different ways of running and being in the institution. I have personally been very moved by longer-serving colleagues' accounts of times when they were able to work out university priorities and plans collectively and democratically (if not always harmoniously), produce at their own pace, read and talk together often outside of their fields, and place students and community interests first. They have helped affirm my own sense that much is wrong with today's university and opened my mind to a range of new possibilities for the university and academic life.

In terms of combating survivalism in the university, we need to re/create an environment in which our places are more stable and secure and in which we are more in solidarity with one another. This is no small feat; however, there are many things that faculty, with the support of staff, students, and especially the public, can do. For example, through our committee work, we can insist that resources be divided equitably between "star" and other faculty and units, and we can defend and employ evaluation criteria that are less heavily quantitative and economically driven and more flexible, sophisticated, and diverse. We can also ensure that we—and others—accord equal respect and consideration to all university workers in both formal and informal interactions and try to resist pressures to treat our colleagues instrumentally rather than with the inherent value and dignity we all deserve. To recover ground lost on institutional governance, we can publicly protest, boycott, and otherwise oppose managerial practices that restrict institutional democracy. We can also work to re-establish, renovate, or re/create collegial bodies and traditions that afford us greater collective leverage over university affairs and allow for much more public involvement and engagement in the institution.

In closing, I admit that I have far greater hopes for the university than those I have expressed here. I would not only like to see some of the old university that changed me restored, but I would like us to move some distance beyond it. I can envision, and long to work in, an institution that is even more open and diverse than it was, more flexible and democratic than it was, more healthy and nurturing of those who work and learn within it, and more responsive to and engaged with the needs of its surrounding communities. I would also like to see our universities adopt more of a holistic and quality-oriented philosophy, such as that which inspires the burgeoning "slow" movement, and become more sensitive and responsive to issues of sustainability in all of their operations and activities. I believe that at this unique transitional moment in our universities' history, when the experience and wisdom of older academics are combining as never before with the energy and creativity of newer academics, the time is ripe to work toward this vision. For this potential to be realized, however, we need first to free our imaginations and ourselves from the constraining mindset and conditions imposed by the corporate university. I hope that this calling card takes us one step closer to making that happen.

Note

1. This view was somewhat idealistic but not altogether wrong, given various struggles in the postwar period to make universities more democratic, autonomous, and public serving.

CHAPTER 2

Beyond Market Self-serving:
Recovering the Academy's Vocation

John McMurtry
Philosopher, University of Guelph

My experience of the university extends over almost half a century. For the first 20-odd years, I was worried the place was disconnected from the real world in self-referential guild specialties. For the next 20-odd years, I have observed the cumulative subordination of the university to corporate-market methods and private-profit projects. Both trends betray the academy's constitutional vocation at collective and individual levels.

How has this happened? On the one hand, corporatization of the academy has undermined it from without by changes that took place in government funding apparatuses from the late 1980s: The terms for funding research shifted from non-profit requirement to for-profit partnership. On the other hand, most academics are so caught up in their own careerist micro-worlds that they are profoundly ignorant of the academy's meaning as an institution of higher learning. They have come to violate its most basic principles as an everyday necessity of their private self-advancement—the formula for academic corruption.

When I retired from the university classroom and on-campus faculty in 2004, I felt that for the first time I was free to pursue the vocation of higher learning and research publication without such corruption. With my files of current research for contracted publications growing beyond the dining room table I'd already occupied, I started to clean up my filing sites. The first files I came across were records of annotated university rules, issues and deciphered mazes of ever-changing regulations, correspondences, institutional directives, and endless administrative review processes—countless stacked files and volumes of them, including academic confrontations over decades that had already flooded into my basement to occupy more storage space. It was a bit like an end-of-life dream—all the petty angling in the bureaucratic foreground obstructing the university's higher calling.

I felt blessed to be free at last to fulfill the constitutional objectives of the university without diversion—to advance learning and disseminate knowledge for the betterment of society as my final purpose without obstruction by the corporate academy.

One great confusion has undermined the university's work for the last 20 years. The objectives of the academy have been submerged in a global market worship that cumulatively overruns planetary life organization itself. "Leave it to the market," "let the market decide," "do not interfere with the market," "bring your knowledge to market"—an idolatrous group mind has come to rule within the academy too. In the words of one professor, deputy minister of education, and head of a major national research granting council over a decade ago: "I contend that the one global object of education must be for the people of Ontario to develop new services which we can offer in trade in the world market."[1] This position is incoherent in principle, but increasingly reigns across the educational system with no notice of its absurdity.

While many faculty slumber in the metaphor of "a market of ideas," they do not penetrate the underlying contradiction between the market's exchanges of private assets for a price and the university's basis in a free community of ideas. Academics have become too busy being specialists to connect across the divisions of their mental labour to the university's shared vocation. I asked a chemical physicist recently why physicists did not challenge the 19th-century model of engineering mechanics assumed by the neoclassical economic paradigm, and he said "the physicists are too arrogant to talk with them." I asked an economist how she could imagine that this lifeless mechanics model could possibly be adequate for human society's development, and she looked at me as if I were from the moon. "Only economists can understand economics," she responded.

Meanwhile students know that going to university is necessary to get ahead, so they do what they must to get ahead in the market. I used to ask my large first-year classes in philosophy "What is the goal of a university education?" There would be a long silence, and then a further question: "Those who think the primary goal of a university education is to make more money, please raise your hand." About 95 percent would raise their hands—more and more after Ronald Reagan became popular as the U.S. president with a credo of "American freedom is the freedom to get rich."

University presidents, campuses, and academic units have followed the market agenda. The presidents are reduced to cap-in-hand fundraisers in the CEO sector, the campuses have become pervasively festooned with corporate ads and brands, student market surveys have long decided the ratings of teaching performance, common academic spaces morph into sites for commodity sales, and multinational corporations control the textbook and journal production system in accordance with profit-first values. Who notices? In the climate of opinion in which we live, the response is likely to be "It is time anyway that the university was connected to the real world."

While it is difficult not to agree that the university should be linked to the real world, corporate marketization moves in the opposite direction of the academy's objectives. First of all, the *academy's purpose of critical search for truth* is a goal that opposes the *corporate market's final goal of financial self-maximization*. For example, it makes no sense in the global market to oppose slavery or 80-hour work weeks as long as they reduce costs for investors and consumers by these forms of labour purchase. On the other hand, good reasoning and research require educators and researchers to consider life-destructive practices independently of their money payoff to private investors, and even in opposition to them. They may even know that it is irrational in market terms to devote long hours to research and rewriting if it simply adds costs to the producer and does not sell, but this is what original research in the academy demands.

Unfortunately, senior academic administrations are now unlikely to defend the advance of knowledge when it is not profitable to do so, but actually assist wealthy corporate interests in silencing academics if they compromise these private interests who direct increased funds to university administrations. Here is an example of a true claim that my university refused to print, which I presented in a paper to address this problem. I was referring specifically to the case of Dr. Nancy Olivieri whose struggle with the pharmaceutical company Apotex and the University of Toronto in the 1990s caused widespread alarm in the academic community and drew international attention. I wrote:

> In the case of University of Toronto, Dr. Olivieri's censure occurred
> while the President, Robert Pritchard, was in the midst of negotiations

to receive a multi-million dollar donation from the corporation trying to silence Dr. Olivieri. Administrators who presided over false attacks were promoted to more lucrative positions—including the current President of University of Toronto. On the wider government plane, the incoming federal administration of 2004 campaigned on the "tripling of the commercialization of university research," which, Paul Martin proclaimed as he became Prime Minister, was "not nearly fast enough."

My observation was not contested because I presented documentation on every point. But my university's administration would not print these sentences in the campus bulletin reprinting my address. The reason given was that external commercial legal counsel advised that it not be printed even if the statements were perfectly true (and truth is an absolute defence against libel). Here we may see how the values of the corporate market and the academy conflict all the way to the publication of reports of the conflict itself.

A second level of contradiction between market and academic models is between the methods of dissemination. The control of all knowledge that corporations can copyright or patent is a principle that ultimately regulates the global market. Indeed, this right to market monopoly of ideas is pursued and extended to the utmost by 20-year patents on life-saving remedies, control of seed varieties, and corporate copyrights on journal articles and texts—all typically discovered within universities themselves. My own university library has stopped me from putting relevant article and chapter publications on reserve for students even when I am the author of them.

This is the extent to which the university has gone in not only accepting the corporate agenda of education as its own, but in enforcing this agenda on the academy's faculty and students against their learning interests. It is now a general fact that academic journals themselves have become copyright-controlled by private corporations buying up the journals, and then multiplying the prices for their purchase and use by university libraries whose own faculties have created the material for no cost to the corporations. Indeed there is a standard copyright form required to be signed by faculty authors whose work is produced and refereed free for corporately owned journals, and these forms demand exclusive world copyright in perpetuity to the private corporate proprietor for no returns to the author, the university, or the public who support both. I always add a specific condition removing this exclusive world copyright, but typically risk or am threatened with non-publication. There has been no such resistance to signing these forms, I am told, by other academic authors.

Thus the public, the students, and the universities pay for faculty to research and publish and for all the university resources to support them, while private corporations buy the vehicles of publication to sell them back to the university communities who have created them. This market game generates private profits to the corporations, which have paid no costs of creation for the products sold, and charges university libraries increasingly unaffordable prices for journals and texts. The extent to which the academy's freedom of knowledge dissemination has been usurped is a measure of its collaboration with the invasion of its learning foundations, yet few notice the undertow pattern—least of all university administrators and government funders who increasingly press for more commercialization of university knowledge creation. When such hijacking of publicly funded academic resources for external private profit is not protested or flagged, one wonders as to the intellectual competence that remains in the academy's ranks.

On the level of practice, fleecing universities of their own creations by exclusive corporate copyright extracted from university authors as a condition of refereed publication is systematic extortion by external agents paying none of the costs. On the level of academic integrity, the university's method of *free and open dissemination* of ideas is the very opposite in principle to exclusionary copyright for private profit that blocks the free exchange of ideas.

The betrayal of the academy's vocation seems to have reached into our very identity as people and academics. Development of abilities of *autonomous thought and action* is what the academy promises and is tax supported to provide. In direct opposition, *consumption of ready-made commodities* is what the corporate market provides to those alone who can pay for them. We know that if anyone tries to buy his or her way into or through university, she or he is liable to expulsion as a cheat. But if the academy follows market values, why shouldn't students buy their papers from sellers of their choice? If all that is involved is an exchange to get what you want for the least price, the free market way, why is buying academic papers wrong? The rising epidemic of Internet plagiarism is not anomalous, but symptomatic of the increasing dominance of market values in the academy.

The ultimate assault on the university's vocation is at the level of truth-seeking itself. The university is constitutionally committed to critically reasoned inquiry, which goes wherever the quest for truth leads it. The truth is not an end state, but an open process in which partialities are continually exposed by thinking through assumptions, evidence, and connections. This thinking through is the nature of learning and knowledge. Reason's movement is always by *a more inclusive and coherent taking into account that is open to shared counter-evidence and argument.* This inner logic governs all disciplines—from the problem of self and other in philosophy, to the nature of tropes in literature, to the hypotheses of subatomic waves and particles in physics. In one way or another, the critical search for more comprehensively conscious understanding leads the academy in every domain and the human condition itself.

In direct contradiction, market enterprises and corporations succeed by *one-sided conditioning of buyers' unconscious desires to maximize sales of products for private monetary returns.* The truth is what sells. If sales increase by imaging and commercials that stimulate primeval appetites of lust and violence, then these appetites are deemed right so far as they promote profits and sales. "We are only giving the people what they want" and "no one is forcing anyone to do anything" are the rationalizations. How does one confront such a reversal of cultural evolution? One can only go to the more basic value of conscious understanding that enables human life to be human. This is the vocation the academy exists to forward, but its mission has been sold out to a life-blind regime that depredates as it invades.

After over 40 years in the university, I see it morphing into a garage sale of the mind. While I directly experience the university's vocational core in my life, research, and publication with all the academic resources I require, I increasingly find this vocation blocked within the institution itself so that it has become marginalized. My own university is a paradigm case. It is repeatedly chosen as the best comprehensive university in Canada, and has internationally leading research complexes devoted to, in particular, the sciences of food production and consumption—biological, economic, veterinarian, and agricultural. "But organically nourishing foods or products is neither a stated or implied criterion in any one of its schools, programs, or mandatory courses." This condition becomes more debased as it totalizes.

As with every other university in Canada I know of, for-profit food services for students specialize in junk foods, rich leases are granted to monopoly

. providers, and competing commercial propaganda sites increasingly pervade the academy's field of meaning. Virtually all of the university's administrative coordinates select for money-return value over enabling conditions for learning. Corporate-ad vehicles and pecuniary alliances are the dominant frame of reference at the management level, and programs follow suit—for example, by administration rebranding of courses into interdisciplinary clusters with no new faculty capacities but more administrator offices and perquisites. Since central administrations adopt market and corporate management techniques as their model and hold the academy's purse strings as their exclusive preserve, they are governed by no academic code of allocation and are rarely held accountable to any academic authority. To distinguish knowledge from self-enriching falsehood is not possible within a totalized corporate culture, and its conditions are already largely established.

Are universities now deprived of their bearings of truth and moral compass? Not at all. Their instituted objectives of advancing learning and disseminating knowledge and the betterment of society remain the academy's given common ground and direction. They are the vocation of the university and of human civilization itself. But living up to them is what has been lacking.

Note

1. Quoted by William Graham, "From the President," *Ontario Confederation of University Faculty Associations Bulletin* 6 (1989), 15.

CHAPTER 3

The Risk of Critique:
Voices across the Generations

BARBARA GODARD

English Scholar and Humanist, York University

I was jolted twice recently by signs of the deep penetration of technology into pedagogical relations and scholarly research in the increasingly corporatized university. I was shocked first when the bright red object on the cover of the latest issue of my professional magazine, *English Studies in Canada*, turned out to be a hot chili, much coveted as a sign of student approval by professors contributing to a "Readers Forum" about RateMyProfessors.com, a commercial online rating system. The second shock came at summer's close on receipt of an email from the university library inviting professors to attend Research Frontiers Day during which the opening session would focus on using Facebook, del.icio.us, and other online social networking tools to "plug in" to research networks, organize research, or connect with other researchers. Together these incidents are symptomatic of the profound changes occurring in the university today with the commodification and privatization of knowledge and decline in social commitment, which have followed the extension of corporate control over the university's key functions. In this essay, I reflect on these issues and comment on what might be done to address them.

Transmitting complex knowledge across generations has long been a responsibility of the university. Through its traditional roles of teaching, research, and community service, the university has generated and shared critical knowledge to sustain the public good. There are signs today that the university is no longer fulfilling its historical function, even as the media proclaim the need in our contemporary *knowledge society* for more graduates. Troubling in the university today is the commodification of knowledge along with a loss of collegiality and social commitment, which are the results of the private sector's increasingly direct control over the university's operations. What disturbs me most is professors' complicity in for-profit digital networks that displace the university's key activities of knowledge creation and transfer them outside itself in ways that limit the practice of publicly engaged inquiry and the dissemination of critical knowledge. Such acceptance of the corporatization of university culture as an inevitable reality abdicates the traditional "self policing"[1] of the teaching profession in resistance to encroachments on its pursuit of free inquiry in the broader public good. Collegial critique interrogating academic practices will wither in the mediatized consensus of a bureaucratized culture unless another generation of university scholars becomes engaged in renewing collective responsibility to continue the struggle for emancipatory knowledge against the creeping credentialization of professional accomplishment.

Already in the post-Sputnik era of the 1960s, the university under rapid expansion was criticized for its dehumanization of learning in the knowledge factories of the military-industrial complex. However, the 1960s was also an era of increased government funding for higher education, especially for basic scientific research, which provided universities with a margin to manoeuvre outside the logic of the market. Government support might well have increased the "large-scale marketing of facts"[2] rather than the traditional training of judgment, but its intervention introduced necessary balance to enable the university to escape the domination of any one group's monopoly of knowledge whether that of the Church, as in the past, or commerce, as in the future. Moreover, students and faculty actively resisted the transformations underway and challenged the increasing utilitarian emphasis in the name of a more egalitarian "community of scholars" whose proper function is to be a "creator and destroyer of ideas."[3]

In the 1990s, under the neo-liberal transformation of public post-secondary education, credentials came to replace ideas. Decreases in government funding led to steep increases in tuition fees as well as in class sizes, turning students into clients for whom a degree was linked to the promise of jobs. Diplomas came to be viewed as a purchasable right. Today, universities may still serve as the publicly subsidized testing service for *private* enterprise, but it is less in their 1960s function of producing the knowledgeable with the know-how that enables the corporate state to expand and the managers that allow it to manipulate efficiently[4] than in facilitating the proliferation of the corporate state's cybernetic systems among a compliant clientele. With corporatization penetrating every aspect of teaching and learning, the university has become a mass marketer for the high-tech industries as professors and students groove together on the latest mobile gadgets. Online, on-demand instruction on the Internet, podcasts, chat groups, Facebook, and even virtual classes on *Second Life*, are offered by universities so that "difficult concepts" can be introduced in an "unthreatening way,"[5] making learning easy. Instead of taking students out of their adolescent subculture and establishing a difference conducive to critical reflection, the university interacts with students in their play. Teachers are reduced to mere content providers of infotainment for digital enterprises when students become consumers. "I want them to think psychology is cool," one young professor says about his podcast to a class of 3,000. *Cool tools* is what it's all about in an era of "education for the high-tech savvy."[6] If the burning question of the 1960s was "Knowledge for whom?" today the question might well be reframed as "What's knowledge got to do with it?"

Coolness lies at the heart of students' university experience, I was troubled to read in the Readers Forum on RateMyProfessors.com (RMP). Students value participation in peer culture—"be[ing] cool"—rather than engaging with "issues and ideas."[7] This gap between generations incites professorial interest in student opinion. Introduced as a forum on pedagogy, the essays focus on the quantifiable measurement of outcomes, the performance indicators of the corporatized university, rather than on teaching philosophies or methodologies that might better awaken students' "engagement, hard work and curiosity"—the "stuff of critical thinking."[8] The English teachers repeat the gesture of the young psychology professor in "going over" to the students in their desire for positive ratings: They write about their own "primarily emotional responses" to student comments, most of them negative.[9] With criteria for evaluation as vague as "clarity" or as antithetical to learning as "easiness," RMP does little to elicit responses about the kind of critical analysis or disciplinary methodologies imparted in a course. Without a specific prompt for information about course content, the rating can only indicate tautologically whether there was any static in the communication channel. RMP invites a content-less, phatic, or asignifying interchange, a pure flow of bits and bytes as computers connect to network, linking to the RMP website or downloading a podcast lecture. Only the passionate extremes of high, but mostly low, get registered in RMP's digital realm. With the prize of chili peppers for professors who are hot, pleasure in the classroom is heavily eroticized.[10]

Affect is what circulates in the pedagogical interchange performing "immaterial labour."[11] Contributors to the forum generally overlooked the social relations of power mobilizing this labour in the shift to services and informatization of late capitalism. Instead they relate anecdotes exhibiting the effects of a generalized circulation of anxiety in students' anger and their own abjection that erupt in a "rudeness endemic to the digital realm."[12] For the angry or pleasure-seeking, RMP is a "formidable engine for the manufacture of 'popular opinion'" as it mobilizes affect into "bankable forms of knowledge."[13]

In the face of the pervasive web-based systems for teaching and research, and the enthusiasm of young professors for such *cool tools*, I was disquieted by a change in understanding of both *community* and *scholars*. Any link made by the professors to a history of scholarship in a discipline is outweighed by their desire to make courses not only relevant but also high in the popularity polls. Nor do they invoke broader social values that might assert alternative claims beyond the purely disciplinary or instant connectivity. A modelling of critical thought through long study and attentive mentoring is disappearing in an age that views a university degree on a fee-for-service basis and substitutes the anonymity of distributed networks for face-to-face debate. Contact through an informational flow of digital codes is confused with knowledge in all its conflicts and contradictions necessitating critical judgment. Moreover, the proprietary software mediating relations among users and the intrusive advertising on search engines and websites serve students up to the corporate economy. The extension of property rights over scientific and textual databases multiplies the risk of closing down the information commons and spaces for dissent as publicly funded research is captured for private gain.

The space for critical thought shrinks with the consequent changes in both the inquiring subject and the object of knowledge. No longer does bio-power produce self-regulating subjects with habits inculcated through the confinement of schooling. The "control society" of contemporary capitalism exercises power through the "continuous control and instant communication" of computers in an informational economy that flattens subjects to "dividual[s]" or digital flows.[14] Additionally, the conflicts between political power and its critique, once internal to the modern university, have now been displaced onto a relation with an invasive outside. The responsibility to justice, which Kant posited as central to the university, was caught then in a conflict between royal power and pure reason, which pitted the faculties closest to power, with their applied knowledge of theology, law, and medicine, against the "lower faculties" of the humanities with their critique and history.[15] Today it is no longer possible to maintain this boundary between the "lettered" technicians, instruments of power trained in the university, and the scholar-professors engaged in the free exercise of judgment in the service of truth. With the archive placed outside the university in web-based data banks, the university no longer retains the prerogative of knowledge and arbitration of truth but has surrendered this mission to "trans-State capitalist powers."[16]

Nor can the boundary be sustained within the scholar, in the split between the exercise of the technical functions of one's profession and the obligation as a member of "a society of world citizens" to make "public use of [one's] reason" to criticize the effects of these functions. "Courage," Kant wrote,[17] was required for the scholar to assume this contradiction between action and truth in order to examine reflexively the social conditions of possibility of one's special competence as professor. With the emergence of new technologies, the public sphere for such free exercise of reason has been transformed so that media-savvy publicists ("médiatiques"), masters of the sound bite, have taken on the guise of scholars[18] as the media has absorbed the public sphere more completely into the technocratic functions of corporate capital. The vigilance the professoriate exercises in ensuring its responsibilities are carried out for the general social good derives from the venerable obligations of the scholar. However, the scope of such self-scrutiny has been transformed from the intellectual's philosophizing on social (in)justice for a reading public to the swift emotional charge of the "celetoid"[19] or TV celebrity. In the resulting intensification of connectivity, affect, not reason, becomes the cultural currency, the means by which capitalism in its present form "seeks to sell ... services, and ... to buy activities."[20]

The conditions for the circulation of affect, especially anxiety, have been produced by a number of major technico-political transformations within and without the university. The weight of corporate-dominated boards of governors and behind them, private fundraising bodies, have extended their extra-statutory reach over university affairs to undermine the authority of collegial governance in university senates and faculties. Information flows bureaucratically down from the administration's marketers as a culture of secrecy replaces a "community of dissensus."[21] In such a culture of managed consensus, Facebook might well seem a welcome alternative in which to exchange information. However, such sites favour instant publicity of accomplishments, which promotes a culture of celebrity while enmeshing scholars ever more deeply in the tangles of the corporate economy under the control of its proprietary rules, which regulate access to technology and software.

Underlying these transformations in university governance are policies of the Canadian state that have produced a general climate of insecurity. Aggressively since the mid-1990s, policy changes have redistributed the wealth of citizens away from support for ongoing operations of educational and other social institutions to build capital for the rich through tax breaks for corporations. Cancellation of funding for bursaries with a resulting shift to loans administered by banks has thrust students into the bondage of debt to the corporate sector. Reductions in social transfers from federal to provincial governments with no specific allocations for education have limited funding for universities with a consequent reduction in the number of professors. Class sizes have swelled to the monstrous 3,000 students assigned to the young psychology professor, while university fees have risen astronomically. Any increase in government funding in recent years has been tied to private-public partnerships that have deepened the penetration of corporate culture in university governance. Funds are now targeted for designated fields of research and program development, moves that have impoverished the humanities and social sciences—Kant's "lower" faculties specializing in critical thought.

Other policies advanced in the name of globalization have simultaneously contributed to this destabilization by radically changing the conditions of labour. With the outsourcing of many industries to Third World countries and the takeover of Canadian corporations by foreign owners, the chances for graduates with a B.A. finding a job have greatly diminished, making student debt an ever more frightening burden. At the same time, universities have met the demands of teaching large numbers of students through an increased use of part-time faculty and graduate, or even undergraduate, teaching assistants. The casualization of labour among university teachers has heightened the power of the course evaluation, the sword of surveillance hanging between these exploited workers and the possibility of a coveted tenure track position or just continuing work. Corporate capitalism has everything to gain from lobbying governments to maintain the climate of fear that, in the resulting scramble for work, results in a population vulnerable to manipulation, preoccupied with constantly reorienting itself. Such sudden transformations are the way the control society operates.[22] Students prolong their adolescence as they cling to their peer group, seeking to socialize with friends "to fit in, and to be cool."[23] Teachers struggle between their role as temporary corporate employees and their scholarly responsibility to disseminate critical thought about the politics of insecurity. The chili pepper is a hot item indeed in this precarious world.

Is another world possible? Memories of a different university linger, for not all those members of the 1960s have retired. The rating systems now captive to corporate capital were, before their current use as surveillance by university administrations, once the creation of student activists who first developed counter-calendars in the aim of democratizing the university. Inspired by the student syndicalism that transformed Canadian universities in the 1960s, students understood themselves to be intellectual workers with a responsibility to participate actively as citizens in socio-political transformation. They recognized that student problems, in particular problems of education, have their origin in socio-economic structures. Student critiques of the academy and society asserted the claims of social justice in the creation of more equitable structures. The ethical impulse of the traditional university training in character and judgment was enhanced in this period by the additional exercise of practical ethics in the wider politico-economic interests of society—an effective process of cultural renewal.

Ghostly voices from that era linger, as in a recent CBC rebroadcast of "George Grant: The Moving Image of Eternity."[24] Matt Cohen, then a Combined Universities Campaign for Nuclear Disarmament (CUCND) activist, T.A. and student of Grant, and later a well-known novelist, reminisced about his relationship to the celebrated philosopher and anti-nuclear advocate. What Cohen remembered most clearly is how Grant's teaching flowed seamlessly from the lecture hall through the seminar room and on to his house, where students joined professors and other intellectuals to converse. Their discussions, not only of classical philosophical texts, but of current social and political issues, would take them together to a teach-in or into the streets in protest against the rise of the military-industrial complex. In this kind of mentoring, students were introduced into the world of professors in multifaceted relationships, fostering a wide-ranging, trans-disciplinary education, linking reflective judgment to action. More complex affect informs these interpersonal relations than the distanced digital professor–student interactions of today. A smaller university where faculty–student ratios were more balanced made such relations possible.

Some of the younger generation hear the voices of the past and recall the era of the intellectual worker as a golden age that they regrettably missed. They hope to keep its spirit alive in manifestos for their generation in these "neo-liberal times."[25] Advocating an active response to the climate of insecurity, they embrace "intellectual risk taking" and "publicly engaged scholarly research" so as to invent alternatives to the prevailing "resigned quietism or instrumental careerism."[26] Against the demands of instant electronic connectivity, this slow learning requires a scholarly "practice of intellectual craftwork."[27] Creation has always differed from communication and may, through its possibilities for "transversal organization," help the emergence of new collective forms of resistance to the "control society."[28] Above all, younger generations need to learn to reconnect the socio-political to the economic in order to understand the role of the state in engineering the corporatization of the universities and the economic changes in the conditions of labour at the root of their anxiety. Professors need to remain alert to the tensions of their position, caught between technocratic subordination and the public use of reason. "Courage," as Kant's voice echoes across the centuries to the future, is necessary to assume this dialectical contradiction and take the risk of critique to make public the social relations of power limiting the exercise of reason.

Notes

1. Jane Jacobs, *Dark Age Ahead* (Toronto: Random House, 2004), 24.
2. Harold Innis, *The Idea File of Harold Adams Innis*, ed. William Christian (Toronto: University of Toronto Press, 1980), 268.
3. Ibid., 171.
4. Carl Davidson, "Towards a Movement of Student Syndicalism," *Our Generation* 5, no. 1 (1967–1968): 103.
5. Elizabeth Church, "Higher Education for the High-tech Savvy," *Globe and Mail* (September 7, 2007), A16.
6. Ibid.
7. Heather Zwicker, "They're Just Not That into You," *English Studies in Canada* 31, no. 4 (December 2005): 24.
8. Ibid., 23.

9. Aimée Morrison, "Some Things, You're Better Off Not Knowing … Thoughts on RateMyProfessors.com," *English Studies in Canada* 31, no. 4 (December 2005): 17.

10. In an earlier version, RMP provided a web link to a newspaper article reporting that good-looking and sexy professors get the highest course ratings, an encouragement to students to equate "sexiness with a good education." Katherine N. Hayles and Nicholas Gessler, "Rating RateMyProfessors.com," *English Studies in Canada* 31, no. 4 (December 2005): 7.

11. Michael Hardt, "Affective Labor," *Boundary 2* 26, no. 2 (1999): 93.

12. Morrison, "Some Things," 20.

13. Stephen Slemon, "dot-com agency: The Politics of Knowing," *English Studies in Canada* 31, no. 4 (December 2005): 29.

14. Gilles Deleuze, *Negotiations: 1972–1990*, trans. Martin Joughin (New York: Columbia University Press, 1995), 182.

15. Immanuel Kant, *The Conflict of the Faculties*, trans. Mary J. Gregor (New York: Abaris Books, [1798] 1979).

16. Jacques Derrida, *Eyes of the University: The Right to Philosophy*, trans. Jan Plug (Stanford: Stanford University Press, [1990] 2004), 94.

17. Immanuel Kant, "What Is Enlightenment?" *On History*, ed. and trans. Lewis W. Beck (Indianapolis: Bobbs-Merrill, 1963), 5–6.

18. Pierre Bourdieu, "Universal Corporatism: The Role of the Intellectuals in the Modern World," trans. Gisele Shapiro, *Poetics Today* 12, no. 4 (Winter 1991): 665.

19. Chris Rojek, *Celebrity* (London: Reaktion Books, 2001).

20. Deleuze, *Negotiations*, 181.

21. Bill Readings, *The University in Ruins* (Cambridge: Harvard University Press, 1996).

22. Deleuze., 182.

23. Zwicker, "They're Just Not That into You," 24.

24. David Cayley, "George Grant: The Moving Image of Eternity" (Toronto: CBC *Ideas*, 1986, Rebroadcast on *Rewind*, August 2007).

25. Fuyuki Kurosawa, "The State of Intellectual Play: A Generational Manifesto for Neoliberal Times," *Topia* 18 (2007): 11.

26. Ibid., 21–22.

27. Ibid., 11.

28. Deleuze, *Negotiations*, 175.

CHAPTER 4

We Are Saying Too Much ... and Not Enough

Karen Rudie

Electrical Engineer and Applied Mathematician,
Queen's University

I'd like to come clean: I have written worthless papers that were published. I have worked on industrial contracts that I thought were boring and knew would do little to advance my understanding of the research problems I was working on. I have sometimes taken on the supervision of graduate students when I did not have specific problems for them to work on and when I did not feel comfortable taking on more students. I have used exam questions that I knew were not nearly as good as other questions that I had thought of. In short, I am a professor.

The way I had imagined my life as a professor would be when I was a graduate student is nothing like the way it actually is. It's not merely that I was unfamiliar with the details of academic life. It's also not that I was seeing only the choicest parts of the picture, leaving out the drudgeries that come with *any* job. After all, anyone who's ever practised music or watched someone practise music knows that behind a concert lie hours of repetitive scales, missed cues, and any number of other less glamorous building blocks. As a graduate student I had been inside the inner sanctum of the professor's world; I had seen the hours of scales that formed the final concert. But in the end, there was a concert to be imagined, if not actually performed, a world of music and musicians, a sense of beauty. It is hard to imagine that anyone would bother training to be a musician if there were no concerts to be had. I stood next to the makers of music in my field, and still my work life as it is now does not have the melody that my Ph.D. supervisor's had. I believe that somewhere in the 1980s (in the latter half of which I was a graduate student), a shift occurred. This shift has radically altered the landscape of the university.

As a graduate student, I lived in a land where I could think about ideas without publishing them right away. In fact, my supervisor discouraged us from publishing. The rare graduate student in my field published more than one journal paper prior to thesis defence or more than two papers arising from thesis work even post-defence. This was as it should be: Scholars in training are still shaping their thoughts. We should give them the time and space to do so.

My Ph.D. supervisor regularly held informal summer learning sessions for students he was supervising—non-graded courses, close in flavour to advanced-level graduate courses. They required much work and time on my supervisor's part. Struggling with the material and working with other graduate students brought me closer to the experience of scholarly inquiry than any other official graduate course did. As a professor today, I cannot imagine doing additional graduate teaching. At best, most of us do only a decent job of teaching what we are *forced* to teach.

Here's what my life is like as a professor. First and foremost, I'm always tired. Every professor I know is tired. Teaching feels like a chore. I spend too much time being a nag in class—"Please be quiet," "Please don't copy your assignments"—and too much time answering non-essential emails from students with questions that have nothing to do with fostering student learning. Instead, they have everything to do with anxiety and fear: "Will this section be on the exam?" I spend precious weekends making up new assignments and quizzes and exams when the ones I made up the fifth time ago that I taught the course were much better than whatever I'll come up with now. That is because then, I put thought, care, and countless hours into developing assignments to help students practise and learn. Creating tests was part of a considered and researched examination of what were the quintessential good problems that *should* appear on tests—problems that would truly fairly measure a student's understanding. Now, I dispense with the obvious, fundamental problems and questions that I once considered an appropriate test of what a student knows. I start by tossing away the very best of my teaching knowledge. I take it as a given that all my students will have memorized how to solve these problems since they will have diligently downloaded all past exams in the course (officially posted by my university). I also presume that most of them will have copies of every past assignment question I have ever given. So my efforts focus on coming up with more and more obscure exam questions and I balance these efforts with equal measures of energy and worry, trying to rework, remake, and mould these questions into ones that are at least fair enough that I can, in good conscience, put them on the exam.

In my research life, I feel a constant pressure to publish. I feel an overriding sense of being wanting and no sense of being part of an exciting collective of people who are trying to discover the world of science—not at odds with each other—linked by the world of mathematics to engineering problems. In the past couple of years, I have managed to feel less worried about my publication rate, but oddly, in some Osmotic Law of Preservation of Anxiety, my graduate students have pulled me back in line by pushing me to send our joint work to conferences and journals as soon as possible. At first, I dismissed their requests, newly ensconced in my sanctimonious cloak of crusader for the under-published and upholder of scholarly purity. However, I soon heard their pleas as legitimate concerns for their careers. They told me that NSERC (the Natural Sciences and Engineering Research Council of Canada, the main public funding agency of engineering science work in Canada) weights quite heavily a student's publication record in determining scholarship and fellowship awards. As a result, I have submitted papers that I did not feel comfortable submitting. Even more scary, some of these papers have been published.

How can it be, you might ask, that a paper that is either too preliminary in thought or too unfinished or too vague gets published? I believe the answer is that reviewers are too tired, too overworked, too junior, too awed by an author's name or their supervisor's name, too undiscriminating, and too uncoached. Not surprisingly, a decline has resulted in the overall quality of published scholarly work. Not that there aren't gems to be found, true beauties in the overflowing stacks of published papers. Also to be found are many papers that—even if not of gem quality—make interesting, useful contributions to my field. The problem now is how to find them. How do we even know which ones they are? The days when the mere presence of a paper in a top journal signalled its importance are over. We no longer have useful markers to help us negotiate the plentiful world of academic work.

Paper counting is not the only enumeration that is going on in scientific fields these days. The other quantifiable measure common in engineering is the number of dollars of research funding. My most memorable encounter with being chastised for not having enough funding was during a year when my department instituted the following scheme for assessing research performance and allocating the associated merit increases in salary. Of 40 available points for research, 10 were based on our funding level and were determined by a scale whose key features were that you got 10 points for funding over $300,000 and one point for funding under $30,000. In other words, you could be an outstanding researcher, you could even win the best paper award at the top conference in your field, but if you had no industrial funding that year, you could not get a merit score on your research of better than approximately 75 percent (i.e., 1/10 for funding and 30/30 for all other aspects of research).

This marking scheme was problematic in several ways. Most significantly, it did not assess the scholarly value of the research. It did not evaluate the contribution of the research to knowledge, the importance of the research results, the value of the research to society, or the difficulty of the research. More insidiously, this form of assessment sets the stage for phasing out theoretical research from the university and doing so without debate. By giving a quiet death to non-applied research, it attempts to avoid what I believe would be a public outcry if the university declared that from here on, professors will pursue only those ideas mandated by private companies. If removing theoretical research from universities were on the table as an issue of debate, I could respond to it. And here's what I'd say: I would not want to fly in an airplane whose control systems were based only on theoretical research done at the university in the last year—research that has not stood up to practical-application testing. But I would no sooner want to ingest medicine tested by researchers at the university in clinical trials that were being funded and directed by the very company that manufactures the medicine. Sadly, though, I don't get to weigh in on this topic because the shift toward devaluing basic research and valuing practical applications of knowledge that benefit corporations is being slowly, subtly, and quietly accepted as a done deal by most of us at the university.

So, what has led us from my idealized past to the current day? I believe one of the biggest culprits is the invention and extensive use of the Internet, both in devaluing students' educational experience and faculty's research experience. Because our students have grown up not knowing an educational world in which the Internet has not existed, their mode of learning is deeply impacted by the sense of immediate gratification that comes from Internet use. To know something is to Google it—to have your screen give you information within seconds of asking. Most of my students have not learned how to "sit with" discomfort, with *not* knowing, with confusion, with unanswered questions. It's from the depths of confusion and intellectual discomfort that true understanding can spring forth. Our students have been robbed not only of an intellectual opportunity—discovering and creating new results and better solutions—but also of the psychological journey that constitutes the other part of university learning. We are making it harder for our students to develop the skills of intellectual and emotional self-sufficiency. Furthermore, while on the surface they clamour for greater dependence—"I want your course notes to be on the web"—we are breeding self-loathing and dissatisfaction.

While instant information obviates the need for deep thinking in the undergraduate world, I don't think the same problem exists for researchers. Access to citation information, contact information for other researchers, online articles, and online journal paper submission have, for the most part, been helpful to conducting research. On the other hand, with the easy access to information, journals have proliferated, thus increasing the number of published articles and requests to researchers for peer-reviews of article submissions, and diminishing the standards for published material. Social and professional boundaries have lessened that would otherwise keep people from making overly frequent or improperly considered requests of others. I remember wistfully the days when an editor had to contact me by post to ask if I'd review a paper. Requests were less frequent, more judicious, and more meaningful.

Corporate involvement and funding is the other huge influence on research in the university today as I have already suggested. In electrical engineering this influence plays out in several ways. Companies financially support the graduate students of specific professors and/or give grant money to the professor. In addition, professors may get paid to do part-time work on a contract. Some companies provide equipment or computers in return for naming a laboratory or lounge after the company while others, in return for the donation, may put constraints on the institution's software choices. I do not hold the view that no good can come from a connection between industry and university. In engineering especially it can be scientifically beneficial for a researcher to have an understanding of the practical, technological, and industrial problems that require further development. It is okay for product development concerns to influence or even determine research direction. However, it is not okay for research to be product development work in disguise. We should be mindful of financial relationships dressed up as pure and non-partisan—namely, as research. At another level, most professors recognize that, although using inadequately paid workers to do your work is a time-honoured business strategy for saving money, it is unethical. Yet, in the course of doing industry-funded research work, we professors are selling our time and expertise for a fraction of the going rate we would receive if we were hired company employees.

An extraordinary paradox is at play in the university these days. On one hand, there really *is* pressure to publish and it plays out in annual performance reviews of professors, graduate student scholarship results, and professorial promotions. On the other hand, we've been sold a bill of goods about the need to respond to this pressure. The job security of tenure and faculty salary increases for merit—even for the most prolific professors—are so small that something other than losing our jobs or getting more money must be driving most of us to feel that we will perish if we don't publish a lot. It's like the proverbial bogeyman that parents use to lure their children to bed. After a while, parents don't need to remind their children that if they don't stay in bed, the bogeyman will get them. Children have internalized the fear so successfully that they eagerly hop in bed before their parents can even utter the words "time for bed." We academics have become embarrassingly obedient. Our compliance has taken on a life of its own. We complain that the university is pushing us to publish too much or to spend too much time seeking funding, but then we write letters of reference that focus on numbers of publications, we apply for funds we don't need, and we base our hiring criteria on the number of papers published and the amount of grant money received. We are policing ourselves and each other. Perhaps most sadly, we deny ourselves the comfort of shared commiseration.

In the short term, the fear-mongering initiated by university administrators and perpetuated by us serves the university's ends. We do indeed increase funding, get more publications, and produce more graduate students. Sooner or later, though, professors burn out, drop out, and become disengaged, cynical, and bored. Our graduate students sense this and they too become cynical, disengaged, and bored. Our undergraduates understand at some subconscious level that integrity in writing is no longer a high priority at the university. The erosion of scholarship is visible. How ironic then that we are so incensed by plagiarism at the undergraduate level, but think nothing of submitting worthless material to conferences and journals! Our students do not think that being a professor carries any weight. They are right—it doesn't. We have lost our integrity and spirit. It's happened subtly and initially through external pressure. Unfortunately, we have, over time, internalized the pressure.

In my 16 years as a professor, I have not published a large number of papers and the part of me that developed in the academy of the late 1980s and 1990s feels embarrassed by my publication rate. But the part of me that was born into academia in the early 1980s has a different way of seeing, a way that is liberating, so liberating that when I can hold onto this view, I can (paradoxically) do better research. That part of me says, "Here is what my life is like": I have taught some interesting, fun classes and some that seemed like torture; I have had students who were a struggle to teach, students who were belligerent and close-minded, and I have also taught lovely and engaging and fascinating students; I have given seminars all over the world and sometimes they have gone well and sometimes they have been lacking. Through my experiences as a teacher and researcher, I have learned about my research area and about myself. I have not published a lot and I've lived to tell the tale.

You might ask why I stay in the academy given the picture I've painted. The university is still the place of my dreams. It is where I get to interact with hopeful minds; where sometimes smart ideas push their way through the mire of bureaucracy; where I can dress however I like because most of the people around me care more about my skills than how I look; where I have the luxury to leave my office in the middle of the day to meet with an old friend passing through town; where I have the freedom to reschedule work when my son's daycare calls with the news that he is sick. In many ways, the university of today is as flexible and interesting as the university whose loss I lament. It is also more diverse, more open to women, and better paying than the university of long ago. But for all the good of the current university setting, the changes that have happened in the last few decades threaten both research and teaching. Being swamped in (often unnecessary) committee work, pandering to student panic instead of engaging in true teaching, publishing papers to make someone else happy, spending too much time reviewing papers because there is a proliferation of journals—each of these things at first is a minor distraction, but after a few years, they add up and squelch the soul of scholarship.

How can we change the academy of today? We can write letters of reference for colleagues who have published little but whose publications are interesting; we can award scholarships to graduate students who are too busy to publish because they are engrossed in exciting research; we can send students to conferences even if they are not presenting papers; department heads can reprimand someone who has submitted 15 journal articles in one year (since *no one* has 15 important things to say in one year); granting agencies can evaluate researchers based on the quality of their work rather than on the quantity of papers published. If you're tenured, tell junior colleagues not to waste years doing things that make them unhappy, that life is truly short, that they too will live to tell the tale if they don't have more than 10 journal articles to their name in 10 years. Let us open the closet to reveal that there really isn't a bogeyman there after all. Above all, let us say out loud that the status quo is not fulfilling and if we keep at it this way, there will be no university as we once knew it.

I want to wash my hands in the waters of academia and come away feeling clean. I want to feel that at least part of my day or week or year at work is joyful. In short, I want to be a professor again.

Acknowledgements

I am grateful for the feedback from the editors and from friends who read earlier versions of this piece. Their comments helped to shape my words. I thank Caroline Baillie, Luke Bisby, Richard Day, Lindy Mechefske, Jan Newson, Claire Polster, Tariq Samad, Greg Stewart, and Stan Simmons.

CHAPTER 5

A Requiem for Fundamental Biology

ARTHUR FORER
Biologist, York University

Prelude

I was asked to discuss how being a scientist at York University differs now than when I joined the Biology Department in 1972. The university and the practice of science have changed greatly: As societal pressures increased to evaluate everything in monetary terms, to look out primarily for ourselves, to get ahead regardless of consequences to society, university degrees became job qualifications, students became clients of the university's training business, and faculty became financial encumbrances to the business balance sheet.

Themes

Faculty members teach, do research, and, at least when I was hired, act as members of the collegium that administers the university. All three aspects have changed, but I concentrate on research and teaching. I first explain why I need external funding, and on how that impinges on my university functions.

Universities do not provide the research tools that scientists need to do research. In 1972, York University supplied space and a small start-up award that did not allow even bare necessities. I needed external funding to purchase supplies, to buy equipment, to operate the equipment, and to cover laboratory expenses, including stipends for laboratory assistants and graduate students. Thus the granting system is intimately involved with my university research.

In the 1970s biologists could get grants from the Natural Sciences and Engineering Research Council of Canada (NSERC) and from some private agencies. NSERC awarded operating grants to support research *programs*; I was not required to follow specific pre-vetted research proposals and was free at any time to deviate from my proposed plans in order to follow up recent findings, to pursue what I thought was a better research strategy. To me, this was the best system in the world. I took the chances in choosing experiments and, if successful, my published articles were evidence of my program's success. When I reapplied after three years, my application was judged on the work I had done. If my experiments were not successful, then my grant could be terminated. NSERC funds were reasonably evenly distributed in the 1970s—no grants were really high, and a reasonably high percentage of those who applied were awarded grants (if my memory is correct, around 30 to 40 percent of the applicants were successful). The key point is this: Grants were not denied based on second-guessing the experiments that the applicant proposed to do.

The system in the United States was different: U.S. granting agencies assessed the *proposed* research. These grants were considerably larger than Canadian grants, and were not as evenly distributed: One received a relatively large amount, or one received nothing. (At present, around 10 percent of those applying for grants in the U.S. receive funding.) Consequences of vetting the proposed research are that reviewers direct the research into approved paths,[1] that applicants propose short-term experiments that will result in guaranteed publications in the course of the grant,[2] and that innovation is stifled. Innovation generally is associated with a break from prevailing ideas and since reviewers who established the prevailing ideas are content with them, contrarian proposals generally are not accepted. Albert Szent-Györgyi's career is an example. While in Hungary and without anyone vetting his proposed experiments, Szent-Györgyi received a Nobel Prize in 1937 for deciphering the role of Vitamin C, and then did innovative experiments toward understanding muscle contraction. He moved to the U.S. after World War II. He described his innovative work as Dionysian to distinguish it from Apollonian work, which more narrowly extends lines of research already done. He stated that his "two major discoveries"—his research on Vitamin C and muscle contraction—were at the time rejected by "the popes of the field," and that had he been required to have his proposals vetted, he would not have been awarded grants and would not have done the Nobel Prize–winning research.[3]

Variations

Alas, the Canadian granting system changed. In the 1980s, NSERC started assessing proposals rather than programs. Consequently research may be directed toward committee-approved paths.[4] Grant awards also became more skewed—more grants with higher awards and more rejections. NSERC also introduced Strategic Grants to target governmental needs of strategic importance.

Targeted research now is the norm. My research no longer is deemed fundamental, but rather is considered curiosity-driven. That is, the previous dichotomy of fundamental, basic research *versus* applied, targeted research is now curiosity-driven research *versus* simply "research." Fundamental research has become mere curiosity, an implied pejorative: "Gee, I'm curious—let's study how that ant moves" rather than "I study ant movement because it is of fundamental, basic interest for the following reason." Bob Goldman, then president-elect of the American Society for Cell Biology, considered the Marine Biological Laboratories in Woods Hole, Massachusetts, as "one of the last bastions of untargeted, curiosity-driven research," one of the last places in the U.S. where one can work on fundamental research problems.[5] The work at MBL is not completely unrestricted since those scientists still need grants, which usually require targets, but Goldman's assessment nonetheless points out how fundamental problems have been de-emphasized and targets emphasized.[6] Canadian government research funding often uses public-private partnerships: Government funds are available only to grantees who obtain funding from private corporations. For example, grants from the Canadian Foundation for Innovation, often used to provide equipment for new faculty, provide 40 percent of the award; the rest is from partners. Genome Canada grants also require private partners.[7] Partnerships have resulted in biased conclusions in articles and even had effects on course content. In an article in the *New York Times Review of Books*, Marcia Angel, a former editor of the *New England Journal of Medicine*, describes how the pharmaceutical industry's sponsorship of medical research has led to serious conflicts of interest, undermined the credibility of research findings, and compromised the integrity of medical education.[8]

Another change from the 1970s is that current faculty by and large do not do hands-on research.[9] In 1972 most of my colleagues worked in the laboratory; now only a handful (out of 35) do. Instead most are managers and grant writers: They direct students and post-doctoral fellows and assistants, write grant applications, network, referee articles, referee grant applications, and organize funds, but are not hands-on researchers.[10] Being a manager and being called a principal investigator (PI) instead of a grant-holder, on the other hand, fits in well with universities modelled after businesses in which higher status managers direct the lower status individuals who do the work.

Graduate education has changed too. When I was a student and until my early years at York, graduate students were taught to understand the tools they used; they knew what the various instruments measured, what the experimental bases were behind the assays, and what the various solutions contained (since they made them up themselves). Present graduate students, on the other hand, by and large do experiments using commercially available kits—prepackaged solutions and accessories that come with instructions on how much of what to mix with what, and for how long, and then what colour (or the like) to measure at the end. It's like making chocolate brownies from a prepackaged mix. Kits are proprietary so students don't know what they are composed of or how they work or what exactly they do.[11] They use kits, nonetheless, because they are quick and there is pressure to publish the work rapidly to support the grant.

Journal practices also have changed. Authors formerly could use the Discussion sections of articles to interpret their data freely: When the experiments described in the Results section were done properly and the Discussion neither contradicted data in the article nor ignored counter-data in the literature, the authors could interpret as they wanted. Now, however, referees often reject articles based on interpretations. Further, whereas referees previously told authors about references that were overlooked, now they also tell authors to remove relevant citations. In the past two years, for example, two colleagues independently told me that they knew my work was an important precursor to theirs, but that a referee told them to expunge reference to my work, edicts that were backed up by the editor. I assume that the rationale was to prevent even an oblique validation of my interpretations because, prior to these incidents, another colleague told me that, shortly after he published an article, an eminent colleague scolded him for citing me because it lent credibility to my views. Practices such as these ensure that articles remain consistent with current mainstream views. Scientists generally are too busy writing grants, directing laboratories, and networking to read carefully much of the extensive literature.[12] Many don't want to waste time with oddball articles and, rather, want to read approved, accepted ideas, much as until the 1960s, some journals required that female authors use their full first names to identify them as female, presumably so that busy males needn't waste their time reading articles written by women. I conclude that the gatekeepers of the field restrict interpretations to prevailing viewpoints.

Other examples fit this conclusion. The prominent review journals whose title begins "Current Opinions in" (e.g., *Current Opinions in Cell Biology*) indicate in each reference list those articles that *must* be read: One star (*) indicates articles of special interest; two stars (**) indicate articles of outstanding interest. Each starred citation includes a two- to three-sentence summary of the conclusions from the article; unmarked articles are not summarized. Readers are thus pointed directly to what is considered to be the important work without needing to read the others, and, given the brief summaries, perhaps this starred citation system even obviates the need to read any of the articles. Another example is the for-profit *Faculty of 1000 Biology* bulletins. Chosen biologists— Szent-Györgi's "popes"—describe and evaluate articles they select, providing readers, according to the *Faculty of 1000 Biology* website, with a continuously updated insider's guide to the most important papers within any given field of research, offering researchers "a consensus of recommendations from well over 1000 leading scientists," as well as "an immediate rating of individual papers by the authors' peers, and an important complement to the indirect assessment provided by the journal Impact Factor." It is endorsed with praise: "a systematic tool that organizes and evaluates (the mass of literature) authoritatively like this is just what we need."[13]

Other restrictions have arisen because much scientific work is judged by the *Impact Factor* of the journals in which the work is published.[14] General journals with huge impact factors such as *Nature*, *Science*, and the *New England Journal of Medicine*, with overall acceptance rates of around 10 percent, for a long time have rejected about 50 percent of submitted articles without sending them out for review. The newer phenomenon is that high-impact *specialist* journals now do the same. Acceptance by these journals often is conditional upon further experimentation, within strict time limits, which, if not met, means that the article begins anew as a new submission. These pressures can lead to less-than-careful experiments.[15]

Using impact factors to evaluate scientific merit is reinforced by the societal value placed on efficiency and objectivity and pressures to evaluate everything quantitatively, from numerical rankings of wine to universities to livability in different countries. These pressures extend to students who need high marks to qualify for jobs or the professions.[16] To enter medical school, for example, students need a high average mark—say, 91 percent—before even being interviewed. Students with a fraction of a mark less—say, 90.7 percent—don't get interviewed. In the university of my dreams, the classes are small enough so that faculty can know each student, and the most important evaluations are personal letters from faculty describing strengths and weaknesses: Is the student hardworking or not, able to think or not, independent or not, and so forth. But in real-life York University, first-year biology lectures have more than 500 students per class; second year has 350 per class. How to evaluate the students? We cannot know more than a few, so rely on multiple-choice exams, heavily policed to prevent cheating—not an ideal environment to encourage scholarship. Many students understand that exams and memorizing are not the same as learning; that the number/mark representation of their ability has limited meaning, but they also recognize that marks are crucially important to their careers. Consequently biological education becomes memorizing facts/details culled from a huge volume of knowledge in five courses taken at the same time. The marks become an end in themselves. Making examinations fair, properly weighted, with no cheating, becomes the teaching goal.

A small percentage of students in university always were interested primarily in marks, not in learning, and attended for reasons other than scholarship. What has changed since I started my career is that most students now study solely to get high marks, and that many graduate students do too because that is how they are judged. NSERC offers undergraduate fellowships to work in research laboratories in summers judged solely by grade-point average. Postgraduate fellowships also are judged on marks, so graduate students now fight for marks the same way undergraduates do. Faculty are obligated to define in detail at each course outset what they will use to determine student marks: percentages—to the percentage point—for each item, and a certain fraction of the evaluation must be completed before the course drop date. For us, the faculty, education is an exercise in policing and organization rather than in helping the students learn to think and evaluate for themselves. Consequently students at all levels learn to be passive absorbers of predigested information that is divorced from their thinking and from their lives.[17]

Coda

I have given my impressions of how biology practices have changed since the 1970s. I do not like many of the changes. I enjoy teaching students who want to learn, but not being a marks policeman. I love my research—if not, I certainly wouldn't have stayed at it after being compelled to retire. For those entering the profession now, however, the present is the norm. Were I to start now, with this as the norm, I am not sure I would become a biologist.

Notes

1. In the 1970s I proposed a joint experiment to a U.S. colleague. She replied that she could not do those experiments because that part of her grant proposal was not approved, so she had to restrict her work to the part that was approved.

2. Because "'guaranteed to work' science tends to be favoured over more innovative science," Mary Beckerle, then president of the American Society for Cell Biology, suggested awarding grants for programs rather than for specific proposals: "Increased emphasis on the investigator's training, track record, and vision rather than on the 'feasibility' of a project would encourage high-risk high-reward science." M. Beckerle, "Taking a Risk: Creativity and Innovation in Cell Biology," *American Society of Cell Biologists Newsletter* 29, no. 12 (December 2006): 2–3. See also J. Katz, "Why Cheat?" *Nature* 358, (1992): 10; H.K. Schachman, "From 'Publish or Perish' to 'Patent and Prosper'," *Journal of Biological Chemistry* 281 (2006): 6889–6903.

3. Alfred Szent-Györgyi, "Dionysians and Apollonians," *Science* 176 (1972): 966.

4. In a grant application to NSERC, I argued that chromosomes move because of forces from a "spindle matrix." The committee drastically reduced my grant and told me, essentially, to toe the line, to forget the spindle matrix, and, rather, to base my work on the prevailing premise that the micro-tubules (and their motors) produce the force.

5. R. Goldman, "Transforming MBL Science," *MBL Catalyst* 1 (2006): 12–13.

6. Schachman (2006) suggests changing the standard academic catch phrase from "Publish or Perish" to the more currently applicable "Patent and Prosper." Silversides describes similar pressures in Canada. A. Silversides, "Merchant Scientists," *Walrus Magazine* (May 2008): 66–71.

7. P. Wells, "Our Mad Scientists," *Maclean's* 118, no. 26 (2005): 34–37.

8. M. Angell, "Drug Companies and Doctors: A Story of Corruption," *New York Review of Books* 56, no. 1 (January 15, 2009), 8–12. Accessed from http://www.nybooks.com/articles/22237. See also L.I. Lesser et al., "Relationship between Funding Source and Conclusion among Nutrition-Related Scientific Articles," *PLoS Medicine* 4, no. 1 (2007): 41–46. Available at www.plosmedicine.org.

9. In 1948, Leo Szilard predicted the effects the granting system has had on science— that grant panels would direct research to areas in fashion, that applicants would

emphasize doable projects of limited scope rather than more risky fundamental projects, and that scientists would become lab managers instead of active laboratory workers. L. Szilard, "The Mark Gable Foundation," in *The Voice of the Dolphins* (New York: Simon & Schuster, 1961), Chapter 4.

10. See T.T.-L. Chang, "Persistence Pays Off for Geneticists Conradt," *Dartmouth Medicine* 32 (2008): 4; and J. Durgin, "$6.8 Million Gift Was Inspired by Donors' Struggle," *Dartmouth Medicine* 32 (2008): 11. A new Ph.D. who wanted to continue hands-on research asked me if there were alternatives to academia because it seemed that being a manager and publishing lots of articles was the only way to survive in academia, and that was not an attractive prospect.

11. Post-doctoral fellows often don't either. Some years ago my staining results contradicted the literature. I called the post-doctoral fellow who had done the experiments to ask if the method of fixation might be different: "This is what we used. What did you use?" I asked her. She could not tell me because she purchased slides of cells that already were fixed. The company from which she purchased the slides would not tell her what they did. Thus those details often are not available, even if they were considered relevant.

12. Wells suggests changes to publishing practices to help "all those time-crunched scientists who find themselves skimming papers" because of "the suffocating mass of background literature." W.A. Wells, "Unpleasant Surprises: How the Introduction Has Wandered into the Discussion," *Journal of Cell Biology* 174 (2006): 741. Many scientists also are too busy to review articles for journals: Instead they give the articles to post-docs in the lab to write the reviews, which they then sign. Mole, "Death by Proxy," *Journal of Cell Science* 121 (2008): 129–130. Some editors do not disapprove of this practice because they themselves were part of this system of doing things in graduate school, about which the anonymous commentator, Mole, concluded "Oh Woe, Are We." See Caveman and Mole, "Re: Death by Proxy," *Journal of Cell Science* 121 (2008): 1139–1140.

13. All quotes are from www.f1000biology.com. *Faculty of 1000 Biology* citations are used to indicate merit in curricula vitae, grant applications, and letters of reference.

14. *The Science Citation Index* was originally compiled for scholarly reasons to track how new ideas arose in science. The *Impact Factor* of a journal—the ratio of the number of citations to articles in the journal, divided by the total number of articles published by that journal—was calculated to indicate the most important journals in the development of the field. Now they are used to evaluate journal merit and, by implication, the merit of articles published in those journals. McCook puts it this way: "Lately, academia seems to place a higher value on the quality of the journals that accept researchers' data, rather than the quality of the data itself." A. McCook, "Is Peer Review Broken?" *The Scientist* 20, no. 2 (2006): 30. Raff et al. observe that "Sadly, career advancement can depend more on where you publish than on what you publish." M. Raff, A. Johnson, and P. Walter, "Painful Publishing," *Science* 321 (2008): 36. As well, the Impact Factor data are now supplied by commercial interests—Thomson Scientific Publishing—and are proprietary: The Impact Factor assessment must be purchased, and publishers of journals can

negotiate which articles are counted in the denominator so they can increase their Impact Factors. See M. Rossner, H. Van Epps, and E. Hill, "Show Me the Data," *Journal of Cell Biology* 179 (2007): 1091–1092. Some describe the validity of the Impact Factor data sold by Thomson as so bad that it would be unacceptable for publication if presented in a scientific article. M. Rossner, H. Van Epps, and E. Hill, "Irreproducible Results: A Response to Thomson Scientific," *Journal of Cell Biology* 180 (2008): 254–255. Also see V. Siegel, "The Promise of Peer-Review," *Disease Models and Mechanisms* 1 (2008): 73–77.

15. Mole, an anonymous commentator in the *Journal of Cell Science*, concludes that "researchers are under tremendous pressure to publish on a timetable ... any work that has used up time and resources," and that journals exacerbate this "by demanding additional results that are conditions for publication, usually on even shorter timetables." Mole, "Fake! Part II," *Journal of Cell Science* 119 (2006): 5007–5009. For high-impact journals, "authors are so keen to publish in these select journals that they are willing to carry out extra, time-consuming experiments suggested by referees, even when the results could strengthen the conclusions only marginally" (M. Raff et al., 2008). Reviewing practices complicate this situation (Mole, 2008; Caveman and Mole, 2008).

16. Vincent Lam, *Bloodletting and Miraculous Cures* (Toronto: Anchor Canada 2006), Chapter 1.

17. For example, I used to teach Mendel's first law of genetics in which our phenotypic traits are quantized: Offspring get traits either from their mother or from their father. I ran through the math treatment that arises from this, and then asked the class if they could specify which of their own visible traits came from their mother and which from their father. None ever replied. They didn't understand my asking the question, let alone having thought about what I said in conjunction with the real world: They act as passive absorbers of information that they don't use in the real world or even consider part of the real world.

CHAPTER 6

Idea and Reality:
The University or the Universities[1]

JOHN P. VALLEAU
Chemist, University of Toronto
and
PAUL ADONIS HAMEL
Biomedical Scientist, University of Toronto

Those who dedicate their lives to serious scholarship share a remarkably consistent vision of what a University should be and how it should function. In what follows we first remind ourselves how this idea of the University reflects a structure and set of traditions that are needed to nurture an effective community of scholars and also to protect their activities from the distorting pressures of an outside world preoccupied with short-term concerns and preservation of the status quo. However, today's scholars find themselves in institutions—our universities—that retain only remnants of the envisioned University. For many years universities have been reshaped to serve dominant interests in Canadian society at the expense of academic vigour, and this process is ongoing. We will look briefly at this deteriorating situation. Of course many scholars still manage fine work by fitting themselves into interstices of the new structures, but they cannot fail to know that their own work, and scholarship in general, is increasingly compromised, nor that the long-term reduction of potential benefits to society is severe. What response should we, as academics, be making to this grave threat?

What Is a University?

The University's potential lies in the cultivation of rigorous scholarship, leading to ever-deeper understanding in many fields, and thus, as a long-term by-product, to profound benefits to society. This unique potential can't be ascribed merely to the number of bright and thoughtful people that the University gathers together (that occurs equally elsewhere) but rather stems from its peculiar centuries-old structure and traditions. These particularly include maintaining for the University a certain isolation from the short-term demands that must preoccupy everyday

But this happens less by administrators!

administrative and commercial life. Those who choose to commit themselves
to academia are aware that they are likely foregoing some material and societal
rewards, and that their activities are partly isolating them from the ordinary
discourses of society. But they make the choice because they understand that
the intellectual life can be fully realized only by those in a very unusual setting, surrounded by fellow scholars—the University's teachers, researchers, and
students—off whom to bounce ideas and with whom to trade insights. She (or
he) must be able to reliably expect trenchant criticism, based on standards of
argument and evidence that are unfamiliar, and indeed socially unacceptable, in
ordinary life. The academic must know that the worth of her or his enquiries will
be judged solely on the basis of their rigour and originality, without reference to
conventional norms and perceptions. The scholar must be able, in fact, without
experiencing ridicule or rancour, to pursue ideas that would be viewed as absurd
or threatening in non-academic discourse: This is known as academic freedom.
The University is the structure designed over the years to gather and nurture the
peculiar community in which all this can be relied upon.

But let us pitch this a bit higher: Wherein lies the glory of humanity if not
in our capacity to *reason* and our experience of *imagination*? The core of the
University tradition is precisely to give these things their full expression by
insisting that the application of reason should be totally uncompromised, and
that no *a priori* limits should be imposed on our imagining of alternative ways
of thought and understanding.

This rigour and freedom from intellectual inhibition are far from what we
find in the discourse of ordinary society, where they are easily (and sometimes
correctly) seen as a threat to society's orthodoxies and dominant paradigms, even
to its very stability. To maintain this rigour and freedom, the University needs to
exist as a society in itself, somewhat separated from the values of that around it.

There is a further need: To reproduce itself, the academic community must
continually nurture new generations of scholars by guiding students to the
standards and methods of academic work. Notice that the teaching relevant to
this purpose has little to do with the transmission of a corpus of information,
but rather implies an apprentice relationship in which teacher and student
share intellectual investigation, the student gradually becoming able to contribute more fully. The need for all these special requirements was recognized from
earliest days in the famous 12th-century law school of Bologna, and learned

more fully from the doctrinal disputes that led to Abelard's confinement and the founding of the University of Paris. It led the scholars to defend their *métier* by banding into self-governing societies that could then guarantee the unique conditions required for full academic discourse—and so they invented the University—for it was understood that without such protection, the wider society and its most powerful, preoccupied with their immediate interests and security, would never permit the scholars to explore beyond the bland and palatable: a lesson learned by Socrates more than a millennium before the prosecution of Abelard!

But What's in It for Society?

Certainly the University would not have survived for 850 years solely on the basis of offering a fruitful environment for scholars in the face of its costs and perceived threats to the rest of society. Apparently societies have overall, and however haltingly, judged it worthwhile to tolerate the University and even to devote serious resources to its persistence. It bespeaks a perception that the University may return lasting benefits to a society that supports it and protects it from undue external influence.

What benefits are these? Paradoxically, one benefit must lie in the very activity that raises fear: rigorous analysis and criticism of the practices of the host society—of its mores, its structures, and its technical methods, indeed, of every assumption upon which it functions. However disturbing and exasperating, such criticisms have been recognized as a powerful corrective to the inertia that otherwise will tend to ossify any society.

Meanwhile, it can be argued that the University has, for centuries, acted as the primary source of whatever has been truly *new* in Western culture, and that this constitutes a second apprehended reward for society's toleration and support of the University's pretensions. The argument is curious and nuanced. It is observable that scholars in the University setting, simply by following their intellectual curiosity, constantly generate surprising new ideas and new understandings in every discipline. A modest few of these ideas and understandings prove to offer striking social benefits in the form of profound improvements—in modes of governance or in industrial processes, medical procedures, communication methods, environmental management, or whatever, not to mention simply cultural enrichment. The scholarly creation of profuse novelty follows from intellectual curiosity combined with academic skills, and notably without any societal direction or coercion.

In fact, we contend that the wider society has no idea of how to encourage genuine novelty—rather, it is only *without* such societal direction that anything profoundly new is likely to appear. That is because such direction will surely deflect efforts toward trivial innovations within existing paradigms: One is not likely to create the quantum theory by looking for a better mouse trap! We expect the University to produce entirely new understanding: new paradigms, some few of which will have the capacity to change our lives dramatically. This is the magic that society has sought over the centuries, and that has led to the relative sophistication of Western society since the Middle Ages. What has been less consistent is the understanding that the magic can be expected only if the University is allowed to keep itself largely isolated from the immediate pressures and concerns of the surrounding society. As John Polanyi has put it, "the demand for relevance is the enemy of excellence."[2]

Is This a Moment in History When This Understanding Is Particularly Weak?

Thus the University embodies a paradox, for it generates profound opportunity for society, but also poses a significant threat to the dominant elite, who bene-fit from orthodoxy. Indeed, from the outset, the threatened elements of the social, political, religious, and economic elites have attempted in various ways either to suppress the activities of the University or to divert them into safer (and preferably exploitable) directions. When such agents are successful, the University passes through lean times, tending toward the vacuous and merely decorative (and lending justification to the pejorative sense often given to the word "academic"). So, seen historically, the picture of the University that we drew above is exaggerated and idealized, but we believe it contains the essential truths about the nature of the community *required* to support genuine scholarship. So it remains the model that lives in the minds of scholars and against which they measure the institutions in which they actually teach and study.

How do our universities stack up? Canadian universities are under severe pressures to abandon important parts of the University culture we have described, to the detriment of serious scholarship, and indeed they already depart seriously from elements of that culture. The pressures come from a variety of directions, mostly external—from the financial and business elites and their government allies—but also, regrettably, from within parts of the universities themselves. We can do no more here than mention a few of the issues this raises.

Who Should Teach What to Whom?

It was perceived, soon after World War II, that the emerging economy required a better-trained workforce. One response by our governments was to impose much of the responsibility on the universities; this was enforced by adoption of per-student formulae for university funding. A consequence has been the large increase in university sizes, bringing with it the rigid and hierarchical administrative structures we now experience. Many young Canadians now pass through universities.

 Naturally, not many of these students are seeking to become scholars; indeed they are often impatient with being asked to involve themselves even temporarily in intellectual inquiry. But their impatience, especially when combined with large class sizes, negates the fundamental relationship between University teaching and scholarship and severely limits the extent to which university teaching can retain an intellectual character. The mismatch is severe. For faculty members, teaching often becomes something quite removed from their scholarly pursuits, seen mostly as a duty keeping them from their study or laboratory. The few truly scholarly students become frustrated upon realizing they are receiving thin gruel. And to the extent that teachers try (for the sake of those few and themselves) to inject intellectual challenge, the protests of the other students attest to their discomfort. The principal purpose is no longer the fostering of scholarly abilities and standards in potential academic colleagues, but rather the transmission of relatively conventional material in established disciplines to prepare the student/client to fill roles in economic life elsewhere. In short, our universities function as trade schools, and the corresponding teaching activity has little to do with the intellectual apprenticeship model we pictured within the University.

Now trade schools are valuable, both to their students and to society. Thus it may well be appropriate for governments to ensure their availability. What we question is whether this role should be imposed on the universities, themselves of unique value, if doing so certainly involves dismantling a vital part of the University culture, especially when the universities, in trying to answer discordant needs, are surely not being particularly effective either in their academic teaching or in their trade-school role. Is this pattern sensible? What are the alternatives?

Can Scholarly Enquiry Survive the New Fashion for Relevance?

Scholarly research is driven by curiosity about the correctness or completeness of our theories and ways of thought. But correctness and completeness can themselves never be proven.[3] So the pattern of such research is to test the theory by seeking exceptions and inadequacies—in fact disproofs, which can lead, with luck and imagination, to revised, more fundamental, assumptions—to the creation of new and better paradigms of thought. This process cannot fail to be inhibited or prevented if researchers are mandated to work within current paradigms, for example, with a view to finding their small and easily exploitable developments—in the current jargon, "innovations."

We are in the midst of a highly orchestrated campaign by financial and industrial interests, in co-operation with our governments, to shift university activity away from scholarship toward bolstering the economic and social status quo and especially to assisting Canadian industries to increase short-term profits—in fact toward the very involvements in everyday pressures certain to inhibit real scholarship and the deeper long-term benefits it offers. The campaign has been signalled by a stream of public reports issuing from government and private sources for 30 years or more, with the consistent message that universities must be diverted from their self-defined enquiries into serving as handmaidens to our industrial elites. They are also consistent in stemming from panels of business executives, who are always without serious academic input, but who nevertheless feel free to propose dismantling a culture that they do not understand.

A key example was the 1999 report of the Expert Panel on the Commercialization of University Research, commissioned by the Advisory Council on Science and Technology, with the revealing title, *Public Investments in University Research: Reaping the Benefits*.[4] The "experts" included no active scholars. They recommended that, to qualify for federal research support, universities "must identify innovation [as part of] their mission," "must provide incentives to encourage [researchers] to create intellectual property" [*sic*], must "establish an organizational capacity to carry out its innovation function," and so on. Though profoundly foreign to the culture of the University, the advice was embraced by government officials. Such reports have been echoed repeatedly by the usual economic pressure groups, for example, by the 2006 recommendations of the Canadian Council of Chief Executives (formerly Business Council on National Issues) found in *From Bronze to Gold: A Blueprint for Canadian Leadership in a Transforming World*,[5] by the final report of the Expert Panel on Commercialization, released in 2005 by Industry Canada, titled *People and Excellence: The Heart of Successful Commercialization*,[6] by the Conference Board of Canada's 2007 Leaders' Roundtable on Commercialization and Innovation-Based Commerce, *Picking a Path to Prosperity: A Strategy for Global-Best Commerce*,[7] and so on, all without serious academic input, and without examination of the trade-offs implicit in what they propose. We can see that these policies are still alive by looking at the 2007 Federal budget, *Aspire: The Budget Plan 2007*, which says that "the Government will identify the best [research] initiatives based on ... *advice from the private sector*"[8] (our emphasis).

The consequences are readily traced. To take a single example, it is easy to follow how the Natural Sciences and Engineering Research Council (NSERC), Canada's prime research-granting agency in the sciences other than biomedical, developed over the years a bewildering array of research partnership programs: Strategic Grants, University-Industry Projects, Collaborative Research and Development Grants, Industrially Oriented Research Grants, Industrial Research Chairs, and so on. An ever-increasing proportion of NSERC research funding has gone into these industry-driven projects as compared with research grants dedicated simply to scholarly research—that is, to Discovery Grants. This development exemplifies, by the way, the government's principal tactic in reshaping university culture: First reduce scholarly funding until it hurts, then offer relief, but only in the form of grants tied to commercial interests.

Apparently, powerful interests believe that diverting a higher proportion of University research activities toward producing modest innovations will be immediately beneficial to our industrial establishments and political elites (although clear evidence for this is not easy to find.[9] More pertinently, by co-opting the universities, the elites also reduce the threats of damaging criticisms of our current commercial and social arrangements. Unfortunately, the universities' acceptance of such intrusion on their self-direction and self-motivation seems certain to destroy the traditions and protections of the University, which alone, we have argued, make possible the creation of radically new understandings with the capacity to change our lot utterly.

This attempt of government and business to make University research more immediately relevant by having it focus on commercial innovation has turned out to have willing collaborators within Canadian universities, particularly in the senior administrations. That is, promotion of a fundamental shift in the culture of the University has somehow become official university policy![10]

Why Has the University Been So Supine in the Face of These Pressures?

One would certainly have expected the universities instead to be putting up a vigorous resistance to this damaging exploitation. Why is this not the case? One reason lies in the fact that the universities' top governing bodies—boards of governors or governing councils—have come to consist largely of prominent members of the financial and industrial communities, ignorant of scholarly endeavour. A second reason lies in the fact that such governors naturally tend to choose like-minded people as senior administrators, who feel that a businesslike structure is appropriate also for the universities, especially for the large institutions they have become. The scholar is apt to perceive himself or herself as subject to a top-heavy administrative structure, cumbersome and hierarchical, focused on concerns that seem largely irrelevant to academic pursuits. Since the administrators control the lines of communication, they effectively make nearly all internal decisions bearing on academic matters; this is doubly unfortunate because many of them (even those who were at one time academics themselves) have evidently imported not only the bureaucratic and hierarchical structures of the business world, but also a set of values remote from that of the University. This is not how it was meant to be. As Karl Jaspers put it, "only someone who carries the idea of the university in himself can think and act appropriately on behalf of the university."[11]

In short, a coup is underway. One could hope that our faculty members, aware of this attack on the very meaning of the University, would have joined in vigorous resistance. Alas, that sense of community is no longer so available, however. In our sintered and bureaucratic universities, most communication passes up and down through chains of responsibility, always filtered by the administrators at each level. How often do we even have occasion to discuss academic matters with our colleagues from other disciplines?

Nevertheless, the coup must be reversed otherwise space for scholarly work will continue to be eroded and the university further trivialized. The manipulation, stemming from the influential and wealthy, is driving us toward accepting an agenda of contributing to their power and short-term interests. Acceptance of such a role, however, is inconsistent with our pursuing real scholarship, which must be fully independent and deeply critical—one cannot serve both masters. And thus we see our ideals, the culture of the University, being dismantled around us. We as academics best understand the uniqueness and value of that culture, and the prerequisites for it to thrive, so we must lead in its rescue. This means shedding our reticence to speak out in defence of scholarship, of both its importance and its requirements; when we do so, much of our society will understand and renew its support. We must insist on reclaiming a large measure of self-governance in all matters impinging on academic life. That means reconsidering the makeup of our governing bodies and re-examining the place of administrators. We need to envision a reorganization of our institutions to distribute more usefully the tasks we accept (e.g., in teaching), and also to counter the numbing isolation between our narrow disciplines. In short, there are many issues needing attention, and doubtless as many resistances to be overcome. In such matters each of us can accomplish little in isolation, so the first requirement is surely to reinvigorate the vision of our being part of a self-directing community of scholars, willing both to assert and to defend our values as our forebears did centuries ago, and for the same reasons.

Notes

1. The authors of this essay requested that, for conceptual purposes, their convention be retained of capitalizing "University" and using the lower case for "universities" and "reality."
2. Quoted from private discussion with permission.
3. Karl Popper, *Logik der Forschung* (Vienna: Julius Springer Verlag, 1934). Available in English as *The Logic of Scientific Discovery* (London: Routledge, 1959).
4. Available at http://www.llbccat.leg.bc.ca/ipac20/ipac.jsp?index=BIB&term=350898 (accessed April 22, 2009).
5. Available at http://www.ceocouncil.ca/en/view/?document_id=484 (accessed April 22, 2009).
6. Available at http://publications.gc.ca/control/publicationInformation?searchActio n=2&publicationId=288278 (accessed April 22, 2009).
7. Available at http://sso.conferenceboard.ca/e-Library/LayoutAbstract.asp?DID=1660 (accessed April 22, 2009).
8. Available at http://www.budget.gc.ca/2007/plan/bptoc-eng.html (accessed April 22, 2009).

9. D.A. Wolfe, "The Role of Universities in Regional Development and Cluster Formation," in *Creating Knowledge, Strengthening Nations: The Changing Role of Higher Education*, ed. Glen A. Jones, Patricia L. McCarney, and Michael L. Skolnik (Toronto: University of Toronto Press, 2005), 167–194.

10. At the University of Toronto, for example, the Report of Manley Panel on Commercialization and Technology Transfer (available at www.research.utoronto. ca/about/pdf/Manley%20report.pdf; accessed April 22, 2009) makes explicit that the intention is to "change the culture of the University" in order to make it "more receptive to commercialization."

11. Quoted by M. Kwiek, "The Classical German Idea of the University Revisited, or On the Nationalization of the Modern Institution," Research Papers Series, Vol. 1 (Poznan: Center for Public Policy, 2006). Available at http://www.policy.hu/kwiek/ PDFs/CPP_RPS_vol.1_Kwiek.pdf (accessed April 22, 2009).

PART 2

Taking Stock of Personal and Institutional Histories: Calls to Account

CHAPTER 7

A Brief Memoir from the Trenches

ANDREW WERNICK
Cultural Theorist, Trent University

My generation, whose entry into academia as graduate students coincided with the great rebellion of the late 1960s, is now sliding toward retirement.

A certain bewilderment attends this passage. This is not just to do with the ironies of the youth-identified becoming old. In 1969 Rudi Dutschke[1] spoke of a "long march through the institutions." Faced with repression in the streets, the movement should focus on transforming the institutions of civil society, and settle in for the long haul. Evoking the heroics of the Chinese Long March of 1927 was the rhetoric of the day, but it was also the spirit of the day. And, in Canada as elsewhere, for many radical activists who became profs, if the mirage of revolution faded in the cold light of the 1970s and 1980s, all manner of ideals and activisms persisted, including toward the university itself.

Looking back it is as though history played a trick. The guild shattered, with its exclusions, but the university became mass and corporate. Student access became open, but to the point of a drastic educational dilution. An intellectual revolution swept away old paradigms, departmental walls crumbled, and new spaces opened up for critical inquiry of all kinds. But academic development became mixed up with rationalizing, business plans, and fundraising. The ruling rhetoric has come to be that of a service industry delivering education and research. For some the resulting situation is one to lament. For others, there are benefits to the (old) university being now "in ruins."[2] But what, in any case, have post-1960s efforts from below to reform or revivify the university amounted to? And what, if anything, can be communicated out of all this for those now lining up to replace us?

Certainly the context in which one enters the academic profession today is immeasurably different from anything I was fortunate enough to experience. Not only is there a great deal more anxiety about career competition and jobs, the university itself has been transformed beyond recognition. What characterizes the older academic generation today, in fact, is not just the 1960s but that our careers and projects have intertwined with this transformation, and have been deeply affected by the particular forms it took in the places we happened to be.

My first experience of university, in the mid-1960s, was as an undergraduate at King's College, Cambridge. It's the sort of place that marks you for life. Luminaries peer down from the walls. The tone was memorably set in the provost's welcoming address. You are here, he thundered, to think. The intellect! The intellect! The intellect! Never forget that the university is a temple of the intellect. I never did—at least that somewhere within the institutions called "universities" there is a vision and tradition, which some try to keep alive, of the university as an independent site for autonomous thought and intellectual culture. I rapidly learned that the university was crossed with forces pulling in other directions, that the temple was tarnished, that only imperfectly was the hierarchy within just one of thought. If there was a (real) university within the university, moreover, it was more like a monastery than a temple— in Cambridge, a single-sex and highly neurotic one at that. The college next door removed the gas fires to cut down on student suicide.

Other than the annual exams that decided our fate, we were pretty much left to our own devices. As for politics, except for the careerist kind around the party clubs, there were little to speak of. In my first year, two students were expelled for daubing "Hands off Cuba" on King's College Chapel, but it was a lone gesture and their punishment provoked no protest. Cambridge, to be sure, was rife with tension. Modernizing pressures were beginning to strain ossified traditions. There were ugly dynamics to do with class. The Beatles and other sirens filled the air with dangerous song. The mood, though, was repressed, somnambulant, fantasy-ridden, a mirror of Lindsay Anderson's film *If.*[3] The wave of student activism burst only after I left, leading (locally) to the abolition of High Table (the literally raised table to which the fellows would ceremonially process before dinner), and the admission, a first for the male colleges, of women.

When I crossed the waters to go to graduate school I was certainly interested in puzzling out the world (I had switched from history to economics, and now turned to political science), but I could not say that I was being drawn to an academic career. It was a deferral. I had already put off law school. I now deferred again, drawn to the University of Toronto by McPherson, Frye, and McLuhan, and to North America by all that that was *not* going on "beneath the blue suburban skies" of where I came from.

I kept deferring. When it came to preparing for the Ph.D. comprehensive exams, we graduate students abolished them. When I should have been writing my thesis, I was immersed with a multitude of others in building the student movement, and pushing the situation as far as it would go. For a moment the earth moved and anything seemed possible, but the moment passed. The state bared its teeth, the movement splintered, and (at least in North America) the wave receded almost as rapidly as it had built up. The precise moment of deflation in English Canada was the declaration of the War Measures Act in October 1970.[4] I have never seen so many frightened rabbits run back to their hutches. By the mid-1970s the political and cultural winds were blowing from the right and normality was restored.

Yet I did not experience what happened as the mere rise and fall of illusion. The war in Vietnam was stopped. A progressive political agenda was established that—from gender and race to global inequality and the environment—did much to shape the politics of the next 30 years. What I learned above all between 1967 and 1971 was that the order of the world was more fragile than it seemed, that the law could be suspended without barbarism immediately ensuing, and that, given the right combination of circumstances, miracles could be accomplished by a certain kind of collective action.

Inside the university, we shook up the decision-making process and built into it a measure of student power; we defeated the attempt to impose a discipline code; we forced the university to support a parent-run daycare centre; we turned classrooms upside down and spurred on a frenzy of debate. Much of this was in the name of academic reform, or for ultras like me: liberating the university—by which we contradictorily meant making it more democratic, free, and serving the people rather than its masters. It must be said, though, that the new left attitude to the university and what it even ideally embodied was dismissive to the point of hostility. My own zeal was closer to that of a disappointed romantic, but it came to the same thing and remained a blind spot. The University of Toronto simply exemplified the worst of what Clark Kerr called a "multiversity."[5] Bureaucratic, impersonal, intellectually conservative, dominated by professional schools, set in its Presbyterian ways, it was irredeemable. With the world situation in an emergency, there were more pressing things to do than worry about the University of Toronto's real problems or actual future.

Had I looked closer I would have seen that the U of T administration, led by a conflicted humanist, was merrily centralizing power, abolishing an independent senate, diminishing the role of the colleges, pushing research over teaching, and steering the university toward being a beacon of productivist excellence, a Harvard of the North, but none of that was of interest. The continuum of history had shattered. The university—any university—was simply a base of operations, an organizing milieu, a zone in which to experiment with community, pedagogy, and struggle.

A month in England after my graduate scholarship ran out was enough to make me seek an academic job in Canada. With gratitude for the berth, and rebirth, it gave me, I have been a faculty member at Trent University ever since.

Hermann Hesse's *Magister Ludi* tells of an intellectual community beyond the mountains on the edge of a Europe plunged into a dark age. The "bead game" they play, as their central activity, is a mixture of music and mathematics. It involves no reference to the outside world, and the aim is aesthetic. The drama comes from a stranger who has fled the troubles to join the community, but who is torn between the bead game (he becomes the new master) and the moral pull to address the problems of humanity he had left behind. I found this parable useful, not only because it gave me a fix on what was instantly beguiling about Trent, but also because it threw into relief (against Newman's contemplativist "idea of the university"[6]) a tension that I take to be irreducible, and that was as evident at Trent—for example, in curriculum squabbles—as anywhere else.

The Trent I came to was a fascinating experiment in institution-building. Designed to be a string of colleges on the banks of a river in the Canadian Shield, the vision of its founding president, Tom Symons, was rooted in that peculiarly Canadian mixture of liberalism and romantic conservatism known as Red Toryism. Most immediately, though, Trent took shape as an almost point for point alternative to the direction being taken at the University of Toronto.

Where U of T was massive, Trent would be small scale and personal. Where U of T opted for research, graduate programs, and professional schools, Trent would emphasize undergraduate arts and science. Where U of T was stuffy and full of denominational influences, Trent would be secular, have no chapel, and would be tolerant to a libertarian degree. Above all, where the U of T was retreating from its earlier character as a confederation of colleges, Trent would be built around them.

The new university would also exemplify an academic community ruling itself. The board of governors (and the liquor board) would be kept at bay. The division between faculty and administrators would be broken down. Where the University of Toronto was fragmented and compartmentalized, Trent would be at once a village and a total institution. Everything would be educational, from the dons in residences, to Introductory Seminar Week, to the aesthetics of the buildings and furniture.

Some of this was out in space. The instant tradition of green gowns and half the faculty having titles (like assistant college master) rapidly dropped. There was an amateurish edge to the enthusiasm for style and teaching. There was never enough money. However, what marked the project from the start was that it *was* a project. Trent was somehow going to reinvent being a university. Intrinsic to that reinvention, moreover, was the sense that it was something done together, and that participation in the university, even at the micro level of departments and colleges, involved institution-building as a practice in itself.

The grand plan was soon aborted. Capital funds ran out after only the third of what were initially planned to be 12 colleges at the riverside campus, with the two town colleges left in an ambiguous status in Peterborough's north end. More seriously still, provincial operating grants were never sufficient to support the labour-intensive Trent model. In a leaner era of "more scholar for dollar" (as an Ontario education minister put it), the money woes mounted. With rising strains on infrastructure, salaries, and workloads came pressures to normalize. Beginning in 1972 and for the next 25 years there was one financial-cum-political crisis after another. Nor was Trent's alternativeness universally supported from within, with a growing faction of faculty, staff, and administrators favouring a more modest and ordinary path. Trent's second president pronounced "Oxbridge on the Otonabee" dead.

Nonetheless, for two decades, while its student population gradually grew to 3,000, the university maintained the basic form it had assumed by the early 1970s and much of the élan as well. After a defeated attempt to close them down, the two downtown colleges evolved into a conservative and radical bastion, giving the whole college system some life and a connection with the gritty and artist-full city. A highly pluralized student and faculty culture encouraged pioneering interdisciplinary developments. There was a vibrant and rambunctious atmosphere. The academic level began to rise. To a remarkable extent too major decisions were settled in a collective process. Senate, with much student representation, became a kind of town hall. There was even a tacit sense of a social contract between ruler and ruled, violation of which could lead to presidents having to resign. The hardline faction gathering in the board (and in the Ministry of Education) must have thought that Trent's administration had forgotten who was in charge.

It is evident that la-la land couldn't last. Considering the tensions building up, it is remarkable how long the counter-revolution was held at bay. One reason, no doubt, is that recurrent crises sustained a high level of involvement. Noteworthy, in the politicized campus that Trent became, is not only the fabled radicalism and activism of Trent students (about which a book could be written) but also the activation of faculty. I do not know of any other university in which so many of its faculty became so involved for so long in the inner politics of their institution.

Faculty activism flowed through two main channels. The first was the union. Goaded by the threat of layoffs or worse (rumours of Trent closing abounded throughout the 1970s), the Trent faculty were among the first in Canada to unionize. A model financial exigency clause prevented the board from cutting or reorganizing the university by fiat. After strikes in 1991 and 1996 the faculty won its other bedrock demands: a formula that guaranteed average Ontario salaries, guarantees on workloads and hirings, and a better managed pension fund.

The second channel concerned academic decision making. Here, as vehicles for faculty assertiveness, faculty council (mentioned in the Trent Act, but not previously operative) became regularized as a general assembly with its own steering committee. Faculty board, made up mostly of department heads and chaired by the dean, doubled as the executive of faculty council, with the power to refer items to faculty council before they reached senate. At their height, in the early 1990s, faculty council and faculty board became proactive. Standing committees were set up on the university's finances and governance. Weak administrative areas were probed. There were moves for senior administrative appointments to be vetted faculty-wide.

The union and the faculty council reinforced one another in advancing an agenda of faculty power, academic self-governance, and administrative reform. In the event, the faculty victory in the second strike made the board determined to roll back the governance role of the faculty and sweep its reform agenda off the table. By so doing the way would be cleared for executive action to make the tough decisions that too much democracy had made impossible. First in line was chopping the colleges and consolidating the campus. Next would come a repositioning that would bring Trent, finally, into line with its appointed place in the system. Caught in the middle the senior administration resigned.

The details of the ensuing upheaval—central to which was the board's recruitment of a new-broom president with close ties to the Harris government—do not concern me here. Suffice to say that the course taken by the board and the new president led to a collision, as it was bound to, over both the general shape of the university and over governance.

The flashpoint was the proposed closure of the downtown colleges. The one to be immediately closed, Peter Robinson, was the centre of opposition and much else. The board's overruling of senate (which triggered an appeal to the courts) fanned the flames. An epic struggle ensued. However, in an atmosphere of financial panic, disciplinary threats, side deals, and demonologizing, the university split, with whole departments being bought off, and some openly backing the president. After the failure of mass lobbying to do more than delay the consolidation plan, a last-ditch student occupation was broken up by middle-of-the-night arrests and strip searches.

The legal action against the board (which I was party to), with its two years of hearings and appeals, was important in keeping the momentum going. But recourse to the courts was not only a tactic. The dispute was about the ground rules and their arbitrary suspension as much as about the decisions themselves. By winning the legal battle, the board got approval not just for closing the town colleges but for the narrowed interpretation of the Trent Act (with regard to what was in the senate's purview as educational policy) that it needed in order to assert managerial control. This narrowing, in turn, gave aid and comfort to those in other Canadian universities likewise pushing back against older traditions of senate–board joint sovereignty.

The legal issues were not exhausted. The case, on appeal, ended in a split decision, but what it allowed was an institutional atrocity. Besides the immediate damage, the episode not only ended "old Trent," it ended any sense of Trent as a shared project, let alone one dedicated to building a counter-institution that might pioneer an alternative and less alienated academic path.

Whether it was a defeat, however, for the very idea of such a project, or for the politics of defending and extending it, is a quite different matter. Let me leave aside that the Trent story itself is unfinished. The fact that there *is* a Trent story (and many Trent stories) should also be pondered. It is a witness to something remarkable. It proves, in the flesh, the possibility of developing a response to the travails of the modern university that does *not* accept the inevitability of its being ruined: a response that would be active, not reactive; that does not abandon the institutions (or abandon oneself to them), but that fights for them, and within them; that is institution-building, rather than deinstitutionalizing, and comprehends this as an ongoing praxis in itself.

And for the future? The times are not good for founding new universities and beginning afresh. But the experience of being in a university that is not one is widespread: One can build on that. There is no reason to suppose, in any case, that the kind of counter-politics it has been possible to develop at Trent is impossible elsewhere. And still less reason to suppose that, in our now globalized academy, there is not at least one small part of it that can be reclaimed by those for whom, stubbornly, the university (in some authentic sense) is a vocation. Every generation, as Walter Benjamin says, "has its own weak messianic power."[7]

Notes

1. Rudi Dutschke was the leader and charismatic voice of the new left student movement in West Germany. He survived an assassination attempt in 1968, but died as a result of health complications 10 years later in Sweden.

2. See Bill Readings, *The University in Ruins* (Boston: Harvard University Press, 1997).

3. The movie *If*, set in a private English boarding school, focuses on a group of existential rebels led by Malcolm McDowell, who swear a blood oath against the bullying order and imperialist nostrums of the school. It climaxes in a dream-like sequence in which they seize weapons from the school armoury (there was army training for the older boys once a week) and shoot up the annual parents-and-prizes day. The headmaster, mouthing platitudes about order, decency, and how the rebels are throwing away their careers, is calmly shot between the eyes. At the showing I saw, when McDowell pulled the trigger, the mainly student audience roared with approval.

4. The act is Canada's constitutional way of declaring a state of emergency. In the October Crisis of 1970, radical Quebec nationalists kidnapped first the British trade commissioner, and then the Quebec labour minister, who died at their hands. As the crisis deepened—with growing signs of support in Quebec for the FLQ and its manifesto, the Quebec government negotiating with the "terrorists" (they were flown to Cuba), and even moderates talking about the need for a transition to independence—the federal government under Prime Minister Trudeau proclaimed the War Measures Act, and sent in the army. Civil liberties were suspended across Canada, and in Quebec hundreds of activists were rounded up. In English Canada, where there were no such arrests, there was only muted protest and, even on some campuses, flag-waving support for the tough measures.

5. Originally written in 1854, John Henry (Cardinal) Newman's *Idea of the University* argued that the highest mission of universities, from Greece and the Middle Ages, was to be autonomous centres of learning and reflection, and that this mission had to be protected (by "high protecting towers") against political and economic pressure. An educational purist, he particularly opposed a confusion of role between technical and vocational institutes and universities.

6. See Clark Kerr, *Uses of the University*, 5th ed. (Harvard University Press, 2001). The essays forming the core of the book were first written in 1963.

7. The full quote is "Like every generation that preceded us we have been endowed with a weak messianic power, a power to which the past has a claim. That claim cannot be settled lightly." See Walter Benjamin, *Illuminations: Essays and Reflections*, trans. H. Zohn, ed. and intro H. Arendt (New York: Shocken, 1969), 254.

CHAPTER 8

A Career against the Grain:
An Academic Callings Interview

Dorothy Smith
Sociologist, University of Victoria
Interview Conducted by Janice Newson

Newson: Dorothy, your career has spanned a lot of changes in the Canadian university, from the expansion of higher education in the late 1950s and 1960s, to the funding cutbacks of the 1970s and 1980s, to the recent shift toward universities adopting an increasingly corporate and commercial orientation. How has your vision of the university fared under these changes?

Smith: I want to say first that some changes I see as very positive. These are changes that have come about from struggles we have made in the women's movement and struggles people have made against racism. I don't want to idealize the results of these struggles, but if I think back 30 years, the effects have been huge. They are major gains. That a group of academic women recently took the case of women's underrepresentation in the Canada Chairs program to the Supreme Court and won it is both evidence of, and a further step on the way to, making—indeed forcing—universities to adequately recognize what we've achieved as women in academe. The same is happening in the area of race and ethnic relations, although I think we still have quite a long way to go in that respect.

I have serious reservations about other things, though. I did my undergraduate work in Britain in the early to mid-1950s at the London School of Economics. Learning to think was the emphasis of our education, and we accomplished that through producing our own work. We wrote short papers, probably every week, which were discussed in a tutorial. Also, we had government grants to support us, though they were not enough to live on, in London anyway. But at the University of Victoria, where I am now working—and I assume this is true everywhere—I see undergraduate students accumulating serious loans, and taking too many courses in order to get through before their loan accumulates too much and working for 30 or 40 hours a week, so they are precluded from engaging intensely with the focus of their education—theoretical work or whatever it may be. And the more class size increases, the more faculty members move away from essay-type assignments to multiple-choice testing, so there is even less opportunity for them to produce their own work. I think that these changes are very detrimental.

Newson: Some people would argue that what you've just described is partly a funding thing, but also the result of making university more accessible—that we've moved away from a system that was elitist, which drew a privileged segment of students and could provide them this deep, rich education.

Smith: Well, I'll tell you, when I was at the University of British Columbia [in the mid-1960s] I was asked to start a new one-year anthropology and sociology course, which I designed around the principle of working with people's work because I realized that students were coming into the university who were not as well prepared as students had been in the system that I'd been through. This meant that I had to have rich teaching systems to start. I had to be able to work with students in small groups. I put in place a number of things—for example, that students would have the option, if they didn't get the grade they wanted, of taking their work to a teaching assistant, or to me, and we would work with them on how to improve their work so they could submit it again within a definite period of time. Everything was oriented around working with their work.

Undergraduate training today is quite inadequate, I feel, not because the students are inadequate—I think they're good. The federal government is allocating funds in ways that shift financing from undergraduate to graduate training, so problems increase in undergraduate education—larger classes, less faculty time for students, and so on. If you want to actually ensure that a broadly based intake of students is going to produce people who have a less adequate education, these changes accomplish exactly that. I find it distressing that the things from my undergraduate education that I valued so much—and that I learned and have used in my own thinking, my own work, and my own career—are not things to which universities presently attend.

Newson: The federal government has also been shoving a lot of research money into the university. The Canada Research Chairs program is an example, as is the Canadian Foundation for Innovation. By contrast, funding for undergrad education, which primarily comes from provinces, has not kept pace. It's where the cutbacks have been felt.

Smith: Yeah, and as I understand it now, universities have to match the funds that come from the federal government to support graduate education, so where does that come from? It partly comes from reducing a share of funds that would go to undergraduate education, and along with it, the workloads of the faculty have increased. I can see now how very busy I was in my main period at OISE. Even though we were teaching only graduate students at OISE, I had a heavy load of supervisions because I was one of the few feminists teaching, and I was involved in the kind of feminist politics taking place at the universities, but particularly at OISE.

Newson: This would be the 1980s, would it?

Smith: Yes, and [the] 1990s, but busy-ness now is more endemic because the teaching loads that people carry are much greater, not necessarily greater in number of courses, but greater in number of students. You can't work with people's work, which is very definitely a loss. It's almost like a slow tweaking transformation of the university into, well, I don't know what it is! I want to see the whole organization of teaching re-examined, particularly at the undergraduate level.

Newson: You mentioned a few minutes ago that as part of your busy-ness at OISE, you became intensively involved in feminist politics. How did this come about?

Smith: Well, I like to say that I became accidentally politically active. While I was at the University of British Columbia, two people had positions that were not renewed. It emerged that the then head of the department had misrepresented the faculty's decision in favour of their renewal to the dean. It was a miserable business, but basically what I did was to get the head to resign, and in the process, I learned about university politics the hard way. So when I got to OISE, I was like a mean internal politician, meaner than I had to be because

OISE was relatively democratically organized, which was very rare. My department had to come together early on after I arrived because we had to fight a number of battles with the administration, and somehow that set in place a co-operative basis on which the department functioned even though we had disagreements, many disagreements, from time to time. But at the same time, there was this kind of knowledge, if you like—we knew how to work through things so that we could act together as a unit.

I became involved, again accidentally, in the wider politics of OISE because I was on a key committee when funding cuts were being proposed to programs that were important to women. So in the struggle to preserve these programs, I was located where significant decisions were being made. That began my intensive involvement in feminist politics at OISE and also to some extent in the Federation of Women Teachers of Ontario.

Newson: You said that your department had developed a sense of solidarity to struggle with the OISE administration around a number of issues. What kind of issues were they?

Smith: The administration was struggling with us around a number of things. OISE was in this odd position because it had financing independent of the University of Toronto so we had a separate budget. And given that we had a much stronger representation of the faculty in the governing body of the institute, the power of the administration was really quite limited. I remember two recurring issues. One is that the role of students in the democratic process was being reduced. And the second is that the administration was attempting to introduce procedures for evaluating our productivity—I mean our work. But we had a strong faculty association that operated in many ways like a union, and we had a very good contract, which laid down the tenure and promotions procedures that took into account aspects of our work that were not included [in these productivity evaluations]. Nobody could see what these measures were about. They were meaningless.

Newson: That period that you're talking about, Dorothy, was the beginning of the expansion of administration that took place in most universities across the country from the mid-1970s and onward. Administrators began taking more initiative—adopting the approach that a number of people, including myself, have described as managerialism.

Smith: Yes, when Bernard Shapiro came in [the] 1980s, he tried to initiate more administrative interventions, but he was basically ousted by the left. You see, still within the constitution of OISE, you had this very strong, not just a democratic ideology, but also a democratic practice, so faculty had a lot of influence still and that then limited the extent to which even somebody like Shapiro could intervene even though he was probably in tune with the general shift that you're talking about. But I think a lot of the things going on elsewhere that were undermining the role of the faculty were not acceptable at OISE because we were not part of the University of Toronto and that's where they would have been happening. It wasn't until the institute was subdued—by, let's face it, Bob Rae's NDP government that insisted on amalgamating the institute with the U of T—that most of the things that I valued about OISE were aggressively undone. Before the merger, you didn't have total freedom to do anything you wanted, but on the other hand, you could always take for granted that things could be discussed because we still had in place a democratic process.

Newson: So once OISE was amalgamated, you were folded into those U of T processes.

Smith: Yes, that would be in the last three or four years of my time at OISE. So much was being changed and so much was a problem. How are you going to preserve some of the things that seemed to have worked so well in the institute and in our department, in the context of a whole set of practices which are very alien to what, even in its later stages, had been a very democratic place? When you're absorbed into the University of Toronto, your own practices are gone and you have to conform to a very different standard. You couldn't replicate in the University of Toronto the ways in which you had been able to represent the interests and concerns of faculty in the governance of OISE. You become relatively powerless.

Newson: So, Dorothy, in light of these concerns—the deterioration of undergraduate education and this loss of institutional democracy—what are your thoughts toward the generation of academics now starting their careers? How will they be able to address issues like those you have addressed? They're coming into a university that is being, or has already been, transformed by some of the processes we're talking about. Do you have thoughts of how you would go about it?

Smith: One thing I see is that the students I am teaching at the University of Victoria find it fascinating to be engaged with social justice issues. They are asking, "How can we take these things up? What's going wrong with a society for it to have these problems?"

The problem is, of course, in getting research funds to support the work of graduate students. The research that I'm doing at present at the University of Guelph—Rural Women Making Change—is funded through a new Social Science and Humanities Research Council program called the Community–University Research Alliance, CURA. This kind of program has a lot of possibilities if you know how to work with it. Community organizations actually value what you do. Disciplines like sociology normally have a hard time achieving the kind of accountability to the public that the natural sciences can achieve, where it is easier to demonstrate the value of your research. CURA projects can provide us with some of that.

Newson: There's a way in which you've always taught against what is current and conventional and you've survived and thrived. I wonder if you think that that is a viable route for young academics today?

Smith: For me what really made the difference was the women's movement and being part of it. In a way I had an accidental career because it never occurred to me that the kind of sociology that I've developed out of what I learned in the women's movement was going to become interesting to others.

Newson: Yes, your work is part of the tradition now.

Smith: I never anticipated it, but I'm really happy about it because it's really great when people find the work you do interesting and useful. One thing that the women's movement taught me was that writing out of your research and thinking allowed you to use the academic publication milieu to talk to

people and to reach people that you wanted to be in touch with. It gave me a completely different understanding of what academic publishing could be, so I try to give graduate students I'm working with some experience of doing interesting research and translating it into a paper, potentially a publication. I try to get them to see that those things are within their reach.

Newson: It's interesting that you talk about the role of the women's movement in shaping your career and you also said that you had [an] accidental career. It's almost like you were a bit of … the image that I have in mind is of a surfer—you caught a wave.

Smith: That's a good metaphor.

Newson: And that wave propelled you, propelled what mattered to you forward in a way that you never would have imagined.

Smith: But it was a bit more dialogic than being on a wave, I think.

Newson: Okay, but being on a wave is a bit dialogic. You don't just stay up there. I mean, there's a bit of tricky footwork to that, as I understand it. And there is choosing the right wave and also keeping the wave going, so to speak.

Smith: Okay, all right.

Newson: But did you mean that the times had a lot to do with what worked for you?

Smith: Well, one of the things that gets left out of this picture is that I'm really obsessive about doing this kind of work. From early on, I found sociology fascinating. I would have gone on doing it no matter what—it wouldn't have been the same, but it would have been something like it is.

What the women's movement did was to create a place where the kind of work I was doing belonged. Outside of the dialogue within the women's movement, it perhaps never could have belonged or couldn't have developed the way it did, but also it meant that I had a career instead of just a job. For example, I think of the first book I produced. Evelyn Fox Keller was associated in some way with Northeastern University Press and was trying to develop a line of feminist publications. She asked me to put my work together, and so I did. I had never even thought of doing the book, but then, because of its character, women were interested in it. I would never have made a mark or even have been published and sociologists would never have taken it up if it hadn't been for the women's movement. Feminism has made a lot of headway in sociology, not so much in other areas, but in sociology, I think in many ways it's been transformative.

Newson: Before we started the interview, you made a comment about the women's movement not being a salient movement now.

Smith: No, I don't think it is.

Newson: Do you see it recycling—not recycling, but being reinvented perhaps?

Smith: Well, I think it's a double thing. On the one hand, nowadays women's issues can be raised in a much more straightforward way—around sexual harassment and those kinds of issues. But on the other hand, the whole issue of child care and other issues don't get taken up in a way they should be. Domestic abuse is another, but at least it's in the newspaper. At least it's in the Criminal Code. Overall, I don't see the same general level of consciousness now, but maybe what's been achieved is such that women don't need it. Maybe they're not going to run into problems until the next stage of their lives—if they get married, if they have kids....

Newson: I feel that too with the students that I teach. Whether they will be able, as women, to get into law school or do this or that is not a concern because they take it for granted that they will. But interestingly, you can be in a sociology class, largely composed of young women, addressing certain issues, and suddenly they will be expressing intensely their angst and anger toward the men that they know. They don't back off from it. There is no fear about speaking it.

Smith: You see I think that's a kind of big breakthrough. Remember how we had no language, no way of talking about it? We didn't even feel that we could and should. This transformation, at least in Canada, is very real. I'm not sure how general it is. But here I think the movement is strong in that way, so much that we don't even realize what we have changed.

Newson: Some people realize it because they have a history of it, but our 20-year-olds in the classroom don't have that history.

Smith: No and why should they? Thank goodness they don't have to go through it, but it was very exciting to go through. [laughing]

Newson: Yes!

Smith: We had a lot of fun and we had a lot of rage and anger.

CHAPTER 9

Living through Revolutionary and Reactionary Times— in the Wrong Order

Roberta Hamilton

Sociologist, Queen's University

My first response to provide a calling card came quickly, and went like this: My generation of feminists and anti-racist scholars had presented themselves as new claimants seeking access to the same things that those already ensconced were enjoying: high-quality and critical education, good libraries, time for research, and opportunities to engage with students eager to learn. How ironic, then, that in the past two decades, budgetary cuts and the imperative to attract funding (especially corporate funding) have quickly eroded the very university to which we sought entry.

This familiar tale of woeful nostalgia, curiously similar to all such stories about a golden, or at least a better, past does resonate. My own university career would never pass muster now. One must have funding, lots of funding, to do the things that I did and didn't do. I recall my mentor's footnote in his first paper challenging Philippe Garigue's interpretation of Quebec society. Hubert Guindon wrote in his rueful style that "Professor Garigue does not conceive of himself as a soldier in the army of science but rather as a field general."[1] Today this would hardly stand as criticism, but rather as appropriate aspiration. Also, I remember Peter Pineo's joyfully satiric comment as he passed through the lab where I worked as a research assistant following my B.A. in 1964: "There's money in poverty!" And certainly there was, for a time. But money follows political will. There's lots of money in obesity now, and only those of us who are genetically skinny but not anorexic escape approbation by the army of researchers documenting the physical consequences and social costs of what used to be called, rather affectionately, chubbiness. The relationship between poverty and obesity—let alone obesity, corporate profits, and addiction—remains invisible in this research, which shows how knowledge, contrary to the dominant rhetoric, is not cumulative but constrained by the politically charged disciplinary blinkers that generate gargantuan grants.

Pineo might also have said, around the same time, that there was money for higher education. Indeed, we thought that university education would soon be free, a reasonable enough prediction in the climate of the times. How could we have suspected that, on the contrary, parents of primary and secondary students would soon become fundraisers, while school fees disguised as money for extras would become the order of the new day?

Resisting these developments—all of which are part and parcel of neo-liberalism's version of globalization—remains crucial, and invoking some golden yesteryear may be helpful in this endeavour. We need to know how things have been—or could be—better, but we need to situate the university within the broader political, social, and cultural environment. The "good things" about universities in the past were nestled in institutions that enjoyed considerable autonomy because they were poorly funded, and few cared what went on within them. Universities accepted and perpetuated the class, gendered, and racialized exclusions of the broader society, but were seldom, if ever, taken to account for doing so. Figuring out how to reinvent scholarly and pedagogical autonomy in universities today requires imagination and political will, and it will never look just as it did 50 years ago.

In Canada, stoking money into universities and encouraging the scions of all social classes to attend lasted only a few years. In 1964, when John Porter published *The Vertical Mosaic*, he decried the elitism of Canadian universities: In 1961 only 8 percent of those between 20 and 24 attended university (11.3 percent men, 4.6 percent women),[2] and those were largely from the middle class. At this time, he argued that developing a meritocracy where the brightest children from all social classes could develop their talents might ameliorate the entrenched social inequalities that shaped Canadian society. While he lost faith in this vision as he acquired a more jaundiced view of Canadian power elites and their unwillingness to open their ranks, governments did respond to popular demands for more and bigger universities. Still, when I attended Carleton in 1960, my parents paid the fees through five $85 instalments and found it a hard slog. Fees relative to income never dropped lower than this.

But, in retrospect, the next few years were the golden ones. At Glebe Collegiate Institute, a mainly middle-class high school in Ottawa, girls who did well had university on their radar screens, and all of my friends went on. While no one suggested to us that we were off to find husbands, during the same time, and long afterwards, Queen's freshettes found a ribbon on their candle at the welcoming ceremony, the colours representing the faculty from which their future husbands would be drawn. At Carleton the introductory classes were large, but they came with tutorials led by the professoriate or senior undergraduates. We loved university. We worked hard. Fell in and out and into love. My two best friends were beautiful, and I spent many an hour with one young man or another seeking insight into how to be a successful suitor to one or the other (and, in one case, to both of them, sequentially). There were four beauty pageants a year, and the contestants' pictures wallpapered the campus. Lord knows what was in our heads, but looking back, we were being groomed for love and marriage, not graduate school or professional life.

All the girls from my high school who went to university registered in arts or physical education except for Cathie Macdonald. Just before classes started in September, her father brought home an architect friend for dinner, and by the end of the meal, he had convinced her to abandon her friends and go into architecture at the University of Toronto. Clearly her father, with his girls-only family, decided to channel his vicarious ambitions into his truly brilliant eldest daughter. (Indeed, research on this subject reveals that fathers without sons shifted their ambitions toward their daughters, and this helps explain why some girls broke with the dominant trajectory.)

Only in the mid-1960s did the Canadian state begin to fund social science research. But starting in the United States, and escalating with the war in Vietnam, university students decried the hand-in-glove relationship between the military-industrial complex and the academy. Many Canadian university students also became serious critics of all aspects of universities—the courses, the canon, the research, even the age of the professors since so few had the stamina to remain under 30. Graduating in 1963, I missed all this, though my brother, two years younger but possessing a generational difference in perspective, was in the thick of it.

My career as an academic rebel came later. As the mother of three young children, I suffered from the problem with no name, though I never read Friedan's book.[3] Subsequently, I was knocked off my rocker by feminist consciousness-raising, and I returned to university armed with the desire to understand women's subordination. As it turned out, there were thousands of us: Feminist ideas landed seemingly indiscriminately like manna from heaven, and the university became yet another site for the women's liberation movement. In the mid-1980s, sociologist Lorna Marsden told me that someone should write the story of the university as a deeply patriarchal institution and that someone was me. Such memories prevent the evocation of some golden age for universities.

In 1983, while being interviewed for a position at Queen's University, Marie Surridge, a member of the appointments committee and the head of the French Department, took me to lunch. Later I discovered that she had charged herself with discovering what I had been doing between 1963 and 1971 and between 1975 and 1979, years in which there were no entries on my c.v. I had not dared put on my application that I had three children, but things were changing: She intended to argue that having children served as legitimate reason to put academic progress on hold and, in my case, she did so successfully. Her intervention changed my life, but this small event was part of a seismic change: Women could henceforth be mothers and academics, though the unintended consequences of the double day have only intensified with the university's rapacious demand that we all become fundraisers. At that same lunch, Marie looked up and pointed across the floor: "See that group of men over there? They run Queen's University and there isn't a woman near to joining them." Eventually there were: The powers that be looked for safe women—i.e., those without feminist inclinations—and sometimes they chose correctly, other times not. But my own administrative career at Queen's was certainly curtailed: I was not to be trusted and, let's face it, they were right.

Indeed, only (some) White men could be trusted. In 1969, four Black students at Sir George Williams charged a biology professor with racism and the university administrators discovered the price of their deep sense of White entitlement that led them to pay no heed. A computer was wrecked and many lives derailed as the court proceedings indicted and jailed many of the protestors. Their fate garnered much support from the Black community in Montreal. A friend's mother recently told me when I interviewed her as part of my research project on the social history of Montreal's Black community that every day after her work cleaning houses, she went to the courthouse with food that she had cooked for the demonstrators.

I have related these stories to illustrate the truism that universities follow, but don't lead. Far from being protected islands where criticism proceeds vigorously, they are informed and shaped by the dominant societal relationships of social inequality and political imperatives. But—and this is key—those political imperatives include the resistance movements that people bring with them into the academy. As a feminist and anti-racist, my best times have been in struggle with others, but as we now know, there is no linear path. As I told an audience a few years back, I had lived through revolutionary and reactionary times; it was just too bad that they hadn't come in reverse order. Still the university does provide a privileged enclave for struggle—no privileges for students, really, except for those who have cleverly selected affluent parents, but certainly privileged for those who attain tenure if and when they care to use it in that way.

Historically, universities have been elitist enclaves: The 1960s constituted an aberration. Since then they have been caught in a downward spiral: declining state support with increasing tuition to compensate. Higher tuition prevents access, real and psychological, as only those who don't really need loans are comfortable incurring large debts. Making the case for higher taxes to support universities smacks of bad faith when so many people cannot even imagine sending their sons and daughters, especially to professional schools, with their stratospheric fees. Very few academics join student protest about fees. After all, we are the ones who made it, and we're overworked—though not, I would argue for the most part, underpaid, but how long will that last?

High tuition, of course, is not the only means for making up the shortfall. Universities have issued an open invitation, nay a plea, for corporate funding for everything, and this process seems irreversible. But the corporate agenda shapes state funding as well, and researchers find themselves herded more than ever into corrals constructed by others. This suits some, maybe most. My experience at university leads me to urge those who find that this shoe does not fit to struggle collectively and individually to maintain and create spaces for the research and teaching that they really value. Tenure does protect; do not go gently into that dark night!

But tenure itself may be very hard to save. For those decades when most (male) Canadians could count on job security, tenure did not appear truly anomalous. To those who can be fired, laid off, downsized with the stroke of a pen, tenure today means unearned privilege. Perhaps by supporting the struggles of others for job security and decent conditions, the professoriate can resist the move to abolish tenure without appearing merely self-interested.

My personal stance toward tenure and promotion emerged from a critical stance toward universities and their strident insistence on one career path over all others: bring in lots of money and publish many articles in journals deemed excellent. In response, when sitting on tenure and promotion committees, I have tried to make the best case possible for each candidate, including colleagues who give more to teaching or community service than research or who publish in venues deemed to be political rather than scholarly. This strategy requires careful reading of files, including publications, and sometimes, because individuals are not easily boxed, creativity and moral suasion. Also, colleagues en route to tenure sometimes find that their lives—babies, sickness, writer's block—get in the way, and faculty unions as well as those on personnel committees need to fight for them. I am proud of my record here (a record kept only by me in my head). Guindon had warned me: Give your loyalty only to individuals—institutions can't and won't reciprocate. When a dean came calling to discuss the possibility of my being an associate dean, he asked me how I would approach tenure and promotion decisions and I confirmed his suspicion that I was not in lockstep with the values of the university. He still offered me the position, but I was never asked to be dean, though once I was urged by the principal to let my name stand. I never discovered what torpedoed my appointment and I was disappointed not to have had the chance to occupy this position of academic leadership. It would have given me an opportunity to work from the inside for things that many of us cared about. But by my own lights, I have actually been intensely loyal to Queen's, to which I owe much. My loyalty is perhaps to the imagined institution that I have partially evoked in this article.

Although highly funded research has become the *sine qua non* of academic life, one must remember that most state funding for universities comes because we teach students. The lament that teaching doesn't count is only partly true. Students go out and become taxpayers and citizens. Aside from being the right thing to do, treating them properly matters a lot to the future of universities. Certainly all my students have not been happy with me: For some, my lecturing style is too quirky, and lectures don't come in five easy pieces. But one on one in my office, I am guided by the view that students are whole people, and as I am fond of saying to them when they do poorly because they've been jilted, sick, mourning, or chronically depressed: Life does get in the way and that's all right. I have often, with a student's permission, called student counselling on the spot to ensure they don't get short shrift by an overtaxed service. At times, I have invited a student to my office several times for my own rendition of therapy—not often, I'm careful—but those are the students who are most grateful, and perhaps become the most open to seeing the world sociologically. Passion for a subject and a teacher are more intertwined than the pushers of big classes and Internet learning would admit.

Universities are bound to continue to be sites of resistance, but who will resist, what they will resist, and their success in resisting are not predictable. Maintaining and creating spaces for new claimants to enter for critical pedagogical practices, for collegial social relationships, and for the research that incites passion and commitment—all this can be chosen. But—and I underline this point—through all this, academic rebels should be sure to find ways to meet the shifting criteria for tenure and promotion. Deprive administrators of the opportunity to deny you or others. Little will be gained if you swim against the tide and get sent out to sea. Be creative and, when possible, collective in your resistance. For those of us who love to read, write, research, and teach, the academic life offers far more than its competitors, but as with all lives, the meaning of it all is not just there for the asking. Perhaps the corporate pendulum has swung as far as it's going to, but what comes next will in part depend on those who choose the academic life and how they choose to live it.

Notes

1. Hubert Guindon, "The Social Evolution of Quebec Reconsidered," *Canadian Journal of Economics and Political Science/Revue canadienne d'Economique et de Science politique* 26, no. 4 (1960): 539, note 28.
2. John Porter, *The Vertical Mosaic* (Toronto: University of Toronto Press, 1965), 178.
3. Betty Friedan, *The Feminine Mystique* (New York: Norton, 1963).

CHAPTER 10

Force without Reason[1]

GORDON SHRIMPTON
Classicist, University of Victoria

"The Prime Minister was emphatic," President McCready of the Canadian Association of University Teachers reported to a meeting of the association on June 12, 1957 in Ottawa, "... even, a critic might say, long-winded on this point [of the need to increase university faculty salaries], and all who entered the discussion in the Committee of Supply echoed his thought in some degree."[2] As if to show its sincerity, Parliament nearly doubled its financial support for higher education. Background to this generous parliamentary mood is found in the *Gordon Commission Report on Canada's Economic Prospects*, published just the year before (1956) and still fresh in the public memory.[3]

That was 50 years ago. We do not hear unequivocal endorsements of the public funding of higher education coming from Ottawa today, and we certainly do not hear politicians encouraging universities to improve faculty salaries. In fact, scarcely 26 years later in 1983, British Columbia politicians were mounting assaults on the university system on a scale that no one would have believed possible in 1957. This essay recalls some of those events. It has another purpose, however, which is to set the ferocity of the Social Credit attack in the context of the long history of the university itself. Social Credit was a political movement that lasted little more than a decade after its senseless attack on the universities and social programs of B.C. in the early 1980s. Our universities, however, continue to offer rationality and stability to a world that all too often loses its senses.

The university known to us today as a centre for industrial-oriented research (among other things) has existed for hardly more than a century, but if we think of the academy—a group of individuals who come together to learn and debate—the university's roots go back to the 5th and 4th centuries BCE. Then, the academy was a grove outside of Athens where Plato's followers met to study mathematics and debate philosophical questions.

In the 3rd century in Alexandria on the Nile delta in Egypt, the ruling Ptolemies established a library and what they called a Mouseion. The library became the ancient world's "Library of Congress" and the Mouseion became the first centre for research in the ancient world, perhaps in all of history. Its principle interest was in medical and biological research. In spite of some remarkable technological inventions, research in Alexandria generally avoided the technical and, as a consequence, never triggered an industrial revolution. The Romans bought books avidly from Greek collections like that of Alexandria and systemized the curriculum of higher education to include physics, ethics, and dialectic.[4] When the Roman Empire collapsed, the barbarian invaders sacked farms and cities, but showed little interest in the remote monasteries founded by Christians fleeing the turmoil. The scriptures and other great writings survived the invasions thanks to the dedication of the monks.

Charlemagne set about restoring the Roman Empire under the auspices of Christianity in the 8th century CE. One of the first things he did was address the problem of political and cultural cohesion among his subjects. Alcuin, in effect his minister of culture, introduced a simplified script that everyone could read easily. He also established the curriculum for higher education to include the seven liberal arts: grammar, rhetoric, dialectic, arithmetic, music, geometry, and astronomy. We might wonder what happened to law and theology. Clearly the expectation was that dialectic, rhetoric, and the other arts would make people better lawyers and theologians. Through Alcuin's efforts and the policies of Charlemagne, the Church became the keeper and promoter of higher education in the Middle Ages. Most cathedral cities, as a consequence, became university towns. Universities were supported from the tithes collected by the Church and from the tuition paid by the students. Moderns who remember the Inquisition and the repression of the works of Galileo and others may be alarmed at these developments. In fact, the Church generally adopted a policy of non-intervention in the emerging universities.

The idea that universities should be centres of advanced research is scarcely more than a century old. During the 17th and 18th centuries, research directed solely by the investigators and driven by curiosity was conducted privately in the homes of the wealthy. Its results would make possible the largest single expansion of the European economy in all of its history, the Industrial Revolution.

In the 19th century, Cardinal Newman articulated an idea of the university that begins to look remarkably modern—a community of scholars engaged in free inquiry. There would be no interference from the Church: Newman believed that the truths of science, being subject to change and revision, would ultimately harmonize with revealed truth as espoused by the Church.[5]

Institutions of higher education that developed in the 20th century became more than sources of cultural stability, however. They became homes for advanced research, acquiring large appetites for money. And the keepers of the main source of that money, the public purse, naturally wanted to know what they were going to get for their investment. The Gordon Commission, issued in 1956, was satisfied that there would be a bonanza of wealth, but the dilemma of universities now became how to assure governments that their money was being well spent while, at the same time, insisting that the kind of research that promised the best results would have to be self-directed by the researcher and curiosity-driven. In other words, it would be best for the funding agency to accept that it had no business specifying what the focus of research should be.

In 1983, the year I became president of the Confederation of University Faculty Associations of British Columbia (CUFA/BC), the Social Credit government, under Bill Bennett, announced its public sector restraint program. The government wanted to rein in public spending by slashing the budgets of many social programs, if not cancelling them altogether, and by removing tenure from the public sector to make it possible for management to expel "deadwood" from the public payroll. The main target of the Socreds was the civil service, which, according to the initial version of the legislation, was to be reduced by an indiscriminate 25 percent, but the entire public payroll was also in their sights. Universities were threatened with funding cuts, and the now defunct Universities Council of British Columbia (UCBC) applied pressure on them to get rid of faculty. As President Petch of the University of Victoria reported to me, they wanted "Blood on the floor."[6]

The minister for universities was the Right Honourable Dr. Patrick McGeer. I remember sitting in his office and listening in disbelief as he droned on about how far short universities had fallen from the dreams of prosperity that had been touted for them. If universities had helped to generate the prosperity envisioned in the 1950s, Dr. McGeer could not see it. He offered no proof that universities had failed, but the burden of proof lay with us. Universities had been founded and encouraged to grow, and Canada had indeed prospered, but how does one demonstrate to a skeptic that there is a connection between the two developments?

To be sure, the Socreds had accepted the need to increase university capacity over the previous 20 years. In 1963 the MacDonald report on higher education recommended the founding of a second university in the Lower Mainland (and third in the province after Victoria), Simon Fraser, which opened its doors in 1965, with Dr. Gordon Shrum as chancellor. Simon Fraser was supposed to have been the flagship for the Socred fleet of universities. Its library to this day is named the W.A.C. Bennett Library, and the main approach still bears the name of the colourful minister of highways under W.A.C. Bennett, (Flying) Phil Gaglardi.

In 1971, the CAUT censured Simon Fraser University over its perceived reluctance to agree to a normally accepted procedure for granting tenure to its faculty. Most of us suspected that its resistance to tenure was strongly backed by the premier of the province. The administration of Simon Fraser soon capitulated to the demands for faculty tenure, however, and, as if to rub salt in Bennett's wounds, Dave Barrett, of the New Democratic Party (NDP), swept the Socreds from power in 1972.

I became involved in my faculty association at this time, heedless of the possible consequences. I watched with interest in December 1975 as Dave Barrett's compulsive blunder handed an election to W.A.C. Bennett's son, Bill. In the first few years of Bill's premiership, the province enjoyed an enormous budgetary surplus, but I remember sitting in the meeting room of UCBC and listening to representatives of the treasury board telling us that the surplus was predicted to dwindle and become a deficit in a few years. We did not know what to believe, so we just went about our business as if nothing had happened. As it turned out, they were right.[7]

Defending universities was becoming increasingly difficult. As predicted by the Gordon Commission, universities had expanded considerably through the 1960s. By the early 1970s, however, the expansion came to an abrupt halt. Graduate schools had geared up to meet 1960s level demands for faculty, but now that they were in full swing, the need for new faculty simply evaporated. The 1970s became the decade of the overeducated parking lot attendant. The media had a field day and politicians became nervous. What was the good of a university education if it did not lead to fulfilling employment? Why spend all that money on universities?[8]

Through the 1970s many faculty associations elsewhere in Canada had organized as unions and were bargaining collective agreements that were the envy of British Columbia faculty. UBC faculty had organized a union drive only to be bought off by the board of governors, who offered the association an agreement to bargain outside the Labour Code of the province, a framework agreement as it was called. In 1977 my faculty association at the University of Victoria decided to try the same approach to obtain collective bargaining, but Dr. McGeer stepped in to bring an abrupt end to the process. He slipped an amendment into the University Act to the effect that the Labour Code of the province did not apply to the relationship between faculty and their university employers. Without access to the Labour Code, our threat of possible union certification was taken from us and our association was powerless to improve its bargaining position. To many of us, Dr. McGeer's move showed a contempt for due process that did nothing to sweeten the relationship between faculty and the Socred government.

When the Bill Bennett Socreds won a new mandate in May 1983 and planned to bring down a budget in July, few people in the province could have anticipated what was in store for us. The budget that was unveiled on July 7 was more than just a budget. Until 1983 there had been something vaguely comical about B.C. politics. Not much of it made sense, and one got the impression that making sense was rarely a requirement. The restraint package contained in the budget continued that tradition in one respect: It made little sense, at least in its extremism, but there was nothing even remotely funny about it. To name only some of its measures, the legislative package weakened, if not gutted, important human rights legislation. It stripped public sector unions of bargaining rights and the civil service of job security, the budget planned for an (indiscriminate) 25 percent reduction in the public sector payroll, and legislation permitted dismissal without cause and eliminated all rent controls.

The reaction was immediate. From the far right, Michael Walker, of the Fraser Institute, lavished effusive praise on the government in guest editorials published in many newspapers, predicting a quick return to normalcy once people had been given time to recover. From the left and centre a coalition was formed called Operation Solidarity, organized to bring the government to its senses or to its knees. I was the president elect of CUFA/BC and retiring president of the Victoria Faculty Association at the time. I quickly invited myself down to the NDP research headquarters in a dingy part of the basement in the legislative buildings. They had already prepared an itemized list of the key items with a brief synopsis of the implications of each component of the package. I took this list and immediately circulated it in a newsletter to the faculty.

One thing was clear to all of us: At stake were the independence of universities and the freedom of speech and inquiry that guaranteed the integrity of our research. Especially if the government was in a bullying mood, we needed to safeguard our members from intimidation, from extremist pressures to toe anyone's line in the pursuit of their research. We could not allow anyone to be fired except for cause. We had to emerge from this struggle with academic freedom and tenure, its safeguard, intact. It was not clear whether the Socreds meant to abolish tenure only in the civil service or in the public sector generally. We were reluctant to ask for fear that we would provoke a firestorm that we could not control. The government actions and statements suggested that the civil service was their primary concern, but in press conferences the premier made declarations suggesting that he took the broader view.

Our position was not strong. Without access to the Labour Code we had no protection if we withdrew services. Even if our membership were angry enough to walk out, we would probably have to advise them against doing so. This left us with a fine line to walk. To us, the weapons of faculty were our ability to marshal facts and show in reasoned statements how far the government was from behaving with good sense, but since good sense had long since gone out the window, we were unsure how far the sweet voice of reason would take us. Undeterred, we called press conferences and sent letters to newspapers explaining tenure and criticizing the extremism that threatened to tear the province apart. Strong support came from the Canadian Association of University Teachers (CAUT), which organized a letter-writing campaign in which faculty from all over the world warned the Socreds of the folly of abolishing tenure—that it would destroy the reputation of B.C. universities as high-quality institutions.

 In retrospect, it looks as if the Socreds had misread the mood of university management. They must have expected that our administrations would thank them for the opportunity to get rid of deadwood and clean up the province's institutions of higher learning. No one did, and as long as no one was being fired, the government's legislation was meaningless. Tenure was intact as long as faculty were not being directly intimidated or dismissed by our administrations.[9]

None of us had been prepared for the onslaught of the restraint program, coming on us as suddenly as it did. From this time CUFA/BC turned to the strengths that faculty possess: the ability to dig out, digest, and report the facts effectively. We decided that we needed to know what the public thought of universities and the issues over which we had fought. At considerable expense and with help from CAUT, we generated professionally a set of questions to be used in a public opinion poll throughout the Lower Mainland and, subsequently, the entire province. The results were more positive for our cause than we could have dreamed and the old voices of opposition to universities were silenced.

Unfortunately, new ones were emerging as we enjoyed our short-lived success. The Bennett Socreds held onto office until 1986 when Bill Bennett's retirement prompted a leadership convention. The surprise winner was William Vander Zalm. He seemed to promise a distancing of the party from the confrontational approach of the restraint program. As a consequence, he won both the leadership and the subsequent provincial election. He remained premier until 1991, essentially the dominant spirit in the early period of high interest rates.

Interest rates presented faculty with a new set of problems. According to figures from the finance ministry, the federal government's debt peaked in 1996–1997 at $583.2 billion (not quite the $600 billion and counting that was repeatedly reported in various news media).[10] In the midst of the hysteria, few public commentators made an effort to put the debt into perspective. The country's ability to generate wealth and service debt is measured by its gross domestic product (GDP). At the peak of the crisis in 1996–1997, the finance ministry reported that the ratio of debt to GDP was 70.7 percent. By 2001 not only had the debt shrunk by nearly $40 billion, but the GDP had risen so that the ratio was now down to a very manageable $51.8 billion. Since that time it has continued to fall.

Canada's debt and deficit problems were variously explained through homey stories in the popular media in terms of costly social programs and foreign borrowing.[11] The perceived problem created such panic that politicians all chorused the need to lower support for higher education and health care. "Of course we believe in those things, but those interest rates! There just is no money. We cannot justify more borrowing given the staggering national debt."[12]

The homey stories never included one obvious option that any householder would at least consider when faced with soaring costs: Find a better-paying job. The government could, of course, increase taxes, but that was seen as counterproductive and perhaps it would have been, causing the economy to shrink when it needed to grow. But longer-term thinking should at least have suggested a strategy aimed at stimulating an increase in the GDP. As the GDP goes up, the seriousness of the debt goes down because the debt falls into the manageable area expressed as a percentage of GDP. If it is true that universities help to generate wealth, then supporting them should have been a key part of any debt management strategy.[13]

What tends to happen in politics is that vision disappears when it is needed the most. Universities have a history in the Western world that is older than most of our major religions. Though universities help to promote political, cultural, and economic stability—even prosperity—they are all too easily attacked in the panic of a perceived crisis. In the case of the so-called debt crisis, for example, to me the key question was: In the event of such a crisis, what sort of people do we want Canadians to be? Who will face the crisis with the greatest resourcefulness, and who will have the best chance of finding a way out? Would we rather have a population in questionable health and undereducated, or a robust populace, educated, with a good understanding of the situation and full of ideas with which to manage it?

Notes

1. The title is based on a rough translation of a remark made by the Roman poet Horace: *vis consili expers molle ruit sua* ("Force without reason collapses under its own weight"). It refers to power politics in the 5th century BCE, but I found it enlightening in 1983 when the universities in British Columbia challenged the restraint program of the newly elected Socred government.
2. Canadian Association of University Teachers, "Minutes of Meeting, June 12, 1957," Canadian Association of University Teachers Archives, Ottawa, Canada.
3. The Gordon Commission was struck by the Liberal government of Prime Minister Louis St. Laurent in 1955. It issued its report in 1956. Its main concern was with foreign control of Canadian assets.
4. Cicero, *Tusculan Disputations*, trans. J.E. King (Cambridge: Harvard University Press), 5.24.

5. In general, see Richard Tarnas, *The Passion of the Western Mind: Understanding the Ideas That Have Shaped Our World View* (New York: Ballantine Books, 1991). On Boyle, see Steven Shapin and Simon Schaffer, *Leviathan and the Air Pump: Hobbes, Boyle, and the Experimental Life* (Princeton: Princeton University Press, 1985). On experimentation and the gentry, see David Bodanis, *E=mc2* (Toronto: Random House, Canada, 2000), 55–69.

6. Warren Magnussen et al., *The New Reality: The Politics of Restraint in British Columbia* (Vancouver: New Star Books, 1984).

7. But not completely. It was a half-truth that the province was headed for a serious deficit. Gideon Rosenbluth and William Shworm, "The Illusion of the Provincial Debt," in Warren Magnussen et al., *The New Reality* (Vancouver: New Star Books, 1984), 56–74, show that the provincial economy had always been cyclical. They predicted, accurately, that the economy would recover and the deficit would revert to a surplus as it had always done before.

8. Gordon Shrimpton, "The Crisis in Canadian Universities," in *The Political Economy of Canadian Schooling*, ed. Terry Wotherspoon (Toronto: Methuen, 1987), 185–210.

9. In the legislature, vicious legislation backed by outrageous behaviour on the part of the Socreds continued well into 1984. See Jeremy Wilson, "The Legislature under Siege," in Warren Magnussen et al., *The New Reality* (Vancouver: New Star Books, 1984), 114–130.

10. High interest rates made it impossible for governments to meet all debt servicing costs in a given year. As a result, the shortfall added to the national debt. See Department of Finance, Canada, "Canada's Debt Challenge, Update 1997," www.fin.gc.ca/update97/factDEBT-E.html.

11. A study published in 1995 by the Australian Parliamentary Research Service may shed some light on the interest problem of the 1990s with regard to foreign borrowing. In 1984, Canada's net foreign debt, expressed as a percentage of GDP, was 24.8. In 1993 it had risen to 44.4. The nearly 20 percent increase in less than 10 years clearly left Canadian international borrowers exposed to outside pressure in the event of a decline in the value of the dollar, which did in fact occur. Of this 44.4 percent, 23.4 percent was "official," which means government borrowing. Clearly, the foreign debt problem lay at the door of NGOs such as major corporations and chartered banks: Tony Kryger, *Research Note, November 10–2 March 1995* (Parliamentary Research Service, Australia, ISSN 1323-5664) (accessed online at http://202.14.81.34/Library/pubs/rn.1194-95/95rn10.pdf).

12. The debate over spending and social programs came to a head in Canada with Linda McQuaig's *Shooting the Hippo: Death by Deficit and Other Canadian Myths* (Toronto: Penguin Books, 1995). The review by Anthony Wilson-Smith in *Maclean's* (April 10, 1995 [accessed online at http://www.thecanadianencyclopedia.com/index.cfm?PgNm=TCE&params=M1ARTM0010336]) is revealing. Wilson-Smith dismisses McQuaig's argument as "wallowing in nostalgia." Curiously, Wilson-Smith buys without criticism the right-wing line that Canada's debt problem was the result of overspending. He does not consider the effect of inordinately high interest rates, which, arguably, were the real cause of the problem.

13. See Stephen G. Peitchinis, "Government Spending and the Budget Deficit," *Journal of Business Ethics* 9 (1990): 591–594. While it remains difficult to show by simple number crunching that universities help to generate wealth, there is abundant, incontrovertible evidence that higher education improves employability and earning power for Canadians. See the StatsCan report: www12.statcan.ca/english/census01/products/analytic/companion/earn/canada.cfm.

CHAPTER 11

Two Hours Left
and Nothing to Say

BRUCE CURTIS
Sociologist, Carleton University

Recently a colleague, now at retirement age, was asked by his second-year and third-year sociology students if there was much homework in a course he was teaching. The question startled him. It confirmed a change in students' understanding of the relationship between university course work and scholarship. Over his university career and mine, it seems that direct personal engagement with the substance of texts as powerful objects in their own right has declined, in many courses, in many disciplines. It has declined both as a practice of students and as an expectation of their teachers and university administrators.

The notions that university education is an intellectual apprenticeship entailing substantive mastery of texts in scholarly traditions, and that texts are sources of insight, enlightenment, and power face stiff competition from increasing numbers of students who see texts as things to be gotten through on the path to earning a credential; from administrators concerned with flow-through rates and revenue streams; and from faculty delivering prepackaged instruction to large classes.

For the students, good courses have few texts or texts that can be gotten through quickly, leaving time for more enjoyable pursuits, or for the paid work in which most students must engage to pay the high cost of university education. Administrators now can less afford to have students who cannot master texts fail or drop out. For teachers facing increasingly large classes, careful scrutiny of texts is a ticket to exhaustion, low teaching scores, and fewer of the publications valued for career advancement.

Over the last several years, I have begun to find fourth-year undergraduate majors committing the academic offence of plagiarism in entirely good faith. They have come to see texts as things to be reproduced and the skill of research as that of locating relevant texts on some subject or issue, then assembling and editing them to satisfy a course requirement. Many universities have developed sophisticated techniques for detecting plagiarism. Not only are these techniques imperfect but, more importantly, they do not address the underlying causes of the phenomenon. While the Internet certainly makes it technically easy for students to reproduce a huge variety of texts, a change in the university has occurred in the relation between student and text.

Policing plagiarism effectively is based on the idea that failing to acknowledge the sources of texts is an intellectual property crime, yet the underlying issue is not the theft of texts—after all, they circulate freely. Nor is it the misrepresentation of authorship—assembling, editing, and reproducing can be seen as authoring. Rather it is the failure or refusal to *recognize* texts. Recognize in the technical sense of re-cognizing, of thinking through again, of making the text one's own through immersion in it and critical mastery of it. Recognition is a form of appropriation, but it is not theft. It is participation in scholarly culture. It is also not homework. It is, potentially, life work. Scholarly texts have the capacity to transform their readers. Their capacity to do so is diminished if they are approached as technical manuals. They also do not offer up their power readily to the reader who has no time to contemplate them, yet the transformation of the university into a vocational training institution makes texts increasingly into technical manuals and contemplation into wasteful idleness.

The causes of vocationalization are well known: Decreased government tax funding and universities' dependence on student fees; government pressure to increase the university participation rate; government concerns about measuring universities *objectively* through performance indicators, such as time-to-completion and completion rates; dramatically increased student–teacher ratios; the professionalization of university administrators and the bureaucratization of administration; teachers' and administrators' acceptance of instructional shortcuts; fewer incentives for professors to be teachers first and foremost; students' paid work, even full-time paid work; credential inflation; politicians' preferences for the scientific, commercial, and technical disciplines over the humanitarian, cultural, or political ones, and so on.

My career experiences are interwoven with these changes, and the brief academic autobiographical essay that follows recounts these experiences. It highlights my efforts, in the face of a tight job market and contentious university politics, to hold to the value of texts, the importance of good teaching, and commitment to research even as vocationalization has advanced in the Canadian university system. Even though one risks appearing as the hero of one's own life, in autobiography some of the changes in the more general climate are refracted.

The first university course I taught was the Sociology of Urban Relations at McMaster University in the 1978 fall session. It was a third-year night course with an enrolment of about 50. I was starting my fourth year in the sociology doctoral program at the University of Toronto, poor because my scholarship had not been renewed, and without experience in urban sociology, except for having tutored a third-year course with my Ph.D. supervisor, Jack Wayne. I arrived the first evening, clutching my six pages of handwritten notes, prepared to present a lecture on Marxist approaches to the city, using Engels' *The Housing Question* as a text. I got through the notes in 45 minutes, after which I had nothing prepared to say. I spent the rest of the class striding up and down and recounting frenziedly everything I had ever learned from grade school to the third year of the Ph.D. There were 10 lectures left.

I scrambled, but managed to make my course a success, and when a two-year contract came open for July 1979, I applied. The prospect of a real job and a real income (starting salary $17,500, three times the value of an Ontario graduate scholarship) was exciting for me at age 29, but the department at McMaster was deeply divided and matters were about to get worse—things about which I was blithely unaware.

In the late 1950s and early 1960s, several members of an earlier generation of male, quantitatively oriented sociologists of work and social stratification, being progressive in their sociological politics, had created an opening for younger teachers, like myself, who were doing neo-Weberian and neo-Marxist versions of political economy, labour studies, symbolic interactionism, and feminism. But by the late 1970s, the world had changed dramatically and the elders found themselves furious with their unruly academic children. Partly, this was a well-known story of struggles over succession that disciplines and departments experience, but it was made particularly vicious by the deep personal antipathy felt by some senior male faculty members and by some members of the administration to the department's feminist scholar. It was her job that was on offer. Violations of professional ethics had been involved in her being denied tenure and one promising young member of the political economy group soon left the department in disgust. The level of tension was exacerbated because, as was not uncommon in sociology departments of the period, graduate students had voting parity on key department committees and used their power usually in support of the younger generation of professors.

Feminism was in transition, with a new generation moving away from the late 1960s' and early 1970s' sisterhood-is-powerful moment of solidarity and toward more serious theoretical work and the challenges posed initially by considerations of class difference. The McMaster job was advertised as sociology of women—not sex and gender relations—and I was one of three finalists. It seemed like a stretch that a man who was an urban sociologist would apply, but I had some credentials. I had demonstrated my political sympathies with feminism, having participated in the first meetings of Queen's Women's Liberation Movement when I was an undergraduate (before women voted to meet separately) and engaged in some minor activism. I was familiar with the literature from de Beauvoir, Greer, Firestone, Morgan, to Mitchell, Rowbotham, and the English feminist historians. I was in the group at the Women's Press that produced *Hidden in the Household*, and I was working on the feminization of teaching as part of my doctoral work. Before women's studies was institutionalized, I, along with a few other men, had become engaged with a feminist-inflected Marxist or political-economic analysis of household-family-sexual-state relations as a likely career interest, although most of us learned fairly soon that this was to be a women's domain in the academy. The faculty split violently over the other two candidates, and I got the job as most people's second choice.

My four years at McMaster was a learning experience in many ways. The Sociology of Women course was extremely popular and was soon sectioned. In the first class of my second offering of that course, as I walked down the aisle of a quite large lecture room, a woman in her late thirties proclaimed in a loud voice "A man! It's a fucking man!" and stalked out of the room in disgust. Perhaps she had a point. In a class in Introductory Sociology, which I also taught that year, I met my first and dedicated heckler, a young man who repeatedly got up to denounce the doses of communist ideology that I was feeding him. In one lecture, for instance, cribbed again from Jack Wayne, I discussed Lenin's analysis of the vanguard party as a problem of organizational sociology: How to organize a revolution under conditions of state terror. The second part of the lecture compared Lenin's organizational problem with George Homans's analysis of the

Hawthorne Experiments in industrial sociology. There was a loud blast from the heckler about how these were not scientific problems, this was Marxist ideology. But the intervention made it possible to address the relations between science and politics: very instructive. An intelligent, committed heckler, well managed, is a great teaching tool, forcing one to be clear and specific, to be flexible and adaptive, and often giving voice to things other people in class may be thinking more or less explicitly. This person crossed out "Sociology 101" on his final exam and wrote in "Marxism 101." He was a smart student and got a solid B+ in the course. A solid B+ was a great undergraduate grade in 1980.

I would not be able to teach that Introductory Sociology course in my current university, nor to grade the way I used to do. And any Ontario student who gets a B+ in an undergraduate course in his or her major risks not receiving scholarship money when applying for graduate school. In 1980, it was chalk and talk, writing on the board, no films, no videos, no PowerPoint laying out the three points to copy down and memorize for the exam, no textbook with its coloured inserts and skimpy whiz over the discipline. I made the students read texts in the original, offered a parallel series of lectures, and made them write many short essays. My teaching assistants worked through the texts and assignments in tutorials. I declared an absolute refusal to accept any late papers and then did not enforce it.

The last time I offered Introductory Sociology, students read *The Communist Manifesto*, Foucault et al.'s *I, Pierre Rivière*, Mamdami's *Myth of Population Control*, Meg Luxton's great *More Than a Labour of Love*, and some bit of Erving Goffman, on each of which they wrote something. It was a hard course, but many students like difficult and challenging courses. If the teacher can actually present difficult ideas in ways that are accessible, even weaker students can appreciate the authentic enterprise of scholarship at issue. The course was also a good way to detect future sociologists and intellectuals: Those with sociological promise would gobble up at least one of the texts. And the sociologists-to-be tended to answer the essay question on the Foucault collection—"Was Pierre Rivière Mad? Discuss."—by arguing that one could make a credible case for him being either sane or mad, depending on how one read the evidence.

McMaster was not unionized in 1980, and those of us without job security were subjected by our seniors to constantly shifting performance criteria. If we did not publish, we were lazy and unfit. We were told to publish articles in refereed journals, but when we did, the journals were described as polemical, not sociological. Or if we produced articles, we were told that real scholars produced books, but she who produced an excellent book was told the press in question was political, not scholarly, and it was a bestseller because what could you expect from the average reader? One of the wheezy, chain-smoking, ash-covered grey eminences was heard sneeringly to describe a junior colleague as "a bright boy" who, unusually for the time, had two publications before finishing his doctorate.

Matters became particularly vile in the winter of 1981 when graduate students occupied the department in protest against the removal of their parity voting rights, to be dragged out after several days by the Hamilton city police. The students had the sympathy of a majority of the faculty, two of whom were reading the conflict as a miniature of larger geopolitical struggles: the contras in El Salvador and capitalist restructuring come to Hamilton. One of the latter, in contrast to the eminences who showed up to work in their 1950s suits, often came dressed in a grey coverall, the kind of gesture of solidarity with the janitorial staff that Pierre Bourdieu analyses so insightfully as the condescension that is possible only for the powerful. After the occupation, the two faculty members invited signatures to a public statement, in the name of a democratic and co-operative learning environment, opposing the actions of the university and department administration in removing student parity.

The authors of the statement had tenure. Two people on tenure-track appointments were invited to sign the statement, but abstained from doing so. Another contractual teacher, a good friend, who knew he had no future in the department, signed. I desperately wanted not to be invited to sign. My two-year contract was up for renewal and I wanted to stay in the Toronto area. I was in love. I was getting near my black belt in a martial arts club. I was working in a record collection in the Ontario Archives in all my spare time. I'd been offered a tenure-track job in Halifax and had turned it down, proof to the dean that I was in demand.

I made myself scarce and stayed away from the telephone, but one of the authors tracked me down and suggested that I should sign. I did not want to be caught in the middle of this conflict even though I agreed with the condemnation of the administration's position and with the students' stance. And I was dependent on support from the faction sympathetic to the students for my contract renewal. In the end, I signed.

The decision on my renewal became an occasion to define voting rights in the department. Students and faculty voted to renew my contract by a large majority. The administration refused to accept the result, saying that only faculty members were entitled to vote on appointments. A second vote was held with only faculty members voting and I won that vote by a smaller but comfortable margin. The administration refused to accept the result, saying only faculty with tenure or in tenure-track positions, not contractually limited faculty, could vote on appointments. A third vote was held. There was a tie, which I am sure would have been resolved in the negative by the chair, no friend, but at the last moment the colleague who had recruited me in 1978 came back from sabbatical to vote in my favour. The last vote, as I recall, was in late May. I was informed at the end of the day of June 30 that my contract had been renewed for a further two years from July 1.

The experience was, to say the least, very stressful. Very few sociology jobs were available in Canada in the 1980s. I was a grown-up in principle and responsible for making my own decisions, but power dynamics are involved when people with job security invite people without it to make decisions that may cost the latter their jobs. Now, I take care not to put relatively powerless people in situations where their well-being is threatened. Senior faculty have an obligation to offer constructive mentoring to junior colleagues and to make the standards of performance as clear as possible. At times, I have no personal or intellectual affinity with colleagues in need of mentoring, but justice demands that at least all reasonable opportunities should be offered for them to meet clear norms of academic performance.

The strength of faculty associations over the past 30 years has eliminated many arbitrary aspects to the appointments process that I confronted, including setting fixed calendars for announcing results. On the other hand, it has become increasingly difficult to dislodge clearly incompetent faculty members. University administrators are fearful of discrimination-based lawsuits. The incompetent frequently claim that their rotten teaching scores are due to the stupidity of their students, or that the rarity of their publications stem from their incredibly high quality. Mutual mistrust between faculty and administrators prevents the definition and enforcement of scholarship-friendly and pedagogy-friendly performance criteria.

After some twists and turns, my early academic story ended well. I fantasized about being converted to tenure track at McMaster. I worked hard in the archives, published, and applied for jobs and for a SSHRC post-doctoral fellow-ship (one could apply within three years of graduation, so I was just eligible for the 1982–1983 competition). But the McMaster position was redefined in such a way that I was not eligible to apply, and I did not get another job for the subsequent year. Instead, I got the SSHRC fellowship, which I held at OISE in history and philosophy. It allowed me to spend a full year working in the massive correspondence collection of the Canada West/Ontario Education Office, day after day, turning over tens of thousands of letters, them and me covered in coal dust, eventually wearing a face mask as protection from black lung because the collection had been stored in the furnace room of the Normal School for part of its life. I spent another year exploring the bowels of the Robarts Library, especially the "old class" sections on education and political economy (there were 18th-century books one could sign out!), and reading in OISE's education library, while teaching a course. Then I got a tenure-track job at Wilfred Laurier University, lots of teaching but also lots of time to write. I was promoted to professor in 1993, and thought I would spend the rest of my life there: tolerable, but not stimulating intellectually even with an adjunct appointment in the School of Graduate Studies in Toronto. But then in 1994, wonder of wonders, two senior vacancies opened up at Carleton University in sociology and anthropology! Explicitly to teach and supervise graduate stu-dents! And only six serious candidates! I was one of the successful ones.

I am startled to notice that 30 years have passed between my first course and the publication of this *calling card*. I almost never hear any senior university admin-istrator make a public defence of scholarship for scholarship's sake these days, and the university is less and less geared to produce it, more and more geared to "demonstrable benefit" work. Concerns with removing barriers to completion to protect government grants and a much higher student–teacher ratio have helped gut the B.A. degree. My department abandoned its honours' thesis requirement some years ago as most undergraduates were not able—or faculty had not prepared them—to satisfy it. The proportion of the university's budget in the instruction envelope has declined markedly in comparison to the administration envelope. More administrators make for more administrative work, in a vicious cycle. In most universities, administrators above the department level have no time and little inclination to do serious scholarly work of their own. Their practical interests and the practical interests of students and faculty increasingly diverge.

I find myself surprised that every year a few students make it to their fourth year in sociology knowing how to read, to write, to analyze, and to criticize. The level of boredom to which such excellent students are exposed must have obnoxious effects on many of them. As well, despite conditions that are economically less congenial than they were 30 years ago, I continually marvel at the depth and breadth of the intellectual insight offered by many of the doctoral students I encounter. Not to romanticize—it is still the case in North America that persistence will earn a Ph.D. where imagination won't—but space and resources must be preserved for these often weird, complicated, conflicted, earnest, irreverent, passionate people many of whom pursue doctoral work because, in Weber's sense of a vocation, they cannot do anything else. They keep faculty members like me alert intellectually.

CHAPTER 12

From the Personal to the Political:
Some Reflections and Hopes

JENNIE HORNOSTY

Sociologist, University of New Brunswick

The first decade of the 21st century is nearly over. While the situation for women in universities is different today than when I began my career, the goal of equity for which academic feminists have fought is still elusive. Whereas earlier, the opposition to feminist research and equity policies was senior White men, today it is the corporate agenda of administrators and governments that threatens to destroy the inclusive university we were trying to create. To stop corporatization, it is necessary for those entering academe to be vigilant and critical of the excessive competitiveness and individualism that is becoming dominant in university life.

There is much I want to tell you in my calling card, yet I am hesitant. I have been taught to be objective, how to write research papers and cite others, but this is a different kind of project. How does one tell one's story and make it relevant for others? That is the challenge. Beginning with my early days, I will share my reflections on some moments that shaped my academic life and activities, and talk about my concerns for the future. I write as a mother, a feminist, and a committed faculty union activist, and as someone fortunate enough to have had a tenure-track position for most of my career.

I began my academic journey in the early 1960s at Berkeley. I was idealistic, eager to learn, and ready to embrace the world for all it had to offer. Since I came from a poor family, I had to split my undergraduate years between going away to the University of California, Berkeley, and attending the University of British Columbia in my hometown of Vancouver. The 1960s were heady times. At Berkeley I became involved with the free speech movement and the anti-Vietnam War movement; at UBC I was part of a group of students (the Academic Activities Committee) who had "toga parties" and academic retreats to discuss philosophical and world issues. At the time, I thought nothing of the fact that as a female, I was in the minority. Yet, reflecting back, I realize how those were formative years for both my socialism and my feminism. I believed that we could change the world.

My first academic appointment was in 1968, after I completed my master's degree. I was not prepared for the sexism and sexual harassment that I would encounter. At the time, there was no language to name what was happening, and certainly no university policies against such practices. When a male undergraduate student in one of my classes gave me a note professing his love for me, I was distraught, but had no idea what to do or where to turn for help. The student dropped the course, although I learned later that some administrators blamed me for what happened. When I began my Ph.D. in 1973, I learned quickly through the student grapevine whose classes to avoid and to always be sure that the office door remained open when meeting with male professors. For me, getting through graduate school meant balancing my femininity with my emerging feminism. When I returned to university teaching in 1977, sexist jokes and sexual harassment on the part of male colleagues were commonplace; to complain was to be labelled one of those bitchy women who have no sense of humour.

A transformation of the university began in late the 1960s when women and other traditionally marginalized groups started to enter the academy in greater numbers. In the 1960s, women comprised just over a third of all undergraduates and a mere 8 percent of Ph.D. students; only 11 percent of full-time faculty members were women.[1] In all my years as a student, I had only one female professor. Today women represent 58 percent of undergraduates and nearly half of all Ph.D. students; nearly one-third of full-time faculty are female.[2] Numbers in themselves, however, are only one indicator of the change.

Universities are social institutions and reflect the fundamental values of the wider society in which they are embedded. By the early 1970s, Simone de Beauvoir's *The Second Sex*, Betty Friedan's *The Feminine Mystique*, and Shulamith Firestone's *The Dialectic of Sex* were being read and debated in consciousness-raising groups and newly established courses in the sociology of women. The second wave of the women's movement was gaining momentum. We demanded control over our own bodies and mobilized to repeal abortion laws. Feminism came of age and made inroads into the university. Florence Bird's 1970 *Report of the Royal Commission on the Status of Women* showed unequivocally that gender inequality in all aspects of life was pervasive, including in higher education. Two years later, a coalition of grassroots organizations came together to found the National Action Committee on the Status of Women (NAC) with a goal to advance women's equality in all spheres of Canadian life. It was also in the 1970s that liberal feminism became institutionalized on many university campuses. Despite resistance, courses and programs related to women's studies were introduced. Also, groups of women on many campuses successfully lobbied university presidents to establish presidential/ad hoc advisory committees on the status of women to address gender equity concerns. These committees publicized gender disparities in areas such as recruitment, promotion, and salary through various reports and lobbied senates (often to no avail) for needed policy changes.

Feminist academics across all disciplines problematized deeply held assumptions about science, knowledge, objectivity, and truth. We critiqued the dominant male scholarship to reveal how women and their contributions had been excluded from teaching and research. At the same time, this new discourse challenged the traditional ideas and structures that governed university life, including curricula, power relationships, and institutional culture as being products of a particular hegemonic masculinity. Women and others (Aboriginals, Blacks, other visible minorities, lesbians, and gays) also were making it clear that they were no longer prepared to be treated as outsiders to a sacred grove. We fought for an institution that was respectful of our knowledge, our research, and our lives.

The extent of gender inequity was further highlighted in the 1984 report, *Some Questions of Balance*, by Thomas Symons and James Page, who concluded unequivocally that "the discrimination against women in universities ... is a national disgrace," and that it was the responsibility of the entire institution to correct this inequitable treatment.[3] That same year, Judge Rosalie Abella published her *Report on Equality in Employment*, which targeted women as one of the four disadvantaged groups. In February 1986 the Canadian Association of University Teachers (CAUT) approved a Model Clause on Positive Action to Improve the Status of Women. Faculty unionization at many Canadian universities in the 1970s and 1980s provided female faculty an opportunity to establish status of women committees as a part of their unions. These committees gave women greater input into contract language and collective bargaining, and were often more successful in institutionalizing policies and procedures promoting gender equity than the previously established advisory committees. During the 1980s and early 1990s, women's committees, both within faculty associations and university-wide, pointed to systemic barriers to gender equality and lobbied for employment equity/affirmative action policies and programs to increase the hiring of women academics. By the late 1980s, a number of faculty unions had negotiated into their collective agreements maternity provisions, procedures for dealing with complaints of sexual harassment, and contract language on positive action to hire more women academics. Undeterred by continued resistance, feminists successfully established women's studies programs, which attracted large enrolments, and feminist perspectives were taught in many disciplines. Outside the university, women's organizations such as NAC and the Canadian Research Institute for the Advancement of Women (CRIAW) were thriving. It seemed at the time that the goal of equality for women, both within society and the university, would soon be realized. I'm less optimistic now.

My primary involvement in institutional change was through my faculty union, the Association of University of New Brunswick Teachers (AUNBT) and, for a brief time, with the CAUT. I helped constitute the AUNBT Status of Women committee, which remains an important vehicle for raising awareness about equity issues and reviewing collective agreements through a feminist lens. We lobbied for a non-sexist language policy and a child-care facility, both of which happened. Through collective bargaining, the union improved maternity and parental leave provisions, strengthened sexual harassment policy, established an employment equity committee and a clause on positive action to improve the status of women, and negotiated some flexibility in time considerations for tenure. In keeping with a policy for executive members introduced by the CAUT at the time, my faculty association reimbursed me for child-care expenses when needed if I was travelling for faculty association business. Over a relatively short period of time, things had improved significantly for academic women.

On December 6, 1989, the murder of 14 female engineering students at L'école Polytechnique shattered the belief that universities were a safe and secure place for women. It painfully reminded those of us who were beginning to think otherwise that misogyny was still deeply embedded in our society. A further reminder of how little change had actually occurred was the growing opposition in the 1990s to new feminist pedagogy and equity policies. Opponents, such as the faculty members who formed the Society for Academic

Freedom and Scholarship (SASF), warned that political correctness was compromising scholarly integrity, impartiality, and freedom of expression. They argued that admission standards were weakened and that there was an impending danger of censorship, socially engineered language, and mind control "if feminists had their way."[4]

The debates about what limits, if any, are acceptable on the expression of ideas in universities was falsely construed as being between supporters and opponents of academic freedom. In truth, though, it was never really about academic freedom; rather, the institutional and academic changes that feminists were slowly bringing about provoked a backlash by those seeking to protect male privilege and their place in the university. Working within the faculty union to improve the situation for women has been both rewarding and challenging. For the most part, my male union colleagues were supportive, and together we brought about a number of positive changes, yet sometimes I felt they did not fully understand the problem, as was the case around the contentious "Yaqzan affair."[5]

In sum, then, the 1970s, 1980s, and 1990s were full of challenges, such as the marginalization of feminist scholarship and a climate that was chilly to anyone who continued to push the university to become more equitable in its treatment of women and more accommodating to their presence, yet, through collective action we were able to bring about some important gains. While sexism still exists in universities today, it is no longer considered acceptable. However imperfect, institutional policies against sexual harassment and sexual discrimination are the norm and provide some avenues for redress. Most universities now have human rights policies. Maternity and parental leave policies are much improved and employment equity provisions have facilitated the hiring of more women. Although today there are more women faculty in tenured and tenure-track positions, these gains must be viewed with caution, for gender imbalance persists in certain disciplines. For example, only 14 percent of undergraduate students in computer science and 22 percent in physics are women. Conversely, in traditionally female disciples such as nursing and education, undergraduate women comprise 92 and 76 percent respectively. Only 12 percent of full-time faculty in engineering and applied sciences and 11 percent of those in physics are women.[6] However, on many campuses and nationally there are active Women in Science and Engineering chapters, yet equity entails more than numerical presence. The transformation of the academy is far from complete, but importantly, academic women today are no longer invisible or silent.

My fear for the 21st century is that we will lose the gains we have made, not as a result of patriarchal attitudes and gender inequities still present in academe, but as a consequence of a growing corporate culture that is redefining academic priorities in universities. Corporate values and market principles encourage outsourcing and privatization of non-academic labour, appropriation of corporate language and logos, modifying course delivery with labour-replacing technologies, redirecting academic research toward commercial ends, privatizing intellectual property, and circumventing collegial governance structures, all of which have a significant impact on university life. The university is seen as just another business whose primary function is to satisfy its clients and maximize its profits. This ideology encourages entrepreneurship and sponsored research that can attract private capital and corporate partnerships and, as a result, traditional academic values, scholarship, and teaching are marginalized.

Serving corporate needs and priorities has led to a growing individualism and competitiveness, as well as insularity, in today's universities. Faculty members are reminded to keep their noses to the grindstone and focus on research that has potential to attract major grants and result in numerous publications. The value of their academic work is increasingly based on measurements of output and quality assurance assessments. Not surprisingly, academic conservatism is re-emerging in the social sciences; there is increasing talk about objectivity and value-neutrality as unproblematic concepts. Younger faculty seem less eager to embrace ideas such as liberation, social justice, and equality as fundamental to a discipline like sociology. Many faculty members show little (if any) interest in governance issues or routine faculty association business. They focus narrowly on advancing their own careers, with little concern for the common or collective good. Increasingly the university is managed by business experts who have little knowledge or respect for collegial decision making.

Today, professional student recruiters downplay the idea of a university as a place for critical thought, expanding horizons, and searching for truths; instead entrepreneurial disciplines and skill training are promoted. Since enrolments drive curriculum and staffing priorities, there is a real possibility that, in a corporate environment, courses and areas of study that are not profitable will be eliminated. As I see it, a danger of the commercialization of university education is that many liberal arts, including programs in women's studies and diversity studies, and some pure science courses could be cancelled because of low enrolment. We are already seeing in the current fiscal environment universities threatening to close women's studies programs. A corporate culture also threatens to stifle academic debate about what constitutes scholarship and knowledge and discussion about the role of universities in society.

More women today are in faculty ranks, but they are still disproportionately found in the lower tiers. Many of us once believed that with good employment equity policies and the monitoring of these, it was only a matter of time before women would be equally represented with men across all academic ranks. This hope is turning out to be a hollow dream. The response of administrators today to cutbacks in government funding for education is to reduce costs and increase flexibility with seemingly little thought given to the impact of such decisions on academic programs. Rather than hiring new faculty into full-time tenure-track positions, more appointments are for a limited term, or individuals are hired to teach one or two courses for a stipend. A large majority of those hired into these temporary jobs are women. Employment equity policies still exist, but these are of limited value when there are few new full-time positions. When I had my first son in the 1980s, paid maternity leave at UNB was for eight weeks at 95 percent salary. Today women in full-time appointments are entitled to one year of maternity leave. However, women who teach on stipend are not eligible for these benefits. As well, in today's highly competitive environment, junior faculty in tenure-track positions may be reluctant to take maternity leave for fear that it might jeopardize their funding opportunities and publication record. I'm concerned that the changing landscape of the university will particularly disadvantage women since we are still the ones primarily responsible for juggling home and work. Our "bifurcated consciousness" means that we do not segment our private and public lives in the ways men traditionally have done.

In the next few years, I will leave my full-time teaching career as a sociologist; this also will mean leaving my activism as a socialist feminist in the university and within the faculty association. It is a career to which I have devoted much time and energy and for which I have no regrets. While research continues to show that academic women are less likely to have children than women in other professions, my academic career allowed me the time and opportunity to enjoy raising my two wonderful sons. However, today's decreasing job security for many, demands for greater accountability and productivity, and a heavier workload will make it more difficult to balance family life with a university career. My older son is contemplating an academic career. While I am somewhat ambivalent about his choice given the corporate direction of universities, on balance I believe that an academic career is still one of the most rewarding and challenging careers possible.

Teaching and research continue to be my passion. I have tried to mentor students to become both good scholars and to engage actively in the world. No matter the discipline, questions of justice, fairness, and equity should guide the work we do as academics. During my university career, I also learned the importance of faculty unions, collegiality, and an equitable work environment. Along with the support of my partner, the late Jim Richardson, I was able to juggle my different roles, in part, because faculty union activists helped bring about policy and cultural changes in the academy that made this possible.

As a concluding thought I want to leave you with hope. Despite my seeming pessimism, I don't believe that future directions of the university are predetermined. Rather, human agency is the motor of change. Equity is still possible, but it can happen only if people act collectively to make it so. The challenges for the new generation of academics are different from those of my generation. Our struggle was to change a culture that silenced and marginalized women's voices, scholarship, and priorities. Your challenge, as I see it, is perhaps more difficult: It is to oppose and reverse the neo-liberal agenda and corporate directions that have the potential, to the detriment of us all, to destroy the university as a place committed to scholarship for the common good and academic debate. My plea to you, the next generation, is to be passionate and active: Become involved in university issues and the world around you; be vigilant, demand change, and don't succumb to a neo-liberal corporate agenda. It is only through our collective action that we can create a world and a university that values equity, social justice, and inclusiveness.

Notes

1. M.G. Urquhart, *Historical Statistics of Canada*, 2nd ed. (Ottawa: Statistics Canada, 1983).
2. Canadian Association of University Teachers, *Almanac of Post-secondary Education in Canada—2008* (Ottawa: Canadian Association of University Teachers, 2008).
3. Thomas Symons and James Page, *Some Questions of Balance: Human Resources, Higher Education, and Canadian Studies* (Ottawa: Association of Universities and Colleges of Canada), 201–209.
4. C. Hodgkinson, "Taking Political Correctness Seriously," ed. M. Walker, *In Defense of Academic Freedom and Scholarship, Fraser Forum* (Critical Issues Bulletin III) (Vancouver: Fraser Institute, 1993), 24–32.
5. Matin Yaqzan, a male faculty member at the University of New Brunswick, published an opinion piece in the student newspaper on date rape, which alleged that date rape is an unavoidable (and justifiable) consequence of men's human nature and their normal sex drive (Matin Yaqzan, "Opinion: Rape, Past and Present," *The Brunswickan* [Fredericton: University of New Brunswick, November 12, 1993].) My feminist values clashed head-on with the union's decision to file a grievance against the administration's suspension of Matin Yaqzan. The majority position of the union executive was that the administration failed to establish sufficient cause for the suspension. Some colleagues argued that it was his academic freedom to say whatever he wanted. I supported the majority of women and women's groups who maintained that Mr. Yaqzan's statements created an intimidating and hostile environment for women and that this constituted just cause for dismissal. It was and is my view that academic freedom does not give one licence to intimidate or harass others. Through a negotiated settlement, Mr. Yaqzan no longer teaches at UNB, but it was some time before my feelings of betrayal disappeared.
6. Canadian Association of University Teachers, *Almanac of Post-secondary Education in Canada—2008.*

PART 3

Between a Rock and a Hard Place: Calls to Administrative Leadership

CHAPTER 13

Yesterday and Today:
Universities and the Growth
of the Market Model[1]

HOWARD WOODHOUSE
Higher Education Theorist and Policy Analyst,
University of Saskatchewan

The demands now being made on schools, colleges, and universities are for vocational and professional training and cannot be described as education. A society that measures everything in terms of work done and money earned is not concerned with anything beyond the requisite number of persons duly trained and labeled with the correct diplomas and degrees and ready for use and service.

— Dora Russell, educator, feminist, socialist,
and campaigner for nuclear disarmament[2]

Misplaced Nostalgia

Those of us old enough to remember the 1960s tend to invoke that particular epoch as a time when, in Wordsworth's words, "T'was good to be alive, but to be young was very heaven." Opposition to the Vietnam War, the student movement, the feminist movement, demonstrations against racist speakers on campus, public lectures by the Black Panthers, rock 'n' roll and the counterculture all provided campus life with a vitality that now seems missing. We tend to forget that even though universities were changing and more working-class students were admitted, Aboriginal peoples were largely excluded and members of other ethnic groups often felt marginalized.

Moreover, the very companies that made money from the Vietnam War—Boeing, General Electric, Dow Chemical—still have strong links with universities in Canada and the United States. Indeed, these partnerships have grown. Our efforts to emancipate higher education from corporate control were vociferous, but largely unsuccessful. The process of privatization so obvious now was present in the 1960s. Nostalgia for this or for any other ideal time in the university's past is misplaced.

But what of the leadership provided by university presidents and other senior administrators? Did they approach leadership differently from their counterparts today? Undoubtedly they were concerned with balancing budgets, but I believe their leadership practices were different then because they thought of themselves as academics in administrative positions, not as managers. A couple of personal anecdotes lead me to believe this was the case, at least for some senior administrators.

I met only once with the vice-chancellor of the University of Exeter in the U.K. During my second year of studies for an undergraduate degree in philosophy, I had broken a university regulation forbidding male students into female halls of residence after 11 p.m. Dr. F.J. Llewelyn, a renowned chemist, interviewed me for almost an hour, asking why I had done this foolish act, and making it clear that he had the power to fine or expel me. In the end, however, he chose neither, simply warning me not to do the same thing again or I would be "sent down." It was one of the most difficult meetings in my life, but he resolved the problem humanely and effectively.

During the 1970s, when I was a graduate student at the Ontario Institute for Studies in Education, I met Dr. John Yolton, president of York University. His practice was to leave his office door open in order to encourage dialogue with students, faculty, and staff. Whether or not it worked, it is difficult to imagine such a strategy being employed by any president today. The demands of email and meetings with corporate and government stakeholders preclude it. Yolton, however, spoke passionately of the need to engage with the university community in ways that encouraged collegiality. Once he stepped down from the presidency, he went back to teaching and scholarly writing in philosophy, including an excellent book on John Locke.

I don't know if Llewelyn or Yolton bent over backwards to attract corporate money. Government funds were more generous at the time and perhaps the pressures on them were less. Nevertheless, their concern for the university as a cultural centre in which its instituted fabric of teaching, learning, scholarship, and research could thrive was paramount. Today, by contrast, presidents and vice-chancellors regard themselves as chief executive officers of corporate enterprises with multimillion-dollar budgets.[3]

A Shift in Perspective

Recent statements by two university presidents provide evidence of this drastic shift in approach. Robert Prichard, when president of the University of Toronto, acclaimed the corporate market as the ruling principle governing the university's every activity:

> We need a more market-driven, deregulated, competitive and differentiated [i.e., product-mandated] system ... production of better services to customers. The market model give [*sic*] universities more freedom ... by allowing administrators to set fees higher and ... by aggressively courting private donors.[4]

Prichard revealed the logic of the market in stark terms: Universities *must* deregulate and they *must* compete by bringing more products to market and providing better services to customers. He saw the *discipline* of the market as a source of *freedom* that allows administrators to raise fees and seek funding from the private sector. Peter MacKinnon, president of the University of Saskatchewan, used the same logic when he prescribed a 15 percent raise in tuition fees across the board, 18 percent in medicine and 28 percent in law, in order "to prevent the erosion of quality at the institution": "'We need to have a source of revenue that is reasonably consistent,' he said. Turning to the students to pay a greater share of the cost is the 'best way to sustain—or even advance—the reputation of the university,' he said."[5] In other words, by making tuition fees more competitive with those of other institutions, the quality of the University of Saskatchewan is somehow improved and its reputation advanced as its market price increases. The fact that higher fees make undergraduate education less accessible to large numbers of students does not compute within this logic.

It might be thought that two presidential statements do not a corporate winter make. However, the market model of university education and governance from which Prichard and MacKinnon draw originates in the World Bank, one of the most powerful international financial institutions. The World Bank's privatization manifesto,[6] presented at the UNESCO World Conference on Higher Education in October 1998, asserted that "higher education can not [*sic*] be treated as a public good ... [because it is] often available for a price" (a prime example of begging the question).[7] Accordingly, students as "consumers" should pay "the full cost" of their service and borrow at "market rates of interest."[8] Not content with urging the privatization of tuition fees, the manifesto demands "restructuring ... [that calls for] radically altering who the faculty are, how they behave, the way they are organized, and the way they work and are compensated."[9]

At the same time, the World Bank recognizes that any such program of corporatization proposed by governments will result in widespread resistance:

> In the case of public universities, the faculty have additional means with which to resist threats of radical change and job loss: the idea of the university as a proper bastion of continuity and tradition; *the tradition of academic freedom*; and the army of students, former students, and would-be students, most of whom are articulate, energetic, politically volatile, and generally able to be enlisted [*sic*] in the cause of opposing the government's efforts to radically alter *their* university.[10]

Not surprisingly, the manifesto warns against the folly of such resistance:

> ... the very short-term robustness of the university ... may be its worst enemy in the competition for increasingly scarce revenues ... [since governments will then need] to close down inefficient campuses, or lay off faculty no longer relevant to the needs of students, the economy, or for that matter the university.[11]

The threat is palpable. Unless the entire package of corporate and managerial reforms is accepted,[12] universities face dissolution: tuition fees *must* be privatized, the work of faculty must be tailored to market demand, knowledge must serve the interests of private corporations, academic freedom must be disbanded, students must conform to the will of governments, and the economy must fully determine the operations of the university.

The Market Model as a Value Program

The market model of education, now the dominant narrative of the day, is proclaimed and adopted as though it were true *a priori*: "There Is No Alternative" (TINA). We hear the mantra again and again even though it contradicts rational and critical debate and universities as seats of learning. The market model is based on a closed *system of values* that has evolved into a *value program*. Let me explain the distinction.

A value system consists of a set of "goods" that are affirmed and "bads" that are repudiated in both thought and action. These related goods and bads may be more or less consciously arrived at, and those who hold them are capable of recognizing the worth represented by other systems. At times they may even modify their values on the basis of experience, judgment, intuition, evidence, and argument. A value system becomes a program, however, where its own assumptions about what constitutes worth rule out any thought that goes beyond it.

For example, a value system based on a scientific materialist world view is one whose affirmed goods are the objective measurement, prediction, and control of a universe made up of lifeless matter. Scientific materialism tends to exclude rational discussion about values because they are considered to be subjective and to lie outside the scope of scientific discourse.[13] The most important questions about how best to live and what constitutes a just and equitable society are excluded from meaningful discussion. Thus the value system becomes a value program incapable of thought about the importance or worth of goods that are excluded from its narrow purview. Adherents to such a program fail to recognize it as such, precisely because their assumed structure of worth precludes them from thinking beyond its assumptions.

The value judgments proclaimed by Prichard, MacKinnon, and the World Bank go unquestioned because they are based on the idea that self-maximization is a universal principle of rationality. However, a value system closed to all but its own demands is hostile to education at every level. Moreover, the assumption on which it is based is counterintuitive: We normally consider a rational person as someone who is capable of thinking beyond the confines of self-interest, and who regards others' interests as important as his or her own.[14]

Presidents Breaking the Mould

Some university presidents today are well aware of the dangers to universities posed by the value program of the market model. They recognize the importance of interests other than their own, or of big business, and support the idea of universities sharing knowledge for the common good. Their arguments against the privatization of undergraduate education and the commercialization of research provide hope for an alternative direction in which universities are freed from the overriding demands of the market's value program.

Colin Starnes, former president and vice-chancellor of the University of King's College, has argued that the federal government's underfunding over a 20-year period—amounting to 30 percent on a per student basis—combined with continually increasing student enrolment (more than 60 percent) has resulted in "a rising tide" engulfing universities. Two related currents in this tide—research intensiveness and privatizing undergraduate education—particularly concern Starnes:

> The indirect pressures and benefits of a vastly increased research agenda [have] created a new environment in which undergraduate education must now make its way ... [and] "privatization" in the form of a dramatic increase in tuition at some institutions ... [is] creating a Canadian university system that would look and act much more like that in the U.S.[15]

Starnes warns that the assumption that government support at all levels will continue to decline while individual and corporate donations will increase to fill the growing void threatens the distinctive features of the Canadian university system; namely, its openness, accessibility, and quality.

According to Starnes, it is the federal government's emphasis on the Innovation Agenda, which is producing "an irreversible sea change" toward research that serves the needs of the market. Because matching funds for such research must be "found from the provinces and the private sector ... [each] university [as well as] provincial governments and the private donors will have aligned themselves (*or been coopted*) *by the federal research agenda.*"[16] While billions of dollars have been forthcoming for Millennium Scholarships, Canada Education Savings Grants, Canada Research Chairs (CRCs), and the Canada Foundation for Innovation (CFI), none of these measures addresses the problem of privatized undergraduate education. The explicit goal of the CFI, CRCs, and the Innovation Agenda is "to have Canada move to fifth place in the world—from its position as 14th—in research support" in order to increase economic productivity.

The overriding need to compete with one another in obtaining large sums of money for market-oriented research, according to Starnes, is driving universities to become "engines of economic growth" without a concomitant discussion of "the relationship between undergraduate education and big research" taking place. Undergraduate education is privatized at the same time as its importance is diminished by the scramble for research funding that feeds the economy.

More recently, James Downey, former president of the University of Waterloo, the University of New Brunswick, and Carleton University, argued for a rejuvenation of the university's currently muted role of social critic:

> Through teaching and research the university must cultivate a spirit of intellectual dissent. Not for its own sake, but in the interests of a free, tolerant, enlightened, and improving society.[17]

While Downey omits to mention that knowledge may have value in itself, he understands that universities today are out of balance. Like President Starnes, he is anxious for a public discussion to take place about the "quality and character of undergraduate teaching and learning, for it is there the broader and deeper values of life are shaped," particularly the ability to distinguish between fact and fiction, knowledge and opinion that is so important for "effective citizenship." Unless universities carry out both their functions of social critic and educator, they "are in danger of being drawn too deeply into the economic functionalism of the age, of becoming too much the handmaiden of society, not enough its honest critic."[18]

Starnes and Downey advance their case in ways quite different from those who advocate the value program of the market. Through careful analysis and weighing the evidence, they show the weaknesses in, and provide alternatives to, arguments that favour research intensiveness, privatization, and the Innovation Agenda. This style of reasoned argument contrasts sharply with the proclamations of their presidential colleagues who conceive of rationality as self-maximization. Liberation from the value program of the market enables Starnes and Downey to conceive of alternatives consistent with the distinctive goals of higher education.

W(h)ither the Corporate University?

Rational argument is crucial in providing a critique of the market program, but not sufficient. As intellectuals, we need to utilize the full range of our capacities in order to instigate a sea change in thought and action.

The work of Alfred North Whitehead is helpful in this regard since he conceives of the role of reason as closely related to experience and the imagination. "Reason," he writes, "is a factor in experience which directs and criticizes the urge towards the attainment of an end realized in imagination but not in fact."[19] Put differently, reason operates as an integral part of experience guiding our impulse to imagine alternative possibilities to reality at the same time as providing a critique of the visions we entertain. Our ideals are constantly brushing up against a world in which the potentiality to change the facts may be thwarted. And it is the gap between the goals of the imagination and the facts that propels achievement of the purposes to which we are committed. But the facts themselves do not determine our purposes, they provide occasions for the critical use of reason to direct experience in imaginative ways. The marketization of the university does not limit the direction in which our experience and capacity to reason must proceed. Rather, it provides opportunities for sustaining opposing ideals by advancing and disseminating knowledge in imaginative and rational ways in order for knowledge to be shared freely.

If these ideals are to be realized, there must be room for *praxis*. The intellectual freedom to pursue knowledge is to be buttressed by a freedom of action necessary for the full realization of our imaginative powers.[20] "The essence of freedom," Whitehead writes, "is the practicability of purpose ... [since] freedom of action is a primary human need." Unless we can direct our reason to put imaginative ideas into practice, our ability to effect "prevalent purposes ... such as belong to the very definition of the species" will be stifled.[21] At this point in history, the value program of the market threatens all such freedoms. The task of faculty is to collaborate with others in creating institutions of higher learning free from its demands, thereby providing visions of hope for all.[22]

Notes

1. A different version of this chapter has appeared in my book, *Selling out: Academic Freedom and the Corporate Market* (Montreal and Kingston: McGill-Queen's University Press, 2009), Chapter 7.
2. Dora Russell, *The Tamarisk Tree, Volume 2: My School and the Years of War* (London: Virago 1981), 204.
3. Jan Currie and Janice Newson, "Globalizing Practices: Corporate Managerialism, Accountability, and Privatization," in *Universities and Globalization: Critical*

Perspectives, ed. Jan Currie and Janice Newson (Thousand Oaks: Sage Publications, 1998), 142.

4. Robert Prichard cited in "Congress News," *CAUT Bulletin* (June 2001): A50.
5. Gerry Klein, "U of S Tuition Hike Straps Students: University Cornered by Years of Underfunding, Officials Say in Announcing 15 Per cent Increase," *The Star Phoenix* (May 12, 2001), A3.
6. D. Bruce Johnstone with Alka Arora and William Experton for the World Bank, *The Financing and Management of Higher Education: A Status Report on Worldwide Reforms* (Paris: UNESCO Conference on Higher Education, October 5–9, 1998), 3, 12, 22. For a critique of the World Bank's approach to education at all levels, see Katarina Tomasevski, *Education Denied: Costs and Remedies* (London: Zed Books, 2003), 69–82.
7. Johnstone et al., *The Financing and Management of Higher Education*, 3.
8. Ibid.,12.
9. Ibid., 3.
10. Ibid., 22.
11. Ibid., 23.
12. Claire Polster and Janice Newson make a distinction between managerial corporatism and entrepreneurial corporatism in "Don't Count Your Blessings: The Social Accomplishments of Performance Indicators," in *Universities and Globalization: Critical Perspectives*, ed. Jan Currie and Janice Newson (Thousand Oaks: Sage Publications, 1998), note 189.
13. John McMurtry, *Value Wars: The Global Market versus the Life Economy* (London: Pluto Press, 2002), notes pp. 248–249.
14. John McMurtry, *Unequal Freedoms: The Global Market as an Ethical System* (Toronto: Garamond Press, 1998), 128–129.
15. Colin Starnes, "Core Funding Lost in the Struggle," *CAUT Bulletin* (November 2002): A12.
16. Ibid. (my italics).
17. James Downey, *The Consenting University and the Dissenting Academy: Binary Friction* (Ottawa: Association of Universities and Colleges of Canada, 2003), 16.
18. Ibid., 16, 17.
19. A.N. Whitehead, *The Function of Reason* (Boston: Beacon Press, 1971), 8.
20. John Cobb, "Beyond Essays," *Interchange* 29, no. 1 (1998): 105–110.
21. A.N. Whitehead, *Adventures of Ideas* (New York: The Free Press, 1967), 66.
22. Howard Woodhouse, "A Process Approach to Community-Based Education: The People's Free University of Saskatchewan," *Interchange* 36, nos. 1–2 (2005): 121–138.

CHAPTER 14

A Postcard from the Belly of the Beast

JANICE RISTOCK
Women's and Gender Studies Scholar,
University of Manitoba

The world is a boat and I'm in it
going like hell with the breeze
Important people are in it as well
going with me in the breeze like hell
It's a heck of a race if we win it
On with the next one please
—George Johnston, "In it"[1]

Dear Friend,

So you're a feminist thinking about an academic career and want to know the lay of the land. I am writing to you after attending my first meeting of the Western Canadian Deans. It was an interesting meeting with topics ranging from "Planning for the Pandemic" to "Issues in Animal Research Labs" to the ever pressing and contentious "Space Allocation" issue. These are not topics I have normally dealt with in my life as a professor in women's and gender studies, where my work has been focused on violence against women, lesbian, gay, bisexual, transgender, two-spirit, queer (LGBTTQ) issues, and community-based research. Being a newly appointed associate dean of arts (research) and new to the meeting, I was often asked what my home discipline was, and when I answered, I usually saw a look of surprise, followed by the question "Why did you accept the position?"

It is an interesting question to reflect on. This was not something I had ever aspired to, and as a feminist I have been critical of universities as institutions that move far too slowly on equity issues; that regulate the production of knowledge; and that value and support large, well-funded research projects with corporate links while seemingly ignoring many innovative, non-funded research projects with transformative outcomes. More specifically, for 15 years I was in a small women's studies program that had to continually struggle for its existence, justify a feminist perspective, and explain the value of research with a social change agenda as something more than ideology. I was socially positioned on the edge of the mainstream university. And despite the struggle for legitimacy, resources, and recognition, it was an exhilarating space to occupy precisely because women's studies offers a critical, transgressive, and transformative view of the academy.

So 15 years into my career it was an interesting challenge to be confronted with: Could I take a broader view and consider the needs and issues of a Faculty of Arts? Could I make any kind of difference in this role or was it all *apparachnik* work to keep the status quo functioning? What is the status quo these days anyway? What was the larger research agenda that I would be supporting? What does the new focus on the knowledge economy and fundable research mean for feminist, queer, indeed, any critical work in the academy?

Well, I took the plunge into the belly of the beast and so far the view hasn't been too bad. In fact, I really like what I'm doing at the faculty level. It is an interesting time to be in the dean of arts office since more than 75 new people have been appointed over the last four years, which means that almost a third of our faculty is new. I am excited to have a voice in the planning and visioning for our faculty. I have the opportunity to meet with new faculty members and am encouraged and impressed by the kind of scholarship they are engaged in. So much important work is happening in interdisciplinary areas such a reformative justice, globalization, cultural studies, and political economy.

Plus, the culture that I knew is definitely changing. Where I had often felt isolated and embattled, I now see trans-disciplinary collabora-tive research groups emerging with colleagues working together to bring in speakers, to host reading groups, and to comment on one another's papers. Where I had experienced a climate that often felt like an old boys' club—chilly to women who happened to be present—we are developing a new equity plan for the faculty with an even stronger focus on recruiting and retaining women, Aboriginal peoples, people with disabilities, people of colour, people who identify as gay, lesbian, and transgender, and religious and ethnic minorities. Where I had been cautioned by my Ph.D. adviser not to come out or work on queer research topics until I had received tenure, I now see spousal hirings being negotiated for my gay and lesbian colleagues. Further, given all of the retirements and the competitive environment for recruiting new faculty members, we are working to ensure that we have a respectful, diverse, stimulating, and collegial culture.

Many of the initiatives are small, but they are a dramatic contrast from when I was hired in 1990. The late 1980s and early 1990s was a period of very little renewal or growth within universities. Only two other people were hired into the faculty the year I got my appointment. There were no welcoming receptions, no efforts were made to introduce us to other faculty members, and information on basic policies such as tenure was not readily available. As the first person hired into a tenure-track job in the women's studies program, it was a pretty lonely existence, but now it feels right to be more active from the inside to try to create the possibility of what a university could and should be.

However, beyond the faculty level, my engagement with the changing world of research funding has been challenging. There is far greater pressure for faculty members to apply for research funding from the major granting councils, yet it is increasingly difficult to get funded. For example, the national success rate for the Social Sciences and Humanities Research Council (SSHRC) standard research grants competition was 33.2 percent in 2007, down from 40 percent the previous year. The new president of SSHRC, Dr. Chad Gaffield, recently acknowledged that "while about 20 per cent of his generation thought research funding was necessary, 100 per cent of this burgeoning generation who've been hired know that research costs money."[2] "Research costs money" when it is the kind of research that is valued by government-controlled funding agencies and university administrations that depend on scarce research dollars to supplement meagre operating budgets. Gaffield goes on to indicate that SSHRC does not have the resources to support most of the applications for research funding from this new generation.[3] A further turn of the screw: The scarce research dollars are now being targeted for certain areas of research. In March 2007, for example, the Government of Canada announced it would provide SSHRC with $11 million annually to support additional research in management, business, and finance. According to the SSHRC web page, "this new funding provides a significant opportunity for the research community, its partners and other stakeholders to contribute towards innovative management, entrepreneurship and sustainable economic development practices in Canada through internationally recognized research and training."[4] Despite the optimism of the announcement, this kind of targeted funding is very worrisome for the majority of researchers in the social sciences and humanities whose work does not fit the areas being targeted. It further raises questions about how priority research areas are being established. It of course makes sense for funders to have a mega-research agenda, but research funding is made available only to support the mandate of government agencies, we will lose the deeply critical, curiosity-driven research undertaken by individual researchers. In some disciplines, research funding is being used as the strongest indicator of success for promotion and tenure. How much money would Judith Butler's research cost, or bell hooks's, or Michel Foucault's, for that matter? How do we ensure that we value the scholar who has never received a grant, but who might be making a significant contribution to knowledge and establishing an international reputation?

A quick look at the discourse from research-granting councils and university administrations and we see the efforts to show that university research has value and utility to those outside of academe. Phrases like "excellence" and "innovation" are often repeated. Great emphasis is placed on identifying "major thrusts" and areas of "strategic importance" and the way we work as "collaborators" who foster "synergies" with "stakeholders" and are committed to "knowledge translation." The discourse is trying to construct us as winners—if, that is, we jump on board and accept the terms. On a bad day it all sounds like the "Price Is Right": "Come on down!" Bill Readings, in *The University in Ruins*, makes the compelling argument that the corporate university's "discourse of excellence" is fundamentally empty. He argues "the idea of excellence functions as an answer, as a means of homogenizing, quantifying and closing the question of value."[5]

Further, Darin Barney argues that the current academic climate is leading to the "creeping culture of the player." He writes:

> The bulk of the blame rests on the climate generated by the past two decades of institutional restructuring in our profession: the exaggeration of success in competition for external research funds as a mark of scholarly distinction; chronic under funding of graduate education, which leads us to believe the best we can do for our students is to fabricate projects that will win the funding that puts food on their table, and to "train" them to become players themselves one day; the diminishing value placed on

individual scholarship alongside proliferating opportunities and incentives for "team" research that have us, in the manner of players, developing strategies, making sure we are on the right team and worrying about our profile on the team or whether we should be captain of our own team; and last but not least, the bogus "star" system created by the Canada Research Chairs program and the various university-level analogues it has inspired (for a player, the only thing better than being a player is being a star).[6]

Barney himself is a Canada research chair (CRC) in technology and citizenship, and I am intrigued by the provocative stance that he is taking while in this position and by his challenge to us that we can fight this culture by choosing to remain as workers engaging with the world rather than as players responding to institutional calls. His critique can be extended by also pointing to the underlying sexism, racism, heterosexism, etc., that can be perpetuated within an academic culture that is calling us out as players. The CRC program is a good example. The program, funded by the Government of Canada, was created to attract the best talent and to help universities achieve research excellence, yet several women professors launched a successful human rights complaint against the program because of the underrepresentation among those being appointed as chair holders of women, visible minorities, people with disabilities, and Aboriginal peoples. Just who gets to be a player or a star? There is a new agreement on equity in the nomination process, but will this corrective be enough? As of February 2009, the CRC web page reported that of the 1,831 CRCs who have been appointed, 75 percent are men and 25 percent are women (they do not break down the demographics any further).

In spite of the discouraging statistics on equity, I am aware of the significant and groundbreaking work of researchers who hold CRCs. But the fact remains that the larger research enterprise brings millions of dollars to universities from granting agencies and government and that system, with its emphasis on fundable research and devaluing of any research that doesn't attract dollars, is unlikely to change anytime soon. The message from people like Dr. Gaffield and Dr. Piper, former president of the University of British Columbia, is that we have to stop complaining, "stop being ambivalent about money," and "think big." They urge us to "partner globally with people in other disciplines, other universities and outside organizations."[7] Their point is that social sciences and humanities research is needed in almost every area, even in the science and technology strategy that we are currently seeing emphasized. Thus, we are being encouraged to find the "entrepreneurial advantage" in different areas that may at first glance seem far removed from social science and humanities research. I sometimes have Brave New World–inspired thoughts of Judith Butler being asked to join a multidisciplinary team to study the societal impact (with a focus on gender and sexuality, of course) of their new genetically modified tomato.

I'm not averse to thinking big or to seeing that we might have to consider doing our research in different ways (globally, with multidisciplinary teams, with community partners) or even in subject areas that we may have not previously considered as relevant to our own work. These can be exciting challenges that might push us in new directions. In fact, I am currently on two large interdisciplinary research teams that are well funded and doing what I think is important research in the area of gender and sexuality: One project is focused on two-spirit Aboriginal women living with HIV/AIDS and their experiences when accessing health care services, and the other project is studying sexual and gender diversity with an emphasis on experiences of vulnerability and resilience and health and well-being. These research team experiences do not reflect my Butler tomato nightmares. They have definitely stretched me, introduced me to new kinds of thinking from other disciplines, frustrated me, and enriched my experience as an academic researcher who is more accustomed to doing solitary work. The emphasis on collaborations with community partners and being accountable even fits feminist approaches to research. But what gets left unsaid in the new rhetoric meant to inspire us to keep applying for funding is that university research must include a diversity of research areas and approaches or we risk losing the ability to generate new knowledge in areas that are not of "strategic importance" and that are critical of the status quo rather than critical to it—areas like queer theory, post-colonial studies, and feminist action research.

As Livio Di Matteo provocatively wrote: "Universities are at a point where they need to decide if research is about scholarship or if it is simply just about the money. Governments need to decide if they want universities that are sources of research and scholarship or just fronts for commercialization, innovation and job creation. The public should be concerned if they want universities providing knowledge and education for their children or that functions mainly as regional economic development projects."[8]

These are the pressing decisions that we are all being confronted with. I am well aware that I do not have any real power to make change given the lower middle-manager role that I occupy as an associate dean (or ass. dean as my partner affectionately calls me), but I can be a supporter of my colleagues' important work, I can lobby others to remember the value of research in the humanities and social sciences, and I can facilitate and advocate for new initiatives in my faculty.

Recently my heart sank when a new colleague asked me what kind of research topics I thought SSHRC was most interested in funding. He was willing to change his research focus in order to get the funds. My advice to him is what I would say to you: Keep doing research that matters to you. Don't just try to follow the money. What is unique and necessary in our work as academics is our autonomy to determine what is important and valuable in our teaching and research, and having a critical mass of autonomous, thinking academics who can imagine a different university is the only way we can work for change.

And so, my friend, I wish you were here. The area isn't crowded with women, and there is room for much feminist critical work to be done.

Janice

Notes

1. George Johnston, *The Cruising Ark* (Toronto: Oxford University Press, 1959).
2. Peggy Berkowitz, "Congress Speakers See Strength Emerging in SSHRC Disciplines," *University Affairs* (August–September 2007): 1–2.
3. Ibid.
4. SSHRC, "Research in Management, Business, and Finance." Accessed May 22, 2007, from http://www.sshrc.ca/web/apply/program_descriptions/mbf_e.asp (no longer posted).
5. Peter Cramer, "Review of Bill Readings' *The University in Ruins*," *Workplace* 6 (2007): 3. Accessed July 21, 2007, from http://louisville.edu/journal/workplace/issue6/cramer.html.
6. Darin Barney, "Taking a Shit in Peace: Players and Workers in the New Academy," *TOPIA Canadian Journal of Cultural Studies* 16 (Fall 2006): 131.
7. Berkowitz, "Congress Speakers."
8. Livio Di Matteo, "Central Planning Alive and Well in University Research," *Winnipeg Free Press* (January 11, 2007), A11.

CHAPTER 15

How Can One Be Persian in the Canadian Academy?

Nasrin Rahimieh

Humanist, McMaster University/
University of California at Irvine

My relationship to Canadian post-secondary institutions began in 1977 when I arrived in Canada as an international undergraduate student. I had left my native Iran two years earlier to first complete my last year of high school in the United States, as part of the American Field Service program, and then to spend a year at the American College in Leysin, Switzerland. In those days before the 1979 revolution, being Iranian and travelling on an Iranian passport were not a handicap.

The American Field Service program, founded on the idea of bringing nations closer together by allowing teenagers to experience a culture different from their own, had allowed me to spend a year with an American family in Old Saybrook, Connecticut, and attend high school in New London, where I was first introduced to North American teenagers' anxieties about making the transition from high school to university. The year I spent in Switzerland brought me in contact with people from many different regions of the globe and made me curious about cultural diversity. My decision to study comparative literature was deeply informed by the experience of traversing linguistic and cultural divides. I knew that to understand a new country, I had to learn a new language and a new way of life. Initially I was focused only on basic communication, but the more I learned, the more puzzled I became about the difficulties of moving in and out of cultures.

Canada was not on my radar until my sister opted for attending a Canadian rather than an American university. Being the younger sibling and following my parents' wishes to keep us together, albeit away from our home in Iran, I too ended up at Dalhousie University. I could not have possibly known that I would spend most of my adult life in Canada serving as a professor, an associate dean, and a dean in Canadian universities before leaving Canada to take up an endowed chair and directorship of a Center for Persian Studies at University of California at Irvine.

Like the fictional Iranian travellers of Montesquieu's 18th-century epistolary novel, *Persian Letters*, who travel to France and write home about their impressions of the country's seemingly strange customs and habits, I found myself in Canada in the position of observer of social and institutional settings unknown to me. Learning to settle into the Canadian university system as a student naturally required different skill sets than those I would have to adopt as a professor and later as a university administrator.

In the 1970s I was immersed in my studies. Excelling in my work meant that I received scholarships and felt supported by my mentors and the university system as a whole. Ironically, as the image of Iran was becoming increasingly eroded in the wake of the revolution and the hostage crisis, I, an Iranian on a student visa, was being celebrated for my achievements. The opposition between the support and security of being a student in Canada and the political turmoil of Iran could not have been more starkly marked, and predictably I chose to continue my studies in Canada while awaiting illusory and elusive changes in Iran. Like many of my compatriots, I found Canada's approach to its Iranian student population a far cry from that of the United States. While we in Canada were given the opportunity to apply for landed immigrant status, Iranians studying at American universities often found themselves the target of the country's hostility. It is not surprising that many like me chose to make Canada their new home.

By the time I entered graduate studies, budget shortfalls and competition for a smaller share of resources had become part of university life. The events sweeping Iran had made me associate politics with wars and revolutions, but gradually I learned about campus politics that at first appeared to have less destructive potential. As a sense of crisis began to take hold of the academy, I wondered if it was my fate to lurch from one turmoil to another. Displacing my anxiety and guilt about not having participated in the political life of Iran during one of its crucial moments onto the Canadian landscape, I became obsessed with a commitment to participating in the life of the institution. I considered myself one of the rare lucky individuals to be granted a tenure-track position and I felt it my responsibility to return the gift that Canada and Canadian universities had given me both in the form of my education and a new home.

Throwing myself into my career was a way of keeping other anxieties at bay, but my vision of being able to participate in something constructive had all the hallmarks of naive idealism. Attempting to model my own behaviour on those of my mentors who had contributed to the collegial governance of universities, I was keen to serve on committees and become part of the decision-making process, but collegiality was severely tested in the era of budget reductions, vertical cuts, and restructurings. The neologisms themselves signalled changes that had drastically altered the university climate and sometimes tested the limits of collegial governance.

My first experience of this new ethos was at the University of Alberta in the early 1990s. Feeling isolated as a woman and a minority in a small department, I accepted an invitation to serve on university-wide committees. My desire to prove myself useful to the university community and to overcome the belittlement I had experienced in my home department made me effective at committee work. Gradually I acquired a reputation for being a willing participant in program reviews, facilitating work across units, and what some would term an ideal university administrator. This reputation led to my being invited to serve as an associate dean of humanities.

I found it fulfilling to serve others and to oversee the establishment of new interdisciplinary programs. The long hours of discussion, planning, and negotiation that went into establishing a graduate program in humanities computing, anchored in different disciplinary homes across humanities, social sciences, and fine arts, meant that I could see myself as part of a new collectivity, one that was not necessarily and exclusively focused on my personal academic and intellectual interests. In retrospect, I see this chapter of my career as a different form of detour away from the disciplinary and departmental home whose own aura of exclusivity made me feel like an exile. Not wanting to participate in battles against the new policies on academic and employment equity waged by many of my co-disciplinarians was the motivating force for my venturing beyond departmental solidarity.

The satisfaction I found in administrative service was countered by challenges stemming from the imposition of new modes of administration modelled on business and the private sector. As a new lexicon of public accountability, strategic planning, and downsizing entered our vocabulary, we were expected to conform to new criteria. Many among us who had entered administration as an extension of our public service as educators were faced with new demands for justifying the unique attributes of university administration. These changes resulted in a widening gap between colleagues and administrators who, by virtue of the new structures, were compelled to participate in the new modes of university governance.

My own position as associate dean at the University of Alberta entailed working within these structures, but, like many other colleagues, I clung to the belief that we could not allow wholesale changes to take place. In my view, participation in the process was a means of challenging the new orthodoxies and inserting our core values in what appeared to be a rapidly changing climate. I was not willing to give into the new discourses without trying to inflect them. Standing with colleagues who believed we needed to remain at the forefront of decision making about our future, I shuttled between being a professor and an administrator.

It was against this backdrop that I assumed the position of dean of humanities at McMaster University. Occupying this position did not exempt me from participating in exercises of rationalization, competing for external resources, and finding savings. During my three years as dean, I saw myself hailed at once as a visionary and a villain. I came to view this polarity as reflective of the changing times and I continued to adhere to my belief that I could serve my Faculty of Humanities without abandoning its most cherished ideals of university education. I did not always succeed in translating this vision to all my colleagues. Some would continue to regard me with suspicion, and I, in turn, learned to accept their need for distance. Needless to say, such moments were the most difficult for me to negotiate and made me feel an isolation that threatened to erode my sense of belonging to the community of scholars I had imagined I would serve. The fact that shrinking resources forced me to make difficult choices could hardly endear me to my fellow academics. Being one of them, I could understand their frustration, but I would hold onto the belief that evaluation, ranking, and benchmarking were at the very core of the educational enterprise.

In our careers we constantly assess academic work and assign grades. We submit to tenure, promotion, and peer review and see these types of evaluations as fundamental to the advancement of our work, and yet the transition from individual evaluation to rankings on a collective level is not easily made. The very need to justify an area of teaching and/or research is counter to what we assume to be fundamental academic values. Even more irksome to us is the encroachment of the corporate model of marketing only the best products and, even worse, thinking of a university education as a commodity. University administrators who speak the language of the market economy do so at their own peril. These reservations are well worth pondering, as is the need to challenge the business model. But we need to also find a new language that accommodates our own understanding of the changing patterns of disciplines and areas of study. Historicizing universities and forms of knowledge is one way of translating the discourses of accountability and relevance into a mode of communication true to our endeavours. We have our own preferences for fields and methods of study and we do recognize that these are dynamic in nature. No field or method of analysis is ever going to remain unchallenged, and those of us who roam campuses are the first to celebrate new discoveries and test their limits. One of the reasons I felt the urge to leave my home in comparative literature was my colleagues' unwillingness to open their notion of the world to that which lay beyond Europe and its legacy.

We are certainly best equipped to educate the tax-paying public and governments about the ways in which universities and university education have transformed society, culture, government, and numerous other institutions. In the process of educating others about what we do, we will no doubt have some of our own cherished ideas challenged. Universities have gone through many changes over the years and they have been the instigators of much of that change. Anchoring ourselves in that knowledge is our best bet against permitting even further encroachments on our ability to determine the parameters of future change.

Having left higher administration and re-entered the classroom has been salutary for me and has reinforced my belief in the possibility of serving as an administrator and remaining true to the very ideals that fuelled my interest in teaching and research. It would appear that my career as a university administrator has not made me less attuned to the current debates in my discipline or humanities at large.

Since my move away from administration, many have asked me how I could have survived the years I was associate dean and dean. This question echoes the one the fictional Persians of Montesquieu's novel face. Attempting to blend in with French society, they don European dress and roam freely until someone aware of their identity points them out and reveals them as outsiders. This discovery gives rise to the observation: "What a most extraordinary thing! How can one be Persian?" Those who ask me about how I managed to be an administrator might as well be asking me how I can be Persian. The answer is that I, like the fictional Persians, find it a matter of core identity. I believe that humanists will and must always be the ultimate decision makers about the nature and structure of universities. We teach our students to live by the concepts, philosophies, and doctrines that served as the bedrock of the modern university. At the very least we should rise to the challenge of putting into practice what we teach.

CHAPTER 16

The Paradoxes of
Academic Administration

MARY ELLEN PURKIS,
Nurse and Social Practice Theorist, University of Victoria

Introduction

I am an academic administrator. For the most part, I enjoy this work. The idea of being an administrator within an academic environment is a contentious one—and I'm not sure that you are supposed to acknowledge enjoying the work. Perhaps this is so mostly because the university claims to be something of an "open society"[1]—that is, its values are for open debate, encouragement of diverse thought, and governance through transparent and flexible means. Governance is intended to be collegial—that is, leaders within universities have been drawn, historically, from the internal ranks. There is something about knowing that you will return to the workplace you have a privileged role in shaping that should, theoretically, keep your decisions contextualized within that workplace in ways that are thought to be quite different than in those situations where managers represent a class of workers apart from those at the front line. Nonetheless, universities have not been immune to the trends that have affected other public sector workplaces where an increasing sense of managerialism has been felt since the mid-1980s.[2] For instance, in Canada, there are several search firms that devote their efforts entirely to filling this managerial class—at the department chair level, the decanal level, as well as the executive level. While it is still common to find department chairs coming from within the ranks, the same cannot be said for deans or for members of the senior executive team. Indeed, in a recent issue of *University Affairs*, a Canadian publication that focuses on issues in higher education, a former dean reported on an informal survey he had conducted when, after 3.5 years into his term as dean, he decided to return to his research position. He found only one other colleague who had made a similar decision. Most others had gone on to comparable or more senior management positions.[3]

Of course, it is not only the emergence of a managerial class that generates tension regarding some of the deeply held values within the academic context. The very idea of an academic discipline immediately clashes with any idealized notion of openness: Disciplines are, by definition, about distinction and exclusion. Added to this, administrators in universities are charged with the dual responsibility for ensuring academic excellence and administrative fairness. Where academic excellence comes to be equated with levels of research funding and numbers of articles published, inequities can arise in relation to the distribution of workload within departments. For example, those with higher levels of funding can negotiate a reduction in other forms of academic work (teaching, committee work, etc.) that, over time, can result in legitimate claims from departmental colleagues of unfairness. The work of academic administration requires engagement in these tensions—between openness and exclusion; between encouraging diversity and adjudicating fairly—and I enjoy having opportunities to think through the complexities associated with working in these tensions.

It has been my experience over the past nine years that I have served as an academic administrator—first for my own school (nursing) and now for an entire faculty (consisting of 74 faculty members who are responsible for the education of some 1,300 undergraduate students and approximately 450 graduate students)—that the numbers of people seeking leadership positions within the university is dwindling. The invitation to contribute to this volume provides me with an opportunity to explore the nature of this work within the contemporary university and to urge my colleagues here in my own university, as well as at other institutions across the country, to give careful consideration to this work on two fronts: First, to have those colleagues consider taking on such a role and, second, to have them consider their engagements with those who have taken on these administrative roles.

My own personal approach to this work comes through my professional training as a nurse. I approach this work from at least three distinct locations: with the practicality of a professional practitioner; with the analytic awareness of a scholar interested in the ways in which organizing occurs through relations of power; and with an administrative consciousness that resources can be obtained where coordination and valued impact can be demonstrated.

Puzzling Paradoxes

The challenges of this work can be discovered most vividly in those spaces where organizational segments meet—for instance, between the dean's office and the schools and programs. But they also occur at the junctures between functional activities—for instance, between the work designated as academic leadership work and that designated as administrative leadership work. An example may help to illustrate not only the troubles that administrators encounter but also to explicate some ways of thinking about these troubles that I hope may encourage others to take part in this work—or at least better understand one administrator's motivations for being engaged in this work, and so enhance dialogue across these divisions that can so quickly become impassable gulfs.

Technico-administrative Advances

For the past two or three years, our university has been working on a massive information technology project that involves overhauling a set of somewhat ancient and distinct information systems that have supported the administration of student academic programs. These systems range from initial inquiry through to alumni relations, payroll systems for staff and faculty, tracking of charitable donations, human resource processes, and facilities management. For the first couple of years, the work involved in this massive overhaul has been rather invisible: Every month or so an email would arrive announcing that a new marker of progress had been achieved, but there was no visible change to an interested but naive academic administrator.

Suddenly, however, a new portal appeared on the university's main web page and the background work became much more visible. Lots of advertising told us of the convenience of this new electronic access to the university: Now, rather than having to sign on to each of the former information systems separately, we would (eventually) have access to all of them through a single sign-on process. Initially the only system we could access was the financial accounting system, but now the facilities management system is also online and, this past year, the student services system has "gone live."

I suspect that many universities are investing in this or similar types of information systems. Whether these two events were intended to operate together or not, ours seems to be tightly linked to a new interest in enrolment management. This is the language used in a strident attempt to increase the numbers of students enrolling in our university. The interest in student enrolment comes at a time when the demographic profile of our country is showing what is said to be an alarming decline in the numbers of 18-to-24-year-olds—the population of students that universities have traditionally relied upon to meet enrolment targets. Commenting on initiatives such as enrolment management as contributing to a new type of policy environment in universities, Sheila Slaughter points to the sorts of demands that such initiatives place on staff within public sector locales: "faculty and professional staff increasingly had to expend their human capital stocks in competitive situations. In these situations, some university employees are simultaneously employed by the public sector and are increasingly autonomous from it. They are academics who act as capitalists from within the public sector: they are state-subsidized entrepreneurs."[4]

As an administrator, I am easily convinced of the changing demographic mix that we are seeking to tap into as I take the responsibility of my administrative leadership role to ensure that we meet our enrolment targets each year. At the same time, I ask questions of my administrative colleagues when we have all-day consensus meetings on our current branding efforts about whether, if we did nothing at all (i.e., didn't rebrand ourselves; didn't hold Open Days to invite students and their parents to see what their money will buy), would we be just as far ahead or behind as we will be once we've devoted innumerable person-hours into getting just the right image that will (hopefully) attract those students and their tuition dollars to our door?

Now to the tension: My administrative and faculty colleagues urge me not to be seduced by these sorts of efforts. They challenge me to think about how I am spending my time: They ask me (very good) questions about what my contribution really adds to the shaping of these larger moves the university is making. They urge me to establish (other) priorities that will promote other initiatives that they and I also see as important signals of what the faculty is seeking to achieve.

My response to them, to date, has been that I need to spend time in these environments so that I can begin to understand the intricacies of the values that underlie this work of academic administration. When I ask a question such as the one identified above, even though the momentum feels relentless on the larger project of revamping the university's attractive image—and all its associated electronic functionality—I feel I may be the only person asking that question. And at least the question gets asked. Perhaps it is only when one becomes disenfranchised that one can no longer ask these questions—and this is an association with the work that I try to avoid.

On the other hand, it is also possible that, while I deny any interest in playing this game of internal competition, I am well aware that there is a certain pride that attains to those deans who are acknowledged, at the end of the term, as having met their targets. And this is not an unsubstantial recognition. Budget requests submitted on the heels of a successful period of enrolment are met much more positively than when one has to make the case, for perhaps the third year in a row, that, with just a small increase in base budget, a struggling academic unit could flourish—trust me!

The real paradox here is that while universities across this country will place a great deal of trust in those who are selling enrolment management strategies, they are much less willing to trust a dean who provides legitimate rationale for why she or he cannot meet enrolment targets.

As I engage in this work, I am conscious of the business orientation inherent in the language in use. I am also conscious that it is not only in my workplace that this language fuels particular sorts of activities, but also in homes, in social service agencies, and in most other areas of the public sphere. Knowing this, I am at once relieved to know that the academic world is not alone in being forced to make use of such language to maintain or advance its own position within society, but also, of course, distressed to recognize that neo-liberalism is, after all, pervasive in our society. Effective means of resistance are difficult to find and, if found, to sustain.

Resisting Corporatization—from the Inside

As I contemplate this uncomfortable and contradictory location within the academy, I am drawn to the work of Chantel Mouffe. I have found Mouffe's writings on political economy relevant as I have sought to think through practices of resistance within the context of my work as a researcher interested in shaping supportive health care systems. In the present context, I believe her writings assist in the development of explanations regarding how these administrative relationships can be used to protect privileged spaces where faculty can have time to read about the world and reflect on how that world is changing.

Mouffe proposes a world of "agonistic" relations where

... the task for democratic theorists and politicians should be to envisage the creation of a vibrant "agonistic" sphere of contestation where different hegemonic political projects can be confronted. [...] There is much talk today of "dialogue" and "deliberation" but what is the meaning of such words in the political field, if no real choice is at hand and if the participants in the discussion are not able to decide between clearly differentiated alternatives?[5]

As a contemporary dean, my job seems to be to serve as a dialogical conduit between the senior executive team and my faculty and staff colleagues. My need to attend the seemingly never-ending meetings is, at least in part, my opportunity to absorb the language and the tactics of the modern, competitive university. My reciprocal need to keep my door open—metaphorically and physically—means that again, my own academic interests are often set aside in an effort to hear how that language and those tactics are being experienced by all those who inhabit the university: students, staff, and faculty, as well as the occasional government representative, parent, and donor. How else can I do the work of seeking to distinguish the boundaries between Mouffe's "clearly differentiated alternatives"? I do not claim to have risen well to all these challenges: It is often difficult to hear all the voices—those above as well as those below—in an open way. I often struggle with what I hear in my own voice as being contradictory to what I claim are my values. At these moments of contradiction, people tell me things that I must, in the moment, refuse, set aside, even trash, but there is a trace[6] that remains, a trace that I may, at another time, pick up on and use as I seek to build alternatives. And perhaps it is this opportunity to create an alternative that serves as my strongest motivation for engaging in this work.

The unique value of doing administrative work within the university context is the wealth and diversity of viewpoints that one can so easily access. This too is the challenge. This may, in fact, be the sort of context that Iain Watson describes when he distinguishes critical social movements from other sorts of social movements. For Watson, "*critical* social movements refuse the imposition of intellectual boundary setting by activating across different political spaces and different political times through encouraging a politics of inclusivity and ambivalence"(italics in source).[7]

Watson's musings suggest a space where I can be conscious of hearing inclusively, but I can also live in the ambivalence of what I hear. Ultimately, administering is a personal activity. This does not mean that it is separate in any way from the context within which the work is conducted, but it is work that will be engaged and activated differently by different people.

Each of us engages in our work in the university from a place of values that enables us to hear possibilities in certain ideas that another may not hear. It is those possibilities that can sometimes be linked to wider projects and, in such cases, resources desired by particular academic units can be delivered with a minimum of strings attached. Units that have independent ideas about what they are trying to achieve create a political space of ambivalence for the administrator whose goal it is to create possibilities for using those ideas to help the larger organization also achieve its ends. These are the opportunities I am watchful for. Success, whatever that can be fashioned to look like, is always more likely when groups are already moving in a direction that resources, one can only hope, will speed their progress toward.

At the outset of this chapter I said I would offer some thoughts for my colleagues who are, of course, specific people. I hope these words might also be useful for those others who work within the set of relations I have been writing about here: academic and administrative colleagues all of whom work within these paradoxical relations of governing within the contemporary university. If I can leave a trace behind, it would be to encourage you to maintain a dialogue with those of us who have entered into this work. Maintain this dialogue even where you find that difficult due to structural arrangements of power and authority. Seek out opportunities to express your experience of working within the university. Only through such expressions, which may not always be in the form of words, and sometimes risking advancement within the university context, will we all be contributing to "a politics of inclusivity and ambivalence" and, through such means, resist the totalizing effects that accompany neo-liberal motivations.

Notes

1. Karl R. Popper, *The Open Society and Its Enemies* (Princeton: Princeton University Press, 1950).
2. Gina Anderson, "Carving out Time and Space in the Managerial University," *Journal of Organizational Change Management* 19 (2006): 578–592.
3. Léo Charbonneau, "So You Want to Become a Dean?" *University Affairs* 46, no. 11 (November 7, 2005). Accessed April 20, 2009, from http://www.universityaffairs. ca/so-you-want-to-become-a-dean.aspx.
4. Sheila Slaughter and Larry Leslie, *Academic Capitalism: Politics, Policies, and the Entrepreneurial University* (Baltimore: Johns Hopkins University Press, 1997), 1.
5. Chantel Mouffe, *On the Political* (London: Routledge, 2005), 3.
6. The reference to "a trace" is based on Derrida. See Jacques Derrida, *Of Grammatology* (Baltimore: Johns Hopkins University Press, 1976).
7. Iain Watson, "Politics, Resistance to Neoliberalism, and the Ambiguities of Globalization," *Global Society* 15 (2001): 202.

PART 4

Making Space:
Calls to Open Paths

CHAPTER 17

Academic Activism and Nomadic Paths[1]

Jamie Magnusson
Critical Theorist, Ontario Institute for Studies
in Education/University of Toronto

Following a nomadic path is not a choice. Nomads exist because the state always has an exterior, and it's through this exteriority that nomads come into existence. Because the state is concerned with vanquishing nomads and controlling their migrations, the nomad is, of necessity, a fighter always on the move—a nomadic warrior. Whereas the state tries to appropriate the nomad warrior's fighting skills and knowledge, and codify these as part of the state apparatus, the nomad has no codified knowledge, only paths. Thus, for example, in the martial arts there are many paths rather than one official knowledge. Learning to undo myself in an ongoing process of becoming myself is critical.

As an academic activist, I've been in a constant process of undoing myself, learning and unlearning. I began university studies in music, but earned a Ph.D. in psychology. I worked for a while as a faculty developer, but now I work in a higher education graduate program in OISE, creating courses such as "Academic Capitalism: Higher Education with a Corporate Agenda," "The Ideology of Science and the Politics of Higher Education," and so on, in order to assist students in their own nomadic paths. Together we reinvent ourselves and through our collective knowledge work, we engage state violence that seeks to control and destroy those whose lives are defined through exteriority.

Lesson 1: Public School Education Is Messy Business

I was born into a working-class family in a tiny village in the middle of the Canadian Prairies. Neither of my parents boasted a high school diploma, and they couldn't fund a university education that required a huge relocation and housing budget. Nevertheless, I was pretty much a product of the Keynesian welfare state, and university education was within my limited financial reach, even as an academically borderline student. I was at the tail end of a massive expansion of the (mostly) publicly funded post-secondary sector. Far from intellectual prowess, my main educational gift was having high school teachers compassionate enough in their wisdom to pass me even though I hadn't technically made the grade in all my courses. Recognizing that my grades had systematically degenerated from straight A+s to marginal by the end of high school, they likely couldn't see the value of torturing me further. To these kind souls who peopled the education institution in my tiny prairie village, I humbly nod my head.

They helped me understand something about the beautiful incoherent system we call education. The beauty was not in the institutional structures designed to shape me. Rather, the beauty was in the messiness that inevitably exists when *real people* populate these mythical institutional structures: those teachers, with their own complex social histories, who passed me even when the system indicated that I deserved an F, and who helped me sustain a sense of humour about it all.

Some of my teachers were educated in faculties of education, some in normal schools, and many grew up as working-class kids in prairie villages, just like I did. Some were French Catholic nuns; some were Chinese Canadian; many were avid curlers; some were alcoholics; some were gifted musicians; some were gays and lesbians painfully closeted, yet out at the same time. Not one of my teachers could claim an Aboriginal history, and so colonial history thoroughly saturated my education through constituent absence. These teachers were supposed to have learned how to objectively evaluate me and, through state-sanctioned science, literature, history, social studies, and physical education, were supposed to have inspired the kind of desire-skills-citizenship by which I would simply regulate my own movement through the social landscape.

Instead, they let me write my own curriculum, and seizing the opportunity, I spent the last years of high school playing basketball, composing music on a Lake Winnipeg beach, and reading all the books in the community library that struck my fancy—Susan Langer, Sigmund Freud, literary criticism inspired by Jungian psychoanalysis, quantum physics, electronics, introductory university texts on various subjects, and enough novels to keep me reading each night until 2 or 3 a.m. I was so busy reading fascinating stuff that I forgot to do my homework. Soon after I turned 18 years old, my teachers scanned their registers where they recorded all the assignments I failed to hand in and, looking kindly upon me, allowed me to proceed to graduation.

Lesson 2: Universities Mean Business

I don't mean to gloss over the pain often inflicted on kids by the public school system. I did grow up in the days of corporal punishment after all, and there were many teachers who chose to use ridiculously cruel and humiliating tactics on innocent kids. My point is more that the pain, especially those related to systemic violence, can be greatly alleviated by teachers' conscious political choices. The pain can likewise be greatly exacerbated. My school experiences taught me that teachers' self-conscious choices can be used to interrupt the official curriculum.

When I was admitted to my local university, I left my tiny community of 3,000, and immediately got lost in this massive system within what seemed to me to be an overwhelmingly large city. I was a student of music, and so ensnared in shyness and social anxiety that I really couldn't survive in that kind of fine arts environment wherein public expressive performance was the medium. But thank goodness I had music to get me in on the basis of an audition because the admissions team was quite willing to overlook inferior high school grades if the audition showed promise. After my first year, I switched to a general arts program and chose to major in psychology because, as a working-class kid paying my own bills, I felt I needed to train in a program offering research assistant work and some kind of job at the end of the day.

I didn't fare well. There were fewer *real* people. Let me give you a quick example. My introductory biology class was held in a lecture theatre holding about 200 students, maybe more. The lectures featured several videotaped talking-head professors projected onto a massive screen. No real people. The labs were constrained by lab books with specific assignments monitored and evaluated by a graduate student teaching assistant. The teaching assistant wasn't even available for discussion; he was more like a glorified hall monitor. Videotaped lectures and tightly regulated labs were meant to standardize the curriculum across multiple sections; these and computer-generated multiple-choice tests introduced the machine-like operations by which the academy became open to the masses: the unbendable curriculum.

My graduate training in psychology was similarly unbendable in the sense that there was no space to ask critical questions. The methodological regimes policed by the American Psychological Association declared what was good knowledge (i.e., positivist, quantified, experimental) and could not handle the questions emerging from my increasingly politicized consciousness. I became fully aware of class dynamics in the interweaving of *official* knowledges, and aware of how these intersected with race and gender.[2] I learned some sophisticated statistics, and combined these skills with computer programming to earn my way as a research assistant through graduate training. But the real people who could exercise their authority as professors, editors, and reviewers, to bend the curricula, or allow official knowledges to be critically interrogated, seemed more unwilling to do so than what I experienced in any other level of the schooling system. I'm not merely talking about one university or one department, but the entire knowledge system: whose research is accepted and whose is excluded from conferences and journals, the official venues of academic knowledge. And I can completely understand this in that as a student, I myself was negotiating the rules of these knowledge regimes in ways that would allow me at the end of the day to graduate and secure a job. I imagine that everyone was doing the same in different ways.

I had an idea that I wanted to contribute something to education, but I wasn't sure what that would be. I wanted to provoke some kind of change within what I felt to be a higher education system fraught with problems. My research worked at the intersection of psychology and higher education, and I was completely frustrated by the rules of the research game, which didn't allow me to politically engage changes at all, or even raise interesting questions. I decided to finish up quickly and find a space to do what I thought would be more meaningful work.

My first tenure-track position was as a faculty developer hired to work with new faculty to engage discussions on teaching, learning, and curricula. I thought perhaps this would be a great space to engage institutional change. As I moved further from the discipline of psychology and closer to the field of higher education, I immersed myself as much as possible in literatures that could help me contextualize my weird straitjacket experiences in psychological training and university education more generally.

Lesson 3: Learning Nomadic Activism

So I pretty much became self-taught in a number of literatures that could be put to immediate use in interrupting official curricula for sound political reasons: feminism, anti-racism, queer theory, critical materialism, post-structuralism, and post-colonialism. At that time, still being a very shy individual, I couldn't find a whole lot of people with whom I could discuss these complex literatures. Obviously I would have benefited from more scholarly mentorship in critical social theory. On the other hand, I wasn't beholden to official curricula within yet another department, which would have had its own baggage.

I tried, awkwardly at first, to integrate these literatures into my faculty development practices through workshops on critical pedagogy, working with politically minded feminists and Aboriginal educators on various curriculum projects, and so on. I have to say that this work was never easy. Without going into gory details, I was happy that there was a small but substantial literature theorizing institutional resistance to critical, emancipatory practices. This literature sustained me through some hard times.

Back then, a few feminist scholars were instrumental in helping me learn how to use my academic position to politically engage institutionalized oppressions. These lessons were better than any graduate course on critical theory. Rosa Bruno-Jofre was a more senior colleague within my university who taught me about the ethics of political engagement grounded in her background in South American liberatory movements, including liberatory theology and pedagogies of the oppressed. She also dragged my puppy neck out of murky waters on more than one occasion. Keith Louise Fulton was an inspiring speaker and organizer for women in academia, and was among the first to help set up a program of women's studies in Winnipeg. Although I never had the opportunity to work directly with Keith, her moral courage and political ethics are qualities I've tried hard to emulate ever since. Laara Fitznor, an Aboriginal scholar and activist, worked with me and helped me understand Canadian higher education from a decolonizing frame.

From my experiences with institutional resistance to equity, and from my lessons from feminist scholarly activists, I learned the importance of maintaining a deliberately ambivalent relationship with universities, knowledge societies, and even community and grassroots networks. For example, sometimes putting my energies into a collective feminist project can be important, but when that collective shows its homophobic face, it's time to denounce how homophobia is reproduced through the collective.

Rather, I've found it helpful to keep up a practice of continually rethinking and renegotiating who I am as a public intellectual in relation to my university work—and yes, I still believe in the political viability of public intellectuals. However, rather than *a* public, I've found it more helpful to think about multiple publics. I think about having available to me, through my own social histories, participation in a wide variety of publics or social genres. I have been a working-class kid. I grew in an Icelandic-Canadian village with its beautiful pre-industrial ways and beliefs: To this day I believe in the hidden people (*huldufólk*) who live communally in rocky knolls. I have been a musician. I have been a single mother. I am queer. I am a martial artist. I can draw on all these, and any others I can access, to accent my own life practices in ways that are entirely inventive.[3] That's what I meant earlier in this chapter when I spoke of how education can be a beautifully chaotic space when populated by *real* people: people who are more than their brief, monolithic, and highly institutionalized social histories as trained psychologists, sociologists, or biologists. However, this requires a kind of nomadic practice, but one committed to an ethics of working toward mutually nourishing relationships in the process of dismantling relationships that hierarchize and subjectify.

Lesson 4:
Creating Nomadic Knowledges Oriented to Activism

By the time I was awarded tenure the first time, I was a single mom and sole financial provider. When my application for sabbatical—a normal entitlement in academia—was turned down, I decided to look elsewhere for positions within, between, and outside of academia. There were many reasons why I felt a move was necessary, but sometimes a critical incident can snap into focus a very clear image of what needs to be done. I was hired within the Higher Education Group at OISE and drove to Toronto with my child to start a new life. I began earning tenure all over again.

When I arrived, Ontario, under Mike Harris's newly elected regime, was beginning a comprehensive program of neo-liberal restructuring, and the deleterious effects were quickly evident in every slice of the public sector. I immediately set up a new research program working at the intersection of neo-liberal capitalism and higher education as an aspect of global economic restructuring. This is the area for which I ultimately earned tenure the second time—very far removed from my graduate training in psychology. The tenure task was daunting, not only because I had to develop expertise in more new literatures, but also because I soon had a family of three children (two stepchildren plus my biological child) to care for and a partner whose health began to deteriorate in an aggressive and unforgiving way. I mention this because these life experiences contribute to my politics, which include a strong commitment to women's issues and the politics of the roles we take on. The gender issues related to mothering and taking care of the ill and dying are huge.

I quickly set up courses in areas such as academic capitalism, radical policy perspectives, globalization, critical pedagogy, and the like. A couple of colleagues and I worked together to establish an equity stream within higher education studies that included post-colonial, feminist, anti-racist, class, and queer studies. Since a large proportion of my graduate students are from the health sector, I find it particularly gratifying to work with them in understanding dynamics of gender, race, and class issues in economic restructuring of the health sector, for example. Or with Aboriginal students, developing higher education policy analyses from a decolonizing framework. Or examining current developments in Canadian higher education in connection to international policies enacted through the World Trade Organization, the International Monetary Fund, the World Bank, etc., and, in general the expansion of what is usually referred to as knowledge society economics.

When my students graduate, most will take up positions within professional schools and colleges, and my hope is that through politically informed work as teachers, writers, and administrators, they'll create pockets of countermovements. Hence my work at OISE affords me some degree of political engagement with respect to destructive regimes and their connections with post-secondary institutions.

Lesson 5: Life at 50—Reinventing Myself Again!

I wrote the first draft of this chapter two years ago. Since then my life and its nomadic links to higher education have changed in so many dramatic ways. I now share my life with my new partner, Beverly Bain, who is a women's studies professor and long-time award-winning activist in the Toronto community. Coming from the anti-violence movement, she's furthered my framework for understanding race and its material intersections with gender, class, sexuality, and ableism. I've been inspired by her work as a Black lesbian activist, and how she engages critical pedagogy as community praxis.

Having recently celebrated my 50th birthday, I am anxious to direct this inspiration toward a much more ambitious program of teaching, writing, and activism. Now that my children have grown up, I have much more time to dedicate to this work than I had in the past.

Higher education is a very conservative field of studies. Most research money and career recognition go to those whose work supports conservative agendas. The history of higher education in North America shows how the profit and non-profit industrial complexes work together, within a corporate ideology, to produce a system of universities that prioritize research and technology as their primary mission. David Noble's *America by Design*[4] is an important text documenting this history, and so is Lily Kaye's *Molecular Vision of Life*[5] and a few others. Those of us working in universities as faculty members would do well to read these histories in order to contextualize current developments, such as the expansion of knowledge society discourse and knowledge economics through very powerful international economic organizations, including the World Trade Organization, the World Bank, and the IMF.

Canada can boast of having had a post-secondary sector woven through a public framework. We're now in the process of dismantling this public framework, and without the kind of wide democratic discussion that should take place. Universities have always been about economics and power. However, it's also important to know that universities have been critical in the expansion of democratizing movements: the peace movement, civil rights movement, feminist movement, gay rights, environmental activism, and agitation against neo-liberal capitalism.

In a sense, then, I suppose I can say that the work I do is marginalized within the broader field of higher education studies. However, I can also say that once I began working with my colleagues to open a space for critical interrogation of higher education in relation to multiple systems of oppression, our endeavours were met with immediate success. That is, we began to attract brilliant students who had motivation and drive to work within this kind of space to introduce new perspectives—counter-hegemonic knowledges. I feel as though my real work in this regard is only just beginning. I've just recently had the luxury to begin reading new literatures all over again, and engaging in research that I believe to be politically important. It seems to me the political stakes are much greater at this historical juncture than when I first became a faculty member.

When I first entertained the idea of becoming an academic, I naively thought about a career that was connected to a systematic training in a discipline, and a more or less continuous program of research and teaching. I realize now that in order to be a politically engaged teacher and public intellectual, I need to be comfortable with reinventing myself and having a kind of nomadic practice as an academic. This nomadic practice directs my personal energies away from state, industrial/corporate, military uses of my intellectual work, and toward imperatives woven through social justice. I also had to be comfortable with occupying a marginal space within a broader field of studies, and with the career recognition implications this entails. On the other hand, I have role models who have been a continuous source of inspiration in this regard; many of my role models are, in fact, organizing and contributing to this collection.

Notes

1. My use of the term "nomad" is from Deleuze and Guattari's "Treatise on Nomadology," in Gilles Deleuze and Felix Guattari, *A Thousand Plateaus: Capitalism and Schizophrenia* (Minneapolis: University of Minnesota Press, 1987).
2. I personally experienced the consequences of class dynamics many times in the university system. One example is the sheer number of times my professors suspected that I was plagiarizing, and asked me to perform humiliating exercises to prove I was the author of the work I handed in. Apparently I was marked as someone who couldn't possibly have produced a high-quality essay without having cheated. It seems I was also marked as someone who was morally inferior, and given to thievery. Those low-class kids: Can't trust 'em.
3. I'm working from Bakhtin and Volosonov here, and in particular with how Dorothy Smith takes up their work to develop a *sociology for the people*. See Dorothy Smith, *Writing the Social: Critique, Theory, and Investigations* (Toronto: University of Toronto Press, 1999). I also enjoy how David McNally reads Bakhtin. See, for example, David McNally, *Bodies of Meaning: Studies in Language, Labour, and Liberation* (Albany: State University of New York Press, 2000). See also Mikhail Bakhtin, *Speech Genres and Other Late Essays* (Austin: University of Texas, 1986) and Valentin N. Volosinov, *Marxism and the Philosophy of Language* (Cambridge: Harvard University Press, 1973).
4. David Noble, *America by Design: Science, Technology, and the Rise of Corporate Capitalism* (Oxford: Oxford University Press, 1979).
5. Lily Kaye, *The Molecular Vision of Life: Caltech, the Rockefeller Foundation, and the Rise of the New Biology* (Oxford: Oxford University Press, 1996).

CHAPTER 18

Transforming the University from an Aboriginal Perspective

Jo-Ann Archibald

Q'um Q'um Xiiem, University of British Columbia

The first draft of this article was written while I was on an island off the west coast of British Columbia. From my window, I watched the waves of the ocean roll toward the shore. The first wave made me think of the Aboriginal academics who first worked at Canadian universities during the 1960s–1990s and who are still academics, or have retired, or have passed to the spirit world. They include Marlene Brant Castellano, Joe Couture, Gail Guthrie Valaskakis, Freda Ahenakew, Olive Dickason, LeRoi Littlebear, Carl Urion, Stan Wilson, Verna J. Kirkness, and Eber Hampton. Shortly after the first ocean wave has touched the land, the second wave follows and, over time, the land may be altered by the combined impact of the waves. I position myself as part of the second wave of Aboriginal academics who are now in academe. In this article, I pay tribute to those who made their imprint upon the university to make it more responsive to providing university access and relevancy to Aboriginal learners; highlight the opportunities and challenges of the second wave of Aboriginal academics; and suggest possibilities for the third and subsequent waves of Aboriginal scholars. The cumulative work of the first and second waves of Aboriginal scholars has initiated the Indigenous transformation of the university in a myriad of ways that will be discussed in this article.

First Wave Aboriginal Scholars

Making institutional changes during the decades of the 1960s–1990s was especially difficult given that mainstream universities did not have many Aboriginal students attending, they had very few Aboriginal faculty, and they often did not recognize or value Aboriginal knowledge and ways of knowing. Nevertheless, during this first wave, a number of Aboriginal scholars were engaged in starting or strengthening Aboriginal programs and challenging academic disciplines to consider Aboriginal knowledge and culture in areas such as social work (Castellano), First Nations studies (Castellano, Littlebear, Ahenakew), teacher education and graduate studies (Kirkness, Wilson), Aboriginal languages (Ahenakew, Kirkness), communications (Valaskakis), and history (Dickason). Others attempted to change institutional policy such as mandatory retirement at age 65 (Dickason); took on key university leadership positions such as president (Hampton), dean (Valaskakis), chairs or directors of major programs and units (Castellano, Littlebear, Ahenakew, and Kirkness); created new university entities to increase student access and retention (Urion and Kirkness); and facilitated Aboriginal discourse through editorship of scholarly journals (Urion and Kirkness).

In order to give some personal and contextual perspective to the first and second wave impact of Aboriginal scholars, I will use the University of British Columbia (UBC) as an example because I know that context intimately. The UBC Vancouver campus is situated on the most westerly point of Vancouver. It sits on the traditional and unceded land of the Musqueam people. The waves of the Pacific Ocean greet this land every day.

Verna J. Kirkness was the first Aboriginal tenure-track faculty member to be hired at UBC in 1980. She came to UBC to be the supervisor of the Native Indian Teacher Education Program (NITEP), a Bachelor of Education degree program in the Faculty of Education. NITEP started in 1974, but it had not had any Aboriginal person leading the program until Verna's appointment. Verna created many important changes at UBC during her tenure, from 1980 to 1993. Aboriginal peoples began to develop and teach the NITEP Aboriginal education courses, they became coordinators, and they became the leaders of NITEP. By the time Verna retired from UBC, she had founded an Aboriginal graduate specialization called Ts'kel in the Faculty of Education and a new university-wide unit called the First Nations House of Learning (FNHL) that worked with faculties and schools to develop Aboriginal programs and courses, facilitated student access and retention, expanded Aboriginal student services, and maintained critical links between the university and Aboriginal communities. A beautiful Musqueam-style longhouse was completed in 1993 as a "home away from home" for Aboriginal students and as an important academic, social, and cultural gathering place on the UBC Vancouver campus.

Verna challenged the university to offer Aboriginal-oriented programs; to hire Aboriginal people who, even though they did not have doctoral degrees at the time to teach Aboriginal courses, had equivalent knowledge; and to ensure that Aboriginal Elders participated in key decision-making university committees. She also challenged Aboriginal undergraduate and graduate students and Aboriginal faculty to put education into culture instead of putting culture into education. The emphasis of using Aboriginal culture as the learning framework made us question the status quo of changing or assimilating Aboriginal students to fit into the mainstream Western university. Today, we talk about a decolonizing approach (Smith, 1999; Battiste, 2000). This is what Verna was making us do. When Verna retired, there were three other tenure-track Aboriginal faculty and many more part-time and full-time sessional instructors and lecturers. I was one of the tenured faculty (senior instructor) in 1993.

A Second Wave Aboriginal Scholar's Reflections

Even though I have been at the university for just over 25 years, I consider myself part of the second wave of Aboriginal academics. I have been a sessional lecturer, full-time lecturer, instructor, senior instructor, associate professor, director, and now associate dean. Through these faculty appointments, I have had the opportunity to teach, mentor undergraduate and graduate students, develop courses and programs, develop student services, engage in policy development, gain management experience, do research, and provide community service to Aboriginal communities and organizations and to the university community. From 1981–1989, with a master's degree, I focused on teaching, program development and coordination, and working closely with undergraduate and master's students in my lecturer appointments (sessional and full-time). The rewards were seeing students start a program and achieve success, overcoming numerous institutional barriers and personal challenges such as limited finances, separation from home community, and experiencing racism. For many it was like climbing a steep mountain. Seeing Aboriginal graduates working in their professions and working to improve the well-being of Aboriginal peoples and their communities reinforced for me the benefit of university education that had relevance to Indigeneity. Because I wanted to continue working at the university, I started a Ph.D. in 1989 and was promoted to senior instructor with tenure four years later, based upon my teaching experience.

I began to get a better understanding of the wider university when I became the second director of the First Nations House of Learning after Verna retired. During the 1990s, my FNHL colleagues and I worked with various faculties to develop new programs such as the First Nations Languages Program and the First Nations Studies Program in the Faculty of Arts, the Institute for Aboriginal Health in the College of Health Disciplines, the Aboriginal strategic initiatives in the Faculty of Forestry, and the Aboriginal business education program (now called Chinook) in the Sauder School of Business. As well, we introduced a new undergraduate Aboriginal admissions policy and encouraged the appointment of more Aboriginal tenure-track faculty members and more Aboriginal peoples to serve as Aboriginal coordinators in faculties.

The work of improving access to the university and expanding intellectual space in the faculties for Aboriginal peoples and Aboriginal knowledge has consumed my energies since I started at UBC. As I reflect upon these experiences, there are some defining moments that exemplify the critical changes that have occurred at a university such as UBC to make it a better place of learning, and troubling moments that reveal the challenges that still must be tackled.

First Wave Impact: Opening up the Physical and Academic University Landscape

A grand opening was held in May 1993 for the First Nations longhouse at UBC. Over 1,000 people witnessed this event, which celebrated the co-operative work among people at UBC, the B.C. Aboriginal communities, the provincial government, and private donors. For many years, the Aboriginal peoples at UBC dreamed of having a longhouse that would bring people together to learn, to dialogue, to practise culture, and to make the university a more welcoming place for Aboriginal peoples. Finally, there was a magnificent Indigenous learning facility on the UBC Vancouver campus that reflected the Musqueam traditional-style longhouse. In the words of Verna J. Kirkness:

> We wanted the longhouse to be our home away from home, where children and Elders had a prominent place in the daily lives of the students. We wanted the longhouse to be a place where our heritage would be respected and where our cultures could thrive. We wanted the longhouse to be a place where we could share our knowledge and cultures with one

another. We wanted the longhouse to be a place where we could share our knowledge and cultures with the university community and with the larger society. Today, we gather to celebrate a dream come true, a vision to benefit those with us now and those children who are yet unborn.[1]

Before the longhouse, some of the Aboriginal programs were located in former army huts that were left on the university campus. The longhouse is symbolic of the challenge that Verna gave to us to put education into culture. It is a place of learning that represents a First Nations structure; it is like a theory that guides practice. Even though it is only one building on a large university campus, it is built upon a firm foundation of Indigenous knowledge. It is a building that Aboriginal students, faculty, and community members can be proud of, and it shows that Indigeneity stands firmly within a mainstream university. Most importantly, it is the result of co-operative efforts of many people within UBC and from Aboriginal communities. In 1993, programs such as NITEP and Ts''kel were operating in the Faculty of Education, and First Nations Legal Studies in the Faculty of Law. Movement was happening in the health area with the formation of the First Nations Health Careers unit. Education, law, and health were the first academic areas that had opened academic space for Aboriginal programs, Aboriginal peoples, and Aboriginal-content courses.

Second Wave Impact:
Growing a Corpus of Indigenous Scholars and Indigenous Scholarly Work through Research

Each May, the UBC First Nations longhouse is filled with family and friends who come to witness the graduation of Indigenous students from all faculties. As each person walks through the ceremonial door, his or her Aboriginal affiliation is called out along with the degree. They are proud to acknowledge their Aboriginal identity in the same breath as their degree. Even though the completion of university degrees for Aboriginal peoples is much lower than that of non-Aboriginal people (8.9 percent compared to 24 percent respectively),[2] those who do graduate add to the small but growing critical mass of Aboriginal university graduates who will contribute to making positive change for Aboriginal peoples and their lives. Many of these graduates are the first to complete a university degree in their family. There is another small but growing trend of Aboriginal graduate students at the doctoral level.

In July 2006, a cohort of students pursuing a doctorate of education (Ed.D.) in the UBC Faculty of Education began their program in Indigenous education leadership. This doctoral program is the first of its kind to be offered at a Canadian university. Of the 15 in the cohort, all but two are Indigenous students. They work in leadership roles in K–12 schools, colleges, universities, social services, and the health sectors. In 2007–2008, there were 35 Indigenous doctoral students enrolled in the Faculty of Education in both Ph.D. and Ed.D. programs, representing almost 9 percent of the doctoral student population. Today, there are graduate courses about Indigenous knowledges and education, Indigenous epistemology, and Indigenous methodologies. Indigenous graduate students have more opportunities to develop their own forms of Indigenous methodologies, if they so choose, and their research aims to contribute to the transformation of Indigenous education at all levels. This starkly contrasts with 1989, the year I enrolled in a Ph.D. program at Simon Fraser University, when there may have been only one other Aboriginal person at UBC completing a doctoral degree.

A Critical Challenge to Be Addressed

The memorable moments described above highlight some of the positive improvements that have occurred in academe based on years of constant hard work by many people, yet one of the greatest challenges not yet tackled is changing institutional policy regarding promotion and tenure of Indigenous faculty members. Currently, there are approximately 20 Aboriginal tenure-track or tenured faculty at UBC, which is about 1 percent of the total faculty of about 2,000. These faculty members must not only meet research/publication, teaching, and service contributions, but they usually engage in additional advocacy work for students, develop new programs, fundraise, and establish and maintain Aboriginal community relationships. Any project or initiative that involves or affects Aboriginal concerns is given to them to complete and they often sit on many more committees than other faculty in order to have Aboriginal representation. If universities are to attract and retain Aboriginal faculty, there must be recognition of the extra responsibilities that they carry out.

The Canadian Association of University Teachers (CAUT) has created an Aboriginal working group of which I am a member. In February 2008,

CAUT hosted a national conference for Aboriginal scholars with the second one planned for November 2009. The issue of Aboriginal community work being undervalued as a criterion for promotion and tenure was reinforced by many who attended this conference. University promotion and tenure committees often do not recognize or understand that much time and effort is needed to build trusting and effective educational and research relationships with Aboriginal communities and organizations in order for Aboriginal peoples to feel comfortable with participating and working with university academics. The community-oriented work of Aboriginal academics helps the university meet its goals of increasing the numbers of Aboriginal students and meeting the needs of Aboriginal communities.

What Lies Ahead for the Third Wave?

I believe that we have reached a time in our history when the third wave of Indigenous academics can really make substantial changes to academe, *en force*, to actualize the transformation of university education and research that was begun by their Indigenous predecessors. The first and second wave Indigenous scholars have struggled to create critical but small openings in academe so that Indigenous programs, Indigenous knowledges, and Indigenous methodologies now exist and more Indigenous scholars are being hired by universities in Canada. Alliances with Indigenous scholars from around the world have been created and this international network is becoming stronger. Their advocacy-oriented academic work has often been detrimental to their academic careers, resulting in few refereed journal articles, which is still the prized currency for achieving promotion. They have consequently reduced their chances for promotion to full professors or delayed their tenure and promotion, or have even been overlooked for prestigious faculty positions, such as chairs.

The third wave will have more opportunities to take on key university leadership roles such as dean, vice-president, and even president. Besides making a substantial impact in mainstream universities, the third wave can create and strengthen Indigenous colleges and universities. However, Verna's challenge to put education into culture is a timeless one that Indigenous academics will need to remember. The academic discourse that we use to convey the meaning of this challenge may change over the years, but its implication remains. Another timeless teaching comes from Elders who remind us to keep our Indigenous heart and mind strong, and to do the work we do in education with love in our hearts for the younger and future generations.

Indigenous academics will need to make choices about how much they can engage in transformative academic work and still produce scholarship that will lead to tenure and promotion. From what I have experienced and from the CAUT discussions, these choices represent two different paths. People may change direction and travel on one or the other, but it is difficult to merge them at this time. In order to achieve the timely scholarly success that non-Indigenous academics experience, Indigenous academics may end up compromising their Indigenous heart and mind values, or becoming assimilated in Western academic values, but I remain hopeful that the work of the future academics may change these promotion and tenure challenges. One emerging collective strategy that is taking hold at some universities is the development of an Indigenous academic caucus. Working together in a co-operative manner can reduce the isolation that Indigenous academics face in their departments where they may be the sole Indigenous scholar or one of the very few, and a strong collective stance can be a powerful force for addressing issues such as promotion and tenure.

In the days ahead, I look forward to standing by the shoreline of academe to see the imprint that the subsequent waves of Indigenous scholars will make on universities.

All My Relations.

Notes

1. Verna J. Kirkness and Jo-ann Archibald, *The First Nations Longhouse: Our Home away from Home* (Vancouver: First Nations House of Learning, 2001), 5.
2. Andrew Sharpe, Jean-Francois Arsenault, and Simon Lapointe, *The Potential Contribution of Aboriginal Canadians to Labour Force, Employment, Productivity, and Output Growth in Canada, 2001–2017* (Ottawa: Centre for the Study of Living Standards, 2007), 7.

References

Battiste, Marie, ed. *Reclaiming Indigenous Voice and Vision*. Vancouver: UBC Press, 2000.

Smith, Linda Tuhiwai. *Decolonizing Methodologies: Research and Indigenous Peoples*. London: Zed, 1999.

CHAPTER 19

Engaging Race, Anti-racism, and Equity Issues in the Academy:
A Personal Odyssey

GEORGE J. SEFA DEI

Social Anthropologist and Sociologist,
Ontario Institute for Studies in Education/University of Toronto

In this short essay, I invite readers to join me as I reflect on the challenges, desires, possibilities, and limitations of engaging race, equity, and diversity issues in the academy. My critical focus will be on race, anti-racism, and equity issues—defined broadly to include class, gender, sexuality, language, and religious difference—as seen through the lens of my personal experience. The mere fact that I feel free to embark upon this personal offering calls for celebration.

The personal has often been, and still is, dismissed in academic circles as subjective, biased, and unwarranted. In my early training as a social anthropologist, I often encountered anthropological monographs where the introductory chapter was anything but personal. Only in the preface would the author veer boldly into the personal odyssey of his or her intellectual exploits. Even then, the author would cursorily mentioned his or her personal/subject location as if it were an afterthought.

But the tables are now turned and some of us are free to bring in the personal side of our intellectual stories. Admittedly, personal narratives can be used simply to justify what we write about or engage in, or to validate our arguments in the name of social justice or equity-based research. The onus is on the academy to curtail this danger. Nevertheless, I believe strongly in grounding analyses in the personal as it helps the reader to understand the writer's perspective and social/spatial location. This is especially the case when focusing on anti-racist critical discourse theory and methodology. As a colleague recently noted, to identify our subject position is not just to outline an ideology or an analytical framework, but also to inscribe a personal account of why we write about what we do.

To paraphrase a question posed by an aspiring U.S. presidential candidate: Who am I, and why am I here? Born and educated in my early years in Ghana,

West Africa, I immigrated to Canada to undertake post-graduate studies at McMaster University and the University of Toronto. Today, I am privileged to be teaching in a graduate department of education at a premier Canadian university. My areas of teaching and research interests are anti-racism, minority schooling, international development, and anti-colonial thought. Like many others, my professional and academic work has led to speaking invitations in Canada, the U.S., Europe, and Africa. I consider myself a public intellectual who has taken advantage of radio and television appearances to highlight my focus on strategies for educational and social transformation within Canada and the transnational diaspora.

The university is an interesting place to have been over the past two decades to carry on this work. It is a space that allows us to think and express our ideas on some of the most pressing issues of the day. As a community of learners in this space, we have a collective responsibility for the continued strength and growth of the university as an important cultural tradition. The privilege of teaching in the university requires that we speak out clearly and boldly to make this intellectual space even brighter and more welcoming for all.

However, traces of exclusion remain in the academy wherever we turn. To write and speak about them takes courage, given that the academy rewards silence and punishes resistance. One of my former graduate students pointed out that no one, upon entering institutions of higher education, passes a sign saying, "Welcome to a Eurocentric institution." Yet some of us see and understand this verity not only through actions we witness, but also through observing which ideas are discussed and heralded and which are silenced and left under the sink. I have thus concluded that a scholarly gaze on race, equity, and knowledge production in the academy offers possibilities of extending the intellectual terrain of discursive politics for critical scholars not only to draw upon, but also to carve out possibilities for social change.

It is not easy to bring critical voices that challenge dominant thinking in public and academic discourse. There is a cost in doing this work, namely, that the person doing it is perceived to be always criticizing, angry, and at times not intellectually credible. I take issue with some colleagues who think that those of us who speak out on race, equity, and oppression are ungrateful for this privilege and are repaying the magnanimity of wider society by fomenting problems that do not exist in the first place. On the contrary, the greatest contribution that so-called immigrants to Canada such as myself could make is to strengthen the place we call our new intellectual home and insist that the wider society live up to its ideas of justice and freedom in every sense of the words. Encouraging newcomers to speak their minds and act on their commitment to social equity and accountability may encourage others to give up their silence and finally be heard.

There is speaking, but there is also listening. In writing about race and anti-racism knowledge, I am continually grateful to the listener since oppressed bodies are never guaranteed that they will be listened to or heard. Many times we do not listen to each other because we arrogantly believe that we know already, or because we refuse to hear a different voice for fear that it may challenge our complacency and comfort. We feel comfortable in our cocoons and become intellectually hostile if excellence—that is, our understandings of what is best, acceptable, respectable, or knowledgeable—does not reflect our own image. Another former student pointed out that wisdom, patience, and piety inspire others to know. They also are the ingredients of excellent scholarship. Arrogance and the belief that one knows all the answers have no effect on knowledge production other than to stunt the spirit and disconnect it from the gravity of awakening.[1]

As anti-racist practitioners working for social justice, we should never allow our abilities, our lives, spiritual purpose, and the particular positions and intellectual spaces we enter (or fall) into be subsumed by conventional/dominant ways of producing valid and acceptable knowledge. To this end, I believe scholarship and activism should go hand in hand. Some colleagues may crave the independence of scholarship from activism, but I have a different position. Our institutions are such that we need academic warriors and academics with consciences. Taking stances assumes a huge intellectual risk given the way the academy distributes rewards and punishment and depending on how comfortable we feel with intellectual stances. I do not insist that everyone subscribe to the practice of activist scholarship. Such a practice means imposing values and ideas. By the same token, those who disagree should not impose on me their standards of knowledge production and validation as though they are the only legitimate and objective way of knowing or of producing knowledge.

For me, theory is a living conceptual document. Anti-racist theory must be alive and compel action. It changes us with each passing day. Theory resides in our everyday realities, and a good theory must comprehend daily challenges and offer adequate responses to be felt, understood, and acted upon by an anti-racist ally. In light of the expanding literature on critical race and anti-racism studies, it is disheartening to constantly hear critics obsess over a supposed lack of conceptual and analytical clarity about race and anti-racism. We need to move beyond searching for an objective, scientific, value-neutral exposition of race and anti-racism knowledge production. Not that this is an unimportant inquiry, but it becomes problematic when it forecloses a critical understanding of what is at the core of anti-racism work and theory.

To begin, we need to recognize that race and racism exist in our society. For those who believe race is an illusion—that the term lacks a scientific and analytical status—the question remains how we must account for the power of the illusion. Historically, race has always been central to colonizing relations. Racial supremacist ideas have enforced colonists' domination, and these ideas and practices have continually been reproduced to serve the interests of the powerful. Goldberg attests to how the European colonial project of empire building relied on race to legitimize its domination of other groups.[2] That racism, classism, sexism, etc., have all been at the core of societal dynamics is a fact of life. They have been implicated in power, control, and conditions of oppression and marginalization for centuries.

Those who benefit from the ways in which the processes of racialization accord privilege and punishment find it easy to deny the power of race. But an anti-racism discursive framework works with the idea that race has substantive explanatory power in racialized and racist encounters. So, I ask, can there be racism without race? Can we have racism without racists? Discussions of race and racism invoke strong emotions and opinions. Everyone can position himself or herself within these discussions and indeed needs to. This includes us as educators. We too hold discursive positions that, like forms of knowledge, are neither disinterested nor neutral. We may work with race or deny race depending on our location in the academic setting and how we see the world. Even when we deny our practices, as knowledge producers we are continually invested in what we do. Claiming neutrality and objectivity in the ways we produce and validate knowledge is intellectually dishonest.

From where I sit there is a fierce struggle in the academy about how we produce, interrogate, validate, and disseminate forms of knowledge. As a public intellectual engaged in this struggle, I have learned many lessons about what happens when someone speaks out differently or against the grain of established truths. I recall writing a piece entitled "Speaking out, Differently" for my university newspaper.[3] As the title attests, my academic and political project was to offer a different reading of youth violence than is offered in dominant interpretations. We all have our understandings of what is violence, its root causes, and how to address these concerns, but in the search for solutions, it is important that we allow different and multiple voices to be heard. This way we can interrogate each other, mindful of the power of multiple knowings and the humility of knowing. But it will not get us anywhere to simply castigate youth and refuse to hear voices that call for collective responsibility while simultaneously critiquing systems, structures, and institutions. Those who take credit for success must be prepared to accept responsibility for failures!

To critics of my position, the phrase "Speaking out, Differently" was lost in translation. A colleague who responded to my main arguments reaffirmed for me that there are interests in the academy that would legitimize particular ways of knowing while denying others the right to knowledge or to know.[4] Those who present counter-interpretations of social facts that challenge established truth or beliefs take risks and often experience consequences. Their academic credentials and credibility, if not the merits of their academic discipline, may be maligned. As well, defenders of dominant views will often twist oppositional or dissenting arguments to support their own claims to know. They abrogate to themselves an intellectual logic that defines their ways of knowing as valid knowledge and, in so doing, they become intellectual gatekeepers without realizing it. Camouflaging vested positions as science and objective knowledge while also claiming to be open-minded is to masquerade intellectual arrogance as intellectual authority.[5]

So what are the future possibilities? Reflecting on my personal intellectual journey, I believe we need to create safe and decolonized spaces to engage discussions about race and other forms of oppression within the academy and the public sphere. We also need to connect these discussions to contemporary public discourse and the role of institutionalized ideologies in fomenting a culture of silence around race and difference.

Achieving this is not easy and it becomes more challenging as our universities shift to commercial knowledge production and become obsessed with maintaining the right image to attract funds from governments and corporate clients. This is not an innocent development. Privileging the production of knowledge that puts universities in good standing with governments and corporate funders means that faculty members, students, and staff who engage some of the tough, critical questions of our time may be scrutinized, if not policed, to ensure that their work does not create a moral panic or offend political or corporate sensibilities. The ever-present threat of corporate funds being withdrawn and fundraising campaigns being jeopardized means that faculty members must be careful of what they research, teach, and disseminate. To do otherwise may jeopardize whatever minor influence they may have in decision making in the spaces they occupy.

If the academy is to be an important place for breaking the culture of silence around race, we must work toward creating a truly democratic culture where people can address issues that really matter to them and do so openly without repercussions. Fostering such a culture will require nurturing "multiple perspectives which [would] engage each dialectically in a process of mutual criticism and mutual correction."[6] Dominant groups have used knowledge to [mis] represent the Other to the extent that the subordinate Other finds it difficult to recognize themselves in the discourses that claim to portray their experiences and concerns. Consequently, anti-racism discourse must acknowledge the epistemic saliency of the oppressed in speaking about their experiences of oppression. Producing race knowledge is critical since it encourages racialized subjects to theorize about equitable spaces and communities in which their identities, experiences, and histories take centre stage.

Finally, I urge that we, as academic workers, not merely acknowledge, but also respond concretely to, difference and diversity. Our work must provide communities of learners with opportunities to speak their understandings of diversity and difference and reflect on the strengths and weaknesses of diversity and difference. We must encourage them to ask what it means to claim a community and affirm responsibility to it. That our histories may be divergent and also contingent on each other calls on us to not simply be responsible for what we say, but also share our intellectual spaces.

Notes

1. A. Wahab, personal communication, Department of Sociology and Equity Studies, Ontario Institute for Studies in Education of the University of Toronto, October 7, 2006.

2. T. Goldberg, *Racist Culture: Philosophy and the Politics of Meaning* (Cambridge: Blackwell, 1993).

3. Dei, George J.S. "Speaking Out, Differently," *University of Toronto Bulletin* (May 29, 2006): 12.

4. See John Furedy, "Gun Related Murder Should Be Judged as Evil and Punished Appropriately," *University of Toronto Bulletin* (June 12, 2006): Letters to the Editor section; Philip Sullivan, "A Merit Oriented Approach," *University of Toronto Bulletin* (August 21, 2006): Letters to the Editor section.

5. A posting on a website affiliated with the University of Toronto, which was recently drawn to my attention, further illustrates my point. It was culled from an article in the *National Post*, of July 28, 2005, entitled "Beware the Lure of Afrocentric Learning." (Accessed from http://www.news.utoronto.ca/inthenews/archive/2005_07_28.html.) I missed this article at the time it appeared, but I see it as hate literature pure and simple, and the fact that it is touted on a university website as real news is extremely problematic. The article rebuffed calls for establishing African-centred/Black-focused schools on an experimental basis, an idea for which a few others and I took a lot of criticism in the media and public circles for daring to reignite at a public forum in the fall of 2005. Interestingly, the same debate has resurfaced in the early part of 2008 in Toronto. If anything, it tells us this problem is not going away soon.

The *National Post* article makes the erroneous assertion that a proposal being primarily advocated by two North American academics—Professor Molefi Asante, of Temple University, and myself—to address "the chronic academic underperformance of Black students in Canada" aims to segregate Black students so they can be taught "a special black-only curriculum in special black-only classes or schools." This assertion is intellectual dishonesty at its worst, but in many ways it is not surprising to me. Although we claim to be fair and open-minded in the academy, we can also be least tolerant of ideas that go against dominant views. One way of reacting to people who disagree with an academic position is to miscapture and mischaracterize their key intellectual arguments.

A lot of selective miscapturing of ideas is happening these days, whether it is the misreading of what anti-racism or anti-colonialism is all about, and/or questioning the merits of Indigenous philosophies to counter dominant ways of knowing. The *National Post* article accused me of arguing that "black knowledge is not about rights or wrongs as such, instead it is an organic reflection of the social reality in which the student lives." It characterized Afrocentric learning as a controversial pedagogy that argues that Black students can succeed if they "incorporate the black mindset." Having depicted my argument these ways, the author reasonably asserts that "these theories … strain the bounds of credibility," and that at their core is the ongoing "hateful brand of Afrocentrism that has no place in our schools." The article concludes with an implicit warning: "Those who would radically change the way we educate some of our children, and who would expect all of us to fund these changes, should be confronted with tough questions. They should be asked to explain their views and their writings. They should be required to detail how their plans will avoid leading to divisions and animosity in the future." This is scary stuff, especially since my theoretical position on African-centred/Black-focused schooling is well documented, explained, critiqued, and debated by accredited and well-informed members of the public and the academy. So much for speaking differently!

6. V. Tucker, "The Myth of Development: A Critique of Eurocentric Discourse," in *Critical Development Theory: Contributions to the New Paradigm*, ed. R. Munck and D. O'Hearn (London: Zed Books, 1999), 1–26.

CHAPTER 20

Feminists in Academe:
From Outsiders to Insiders?

JOAN SANGSTER
Historian, Trent University

What are the possibilities and perils of feminism within academe? This was a question I asked myself when the Canadian Committee on Women's History (CCWH) invited me to participate in a collective retrospective, marking its 30th anniversary in 2005.[1] The panel compelled me to reflect on whether, and how, feminism has transformed the historical profession. Admittedly, my take on this question will be personal, but I believe the subjective should not be left to dangle as idiosyncratic, individualist, or relayed as victim/heroic stories, but should be related to the social forces and cultural imperatives that shaped our lives, the choices we made, and the communities we work in. As historians constantly proclaim, context matters!

The very idea of a personal narrative unsettles me for I don't see the historian's role as one of showcasing ourselves, even if our own political, ideological, or theoretical frameworks inevitably influence our research. Since I have written academically about storytelling, the way in which narratives are used to rationalize or justify one's life, or sometimes to create an appealing "I" for public consumption and posterity, I am wary of overvalorizing the personal narrative.[2] Yet, we can hardly abandon them for they can be a powerful means of conveying a feeling for an era, illustrating one's analysis, or connecting personal and political experiences. My compromise is to try to connect one feminist history, my own, to the history of feminism in a small corner of academe.

I wasn't at the birth of the CCWH, founded by a small group of predominantly young, White, female historians in 1975, but as a university student in the early 1970s, I recall, all too vividly, why professional women felt the need to band together, to promote feminist perspectives, and to offer each other some welcome sanity checks. Despite the renewal of a variety of feminisms in the late

1960s, many workplaces, from blue collar to the professional, were unwelcoming to women, and hostile to feminists. Picturing the social context of the 1970s is crucial: When I graduated from university in 1974, abortion was still unavailable to many women; the condemnation of domestic violence was relatively new; help-wanted ads were only recently desegregated by gender; the term "sexual harassment" had yet to be coined; and housework was derided as non-work.

Those of us who grew up in the so-called rebellious 1960s knew that the reality of this decade was more complicated, a contradictory blend of gender conformity and gender rebellion. By the late 1960s, we may have seen images of youthful protests flashing across the news, but we existed in schools, families, and communities where rigid and repressive gender roles, and a completely taken-for-granted heterosexuality, were still stolidly maintained. In my high school, the dress codes and militaristic rules dictated by those in authority were paralleled by a peer culture of immense conformity in dress, sexual mores, social life, and occupational ambitions—or lack of ambition if you were a girl. This was a far cry from hippie or radical youth cultures, though there were cracks in the edifice of feminine conformity as more young women risked sexual engagement (and it was a big risk, since pregnancy and/or social ostracism as "the easy girl" could result), or expressed their dreams to attend university, leave home, and explore the world.

Perhaps these contradictions are well illustrated by one measure of female achievement at my high school: winning the snow queen (beauty) contest. Despite the fact that many girls from this predominantly middle-class school went on to further education, this contest was supposed to define our desires: designation as beautiful, not smart; understood as a sweet person, not ambitious; becoming a caring nurse, never a doctor. When I show photos of these snow queen contests to women's studies students, they are greeted with amusement, but also with a somewhat agnostic, detached interest in their cultural meanings. More recent academic writing, especially that of self-designated third wavers, often portrays strong critiques of beauty contests as remnants of a simplistic, old-fashioned, judgmental, second wave feminism. Having lived through the oppressive conventionality of them, I'm quite happy to declare my sympathies for those simplistic second wave feminists who staged the Miss America protest in Atlanta in 1968, and who, after all, simultaneously denounced racism and the Vietnam War, something often forgotten.

For more privileged young women from White, middle-class, and, to some extent, working-class backgrounds too, the expansion of universities offered hopeful relief from beauty contests and stultifying conformity, yet in the early 1970s, we attended universities that were very much dominated by middle-class, White men in authority. Some universities still informally barred married women who had spouses at the university from teaching positions, and the appropriate persona of a female faculty member was the career, spinster academic, unencumbered by children. Some professors mused openly that females were hardly serious students (a comment I heard), and there was almost no discussion of women in the curriculum. To be interested even in the history of suffrage marked one out as a *curiosity*.

In the early 1970s, to be sure, a student left and feminist presence was evident on some campuses. Whether they were mobilizing against visiting fascist speakers, protesting cutbacks, or creating an alternative feminist culture (I remember hearing Rita McNeil, the singer, in a Peterborough basement in her early feminist persona), radicals on my campus provided a glimpse of political alternatives to those of us who were intellectually, if not actively, sympathetic. Nor were our sensibilities bound only to our immediate locale: Images like that of the Kent State murders created a sense of outrage and connectedness to other student struggles. Still, radicalization is often a process of uneven development. Although I later understood Marxist-feminists' critique of the family, the ultra-politics of smashing monogamy was still rather unsettling and puzzling to me at that point—perhaps I was trapped in high school notions of romance and gender roles.

Even in graduate school in the late 1970s, women were not always welcome, and feminist history was typecast as marginal at best or trendy at worst. Those of us who survived often found sympathetic supervisors, but a refrain I heard from some faculty and students was that women's history was too political, biased, and partial: How could we not study *men's* gender roles as well, we were asked. The "trendiness" of women's history could also be turned back on us with a barely veiled animosity. Was this not why women received scholarships or other recognition? Women were a smaller proportion of the graduate cohort than now, and though we treasured those few, beleaguered, kind women faculty who offered us support, we could also see that they too were the targets of masculine marginalization: Those who stuck their necks out on issues like sexual harassment might be mocked or sidelined.

In other words, a resurgent feminism did not immediately change academe. That was part of a much longer struggle, which was not without its sweet rewards. My most savoured political moment in my 25 years at Trent University was our success in securing a new, state-of-the art daycare, a concrete testament to our political lobbying, and a changing professoriate (or, in this case, administration) that recognized the importance of child care to our professional and personal lives. New hiring and possibilities for women opened up because feminists and their allies struggled hard to make them, but this gendered democratization of universities was ethnically and racially limited. However acute our analysis of the masculine, or even heterosexist university (homophobia was one of our key concerns when we organized the first Women's Centre on the McMaster campus), a critique of the racial exclusions characterizing academe took shape later. And the lingering echoes of traditional gender roles or insecurities echoed in our heads, keeping us prisoners of the imposter syndrome, something that was compounded for women from more marginal class or ethnic backgrounds. Universities may have beckoned feminists with hope and possibility, but always within circumscribed bounds, both social and intellectual.

The cumulative effect of the rhetoric of equality but a reality of sexism, along with political impact of the radical social movements of the 1970s, did have some transformative consequences. We were heartened by a political feeling in the air that things just might be turned upside down. After all, for over a decade, civil rights, class, and anti-colonial struggles, as well as feminism, had been challenging social authority. I emphasize this range of influences because the received stereotype of second wave feminism (itself a flawed term that suggests a trough in feminist politics between 1919 and 1969) needs revision. In one of our more recent ritual women's-studies'-students-criticize-the-faculty sessions, a student equated second wave feminism with the belief that only gender mattered and a homogenized (White, middle-class) woman is at the centre of inquiry. One professor's course, it was charged rather condescendingly, was just "soooo second wave" (even though it actually included many articles on class and imperialism). Make no mistake, this was a putdown, and is there anything more depressing than being consigned to the category of "dinosaur feminist"?

Influenced by a range of political ideals, some of us ended up as feminists or in women's studies not via a one-way route from women's consciousness-raising (nor was a universal sisterhood necessarily our political ideal), but via multiple trajectories. The first book that profoundly unsettled my liberal (and as a child of Trudeaumania, I admit Liberal for one election) allegiances in high school was actually *The Unjust Society* by Harold Cardinal. Another epiphany came when I finally understood the theory of surplus value during a Marxist institute course, though by that time, I was reading and influenced by socialist-feminists like Sheila Rowbotham.[3] And as an undergraduate with no exposure to women's history, my first desire was to be an African historian. Revolutions are often more enticing elsewhere, though after a period travelling in Africa, I reconsidered the possibility of studying radicalism on the home front. Even in graduate school, my politicization was linked as much to union and left friends and political work (organizing the McMaster Graduate Assistants Association [the early CUEW], solidarity work for the 1978–1979 Sudbury miners strike, and Hamilton Working Women) as it was to my participation in the establishment of the first feminist Women's Centre on campus. I don't want to overidealize our politics: There were also tensions, problems, and blind spots, but we did not emerge from one feminist mould.

Still, feminist professional groups and networks like the CCWH were important to those of us working within male-dominated institutions. Even if my identification was also with the left, feminist organizations spoke meaningfully to some aspects of my life. After all, our politics do not fit neatly into one of the trilogy of radical, socialist, or liberal feminism: They are often more messy. Even though we were studying and working within the privileged space of the university, our isolation was still very real. This was symbolized for me at my first departmental meetings (all men) in which the youngest man always addressed us rather augustly as "gentlemen," though I'm not sure he was one when it came to women. Isolation was compounded by the downward plunge in the economy from the late 1970s through even worse times in the early 1980s, when hiring was almost non-existent. Some of my cohort just gave up on academic life.

A collective identification with other feminists in the same boat, if not sharing the same politics, was thus important. I recall the first time I ever gave an academic paper (eight months pregnant, and without a job), confronting my very real trepidation about public speaking, which has never entirely dissipated. Two feminist historians I had never met, Bettina Bradbury and Vikki Strong-Boag, appeared at my side afterwards and said, "Come to lunch and tell us about your research." That kind of reaffirmation was simply a revelation for me. Building this professional feminism did not necessarily entail a mentoring process in which we were counselled on careerism or encouraged to cite our mentors approvingly. It was a more informal, subtle, and personal process that emerged organically because we were still on the margins. Within our own institutions, the joys of feminist friendships were also a wellspring of support and comfort. In the light of later critiques of the race and class limitations of 1970s feminism, we may be inclined to downplay our feelings at the time, but in all honesty, we did feel drawn together by a sense of outrage about women's oppression, and invigorated by an exhilarating sense of purpose, connection, and solidarity engendered in our political work.

When the CCWH emerged, it thus spoke to a new generation of women in academe, archives, and museums; it promoted a new field of study we felt quite passionate about; and it allowed isolated feminists fleeting connections across geographical and institutional distances. Though we were homogeneous in terms of race and our politics were not cut from the same cloth, as a professional organization, we had to find common ground unspecific to left, liberal, or other ideological positions. Our priorities also changed over time: In the 1970s, attempts at inclusiveness were linked to regional participation and, most importantly—given the analysis of Quebec as a colony—the inclusion of Quebec historians, though I think Quebec feminists quite rightly saw that this dialogue usually happened in one linguistic direction.[4]

Assessing the situation in 2009, one can chalk up some successes for feminist historians. The few, much-cited male historians, quoted in the *Globe and Mail*, who offer up derisive views on feminist history, do not represent the mainstream of the profession. Look at the articles published, papers at conferences, editorial boards, executives of professional organizations, routine questions to job applicants (what about gender?), and prizes awarded. Look at power. True, there may be some stray departments and individuals trapped in the past, but the centre of the profession has decisively shifted. Surely we can conclude that a liberal feminist project has scored some points—and not inconsequential ones at that.

This is not to offer up a Whig view of unending feminist progress, as if to say, we have come a long way, baby, and can now rest on our laurels: Aren't we lucky that we now have (real) maternity leaves, anti-harassment clauses, courses on women, more than one woman per department, and women's studies programs, to name a few things that simply did not exist when I began. Even if the gendered face of academe altered, we have to recognize that this did not address other oppressions and exclusions based on class and race. Secondly, sexism has not been completely vanquished; studies, for instance, show that too many women are still systemically clustered in particular disciplines and at lower levels of the profession, but statistics are not the whole story. Feminist organizing has altered academe and, perhaps most importantly, without the larger feminist movement, we *would be nowhere.* Not only did feminist organizing win key gains like reproductive rights, which were crucial to our well-being and ability to stay in academe, but feminist, anti-racist, and anti-colonial organizing also provided political dialogue, inspiration, and examples for us, while also posing challenges to what we researched and wrote about.

Unfortunately, we also found that feminism could accommodate itself to academic life and institutions in reformist, even acquiescent forms; after all, gender equality can be tailored to fit into existing professional hierarchies. Feminism might alter the face of a masculine university, certainly for the better, but it could also take on alarming forms, shape-shifting to become individualist, competitive, careerist, thus absorbing the long-time ingredients of academic life. And precisely because feminism—at least in some forms—became more respectable, it could be used by a very few individuals as a pathway for self-advancement. Universities when I started were ruled by old boys. Now there are dynamic women at the top, yet this has not altered the pernicious influence of a more corporate agenda in higher education. Nor, as I have discovered the hard way, are academic freedom and union democracy automatically guaranteed by having female union leaders. And we have yet to really open up universities to working-class and racialized youth. Moreover, feminism can also be used as a strategy of derision and opposition to *other* politics of emancipation—such as Marxism—that some of us still embrace, putting us in the difficult position of engaging critically with other feminists. While acknowledging that class designations and political typologies are complex, not all brands of feminism are simpatico, and I believe that some feminist strategies for individual advancement *do* have negative consequences for the interests of other, more marginalized women.

Make no mistake: This is not another attack on either the professionalization of women's studies (which brought both benefits and problems, inevitably placing us in a contradictory role in universities) or on women administrators per se. In the latter case, I can identify with the hope of trying to make things just a little better in the institutions where we work, but how do we avoid feminism being trapped within the ethos of individualism and careerism that shapes university life? I hear many radical positions publicly professed by academics, yet, despite their own security, some will then say they cannot take a stand on some issue of principle—however small—because it will be negative for their career: I have to please this person, I can't be shut out of publishing, professional networks, and so on, are the direct, or more often subtle, responses. This is surely depressing. This does not mean I agree for a second with misogynist writers who trash academic feminism as opportunist, antidemocratic, authoritarian, and so on. As an ideal, feminism stands for equality and the questioning of all oppressions, and that is what I believe we should continue to work toward.

Do we still need professional organizations like the CCWH even though feminism has made inroads into universities? I would say yes, as long as gender inequality remains (and it does), and yes, because they represent a historic feminist impulse of importance, because they can connect us to other marginalized groups in academe, and because they can provide a link with like-minded historians across the globe. The use of "woman" in the title may seem a contradiction as feminist writing increasingly explores intersectionality and analyzes multiple axes of power. Perhaps the nomenclature of the CCWH is more symbol than analytic tool: It recognizes that women's historical marginalization brought the organization into being and remains one site of social inequality. The more important issue for me is whether feminism will be absorbed into the existing academic power structures, and whether it can deliver on the broader emancipatory ideals that inspired us 30 years ago. In *After Theory*, Terry Eagleton has recently lamented the disappearance of more utopian, radical hopes for social change within intellectual life. If the universities are now less likely to be engaged in these debates, he says, they nonetheless provide one place where things *might* continue to be turned upside down.[5] I would agree: They remain places of possibility, but also of political confinement. They are places of privilege, and I would never argue that our workplace issues are more critical than those of exploited women service workers in the new economy. Feminists like myself, who grew up in the dark days of snow queen contests, and never even imagined we had the ability, qualities, or especially the right to be here (despite my White, middle-class background), are the lucky ones. To be sure, we have benefited from the flowering of professional liberal feminism and the gains made by the women's movement. The question is whether this will remain the end of the line, or simply a stage along a political road, whether we can maintain a vision of a more comprehensive, transformative politics of liberation, or give in to the comfortable and limited progress that has already been made.

Notes

1. My thanks to the CCWH as my presentation became the basis for this article: "Thirty Years of the CCWH," Canadian Historical Association Meeting, University of Western Ontario, June 2005.
2. Joan Sangster, "Telling Our Stories: Feminist Debates in Oral History," *Women's History Review* 3, no. 1 (1994): 5–27.
3. Sheila Rowbotham, *Woman's Consciousness, Man's World* (London: Penguin, 1973); *Women, Resistance and Revolution: A History of Women and Revolution in the Modern World* (New York: Vintage Books, 1974).
4. Veronica Strong-Boag, *What Is to Be Done: The Canadian Committee on Women's History*, pamphlet published by the CCWH, August 1995.
5. Terry Eagleton, *After Theory* (New York: Basic Books, 2003).

CHAPTER 21

An Ode to Wisdom:
Got, Don't Got, Borrowed, and Sought

Elizabeth (Bessa) Whitmore
Social Work Educator, Carleton University

Dear new faculty member,

I wish I had had one of these letters when I first started in academia. It might have helped me learn some lessons the easy way. Inevitably, I suppose, the trial and error that is life teaches us what we need to know if we take the time to listen. So, I offer some reflections on my zigzag path through academia and through life, and a few bits of advice from the I-wish-I'd-known-that department, from the wonderful vantage point of hindsight.

Gender Counts in Academia, Whatever the Rhetoric
"Someday, Maybe I'll Get into Teaching ...
No Straight and Narrow Path."
In the late 1980s, at a faculty union-sponsored workshop at Dalhousie University, I was asked to talk about my experience as a part-time—as yet untenured—faculty member. I drew a zigzag line on a flip chart, putting in all the detours and obstacles that I had encountered along the road to tenure. While most men seemed to have travelled a pretty straight line from graduate school to a tenure-track position to tenure, my road was full of curves and potholes.

I first got into academia as a social worker with a master's degree and 10 years of on-the-ground experience. I thought that I'd get into teaching, a notion I had had since my own graduate days. I wanted to improve what I had experienced as a patronizing, detached-from-reality education.

Social work is a women's profession; so it is low prestige (and pay) in general and certainly within the university system. But the good news is that, at least back then, seasoned practitioners looking to enter academia were viewed as an asset to schools of social work, most commonly through the field practicum, a standard part of social work education. Thus, ever so naively, I began by agreeing to take on the supervision of a community-based field unit for a school of social work, which was quite an innovative idea since most field placements are in established agencies and organizations. I jumped at the chance.

At the time, I was married and had two small children, so—*of course*—I would only be able to work part-time. Child care was what women did, and besides, my husband had a full-time, tenure-track position. My job was an extra, he thought and, to be fair, so did I, though I knew that being at home full-time with small children was not a good fit for me. I ended up working on contract, part-time for the next 15 years, with four years in the middle to do a Ph.D.

The debate among faculty at the school about how I should approach the field placement was between the micros, those doing individual and small group work—"She should just take the students out to the community and see what happens"—and the macros, the social policy people—"Oh no, she has to make a master plan … get all the key decision makers on side." I felt like the ball in a tennis match!

In the end, the micros won that round, and four students and I found our way to Sackville, a new, fast-growing suburb on the outskirts of Halifax. In this planned community, there were roads, basic water and sanitation systems, and schools, but otherwise there were no social services—indeed, no services at all. No grocery stores, no health facilities, no public transportation, though there were a few gas stations and the occasional corner store. We were astonished to find that the planning documents for the new community contained just one short paragraph about community development. All the rest was basic, physical infrastructure. People living in Sackville, mostly young families, had to go to the city for virtually all of their needs, except spiritual, as there were some churches. And if you didn't have a car, you were stuck. Husbands took the one car to work and it was the women who were left at home to manage.

Where should our field unit, a little group of outsiders, start? We plunked ourselves down in the middle of the community and thought about what to do first. We decided to start by talking to the people who lived there about their lives, concerns, and wishes. To do this, we developed a brief set of survey questions and went knocking on doors. What we found were people—mostly women, as this was during the daytime—who felt isolated, frustrated, and who yearned for the basics of any community, both physical (amenities, services) and emotional (connections, a sense of belonging). Politically, they felt they had little voice or ways to make change as Sackville was just one part, albeit a large and growing one, of a sizable rural county. So we got involved in organizing neighbourhood meetings around these issues and by the end of the four-month field placement, the Greater Sackville Community Council was born and, importantly, we had a lot of fun doing it! What a great way to start a teaching career!

Faculty members were astonished. How had we managed to do this in such a short time? We realized, then, that if we had gone the macro route, and spent our time talking to officials and drawing up some kind of plan, nothing would have happened. Indeed, many of these officials were part of the problem. We were simply the sparks that ignited what was ready to happen—a matter of asking a few questions at the right time. This lesson has stayed with me ever since. Start from the ground up, ask lots of questions, listen, and then act.

As a sequel, the following year, as I continued to supervise this field placement, the community council wanted to hold its first annual meeting. How to get people to come out? At about this time, the city of Halifax was looking for a new dump site and, in its infinite wisdom, decided to locate it in the middle of Sackville. They scheduled a public meeting to discuss this and, as you might imagine, most of the community was there to protest. Here was an opportunity we couldn't pass up, so we borrowed a tactic from Saul Alinsky[1] and held the first annual meeting right after the public meeting. Within an hour, we had signed up 400 people!

Part-time Pay, Full-time Work

I continued to work on part-time contracts at the university for the next 15 years. I soon learned that part-time work demanded many more hours than was reflected in the pay. There were no benefits, however. What did I need benefits for, since—*of course*—my husband would support me. It was only after our marriage fell apart that the reality of this situation hit home. All those dreams, all those promises slowly but surely dissolved and I found myself needing to earn more money to support two children and myself.

So, I picked up other contract work outside of academia, mostly in the social service field. At one point during this time, the faculty went on strike—to its credit, one issue of contention was the low pay for part-time faculty (who were part of the union) and, not surprisingly, most were women. As I walked the picket line one day, I told a business professor how smart I thought I was for having two part-time jobs, one inside academia and one outside. His response was to pat me on the head and say, "My dear, we do this on a full-time salary." Oh.

"If I Can Do This, I Can Do Anything"

After the divorce, I went back to school to get a Ph.D., with two upset children in tow. It was one of the hardest times of my life as we all struggled to adjust to a new life in a new place. Being on 24/7 is what single moms do, but until I went through it myself, I had no idea what this really meant. The daily ups and down, the crises, and the emotional storms that accompanied their father's visits took just about all my time and energy. There were three schedules on the fridge door, one for each of us. All women are jugglers, but single moms are the real experts at this!

By the end of four years, I figured that if I could do that, then I could handle just about anything! At the same time, whole new worlds opened up for me, so while it was hard, it was also exhilarating. I was exposed to so many new ideas and possibilities, ones I had never imagined, such as participatory approaches to research, which fit perfectly with my experience and interests as a social worker. I learned that jumping into the unknown is scary, but it can offer unexpected and life-changing opportunities. One weighs the leap carefully, of course, but after this experience, I did it with less fear and more confidence that I could manage.

What kept me grounded and sane during this time was a small support group of women who met just about every week for four years. We cried, we laughed; we shared our stories, our feelings, and our dreams. We were there for each other through the crises; we did silly things, like skinny-dipping in the creek while eating ice cream cones. It was the women's movement at its best, and it was healing.

Learning about Learning

In the late 1970s, the School of Social Work at Dalhousie University began a B.S.W.[2] program. The first priority was to target those already working in the field, 80 percent of whom were untrained, so our classes were held in the evenings, after work hours, and I moved into the classroom. Fortunately, we were given some training in teaching methods, an opportunity that most faculty do

not have. Since we would be teaching working adults, we learned adult education methods, based on the philosophy of Paulo Freire.[3]

Students worked all day, came to a 5 o'clock class, and then into my class,
which went from 7:30 p.m. to 10:00 p.m. You can imagine what shape they
were in by that point! If I talked at them for more than five minutes, their eyes
were closed, and it wasn't because they were carried away by my wisdom. This
is where I learned experiential techniques, such as action-reflection, out of pure
necessity. Students found a reserve of energy in the interactive exercises and
the dialogue that followed.[4] I have taught this way ever since. My philosophy
of teaching is summed up in the proverb: *Tell me and I'll forget. Show me and I
may remember. Involve me and I'll understand.*

People learn in many ways. In universities, the assumption is that people
learn primarily in only one way—passively, through lectures. The lecture halls
consist of chairs bolted down in rows, and the furniture in classrooms is difficult, if not impossible, to move around. It is pretty difficult to have a dialogue
when one is seated in rows! When the School of Social Work at Carleton
University moved to another building on campus, we had to fight for movable
furniture—this at a time when the university publicity was all about opening
up learning, being creative, etc.

At Least One Foot in the Community Keeps You Grounded

"Stop Using Them Big Professor Words!"

I was conducting a participatory evaluation of a single mothers' prenatal
program in Halifax, and had hired and trained three program participants
to do the evaluation—all aspects, including design, data collection, analysis,
and reporting. It was in the writing up of our report that a mother made this
comment when I used the word "specific." My ordinary word was her big
professor word!

One of the biggest problems we have, as academics, is that we forget how to
talk with ordinary folks. The culture, to say nothing of the publication milieu,
demands a particular kind of language, one that few others can fathom. We talk
to each other and understand perfectly. This creates another difficulty when
we want to partner with community groups or organizations; indeed, instances
of miscommunication and/or alienation are well documented.[5]

The euphemism "ivory tower" is, sadly, quite true in my experience.[6] We are, in general, isolated from the community around us, regardless of the rhetoric in many university mission statements. It has been relatively easy, in a school of social work (and as a long-time community activist) for me to be involved in a variety of community activities. Indeed, my scholarly work has been grounded in these activities, but these are not recognized in the university hierarchy of values, and certainly not when it comes to tenure and promotion.

"For Fast-acting Relief, Try Slowing Down" (Lily Tomlin)

The university throws you away when you retire (unless you are a star)—a sad, but true reality. But now I have time, a commodity I never had as a full-time faculty member. I realize now how much I was always running to catch the caboose—there was always something more to read, writing to do, preparing for class, etc.—and I never felt that I had time to spend just hanging out with family and friends. And life speeds by—cranking out more articles, more publications, more course outlines, reports, and critiques, to say nothing of the endless meetings.

Happiness is not having to set the alarm in the morning. Heather Menzies hits the nail on the head in *No Time*[7] when she talks about the lack of time in the speeded-up world of the corporate university. She describes the fast-forward world in which we produce more and more, but have less and less time to reflect, to *be* with oneself, and for real and meaningful dialogue with others.[8] It's like going through an art gallery on a motorbike—everything becomes a blur. Upon retirement from the university, however, I now have time for that dialogue. I have been able to slow down the pace, to reconnect—with myself and with others—in a way I have not for quite awhile. Isn't this what really matters in the end?

At the same time, the generation gap in terms of technology is ever growing. How much are our worlds and our understandings shaped by the technology and the times in which we live? One story brought this home to me. Recently, I was touring the Pablo Neruda Museum in Santiago, Chile. The museum was Neruda's house, so the rooms were full of many things that one would find in a home. In one room there was a 1930s telephone—one of those huge old telephones, with a big receiver that you held up to your ear. A little boy in the tour group, perhaps 10 years old, asked, "What's that?" The guide explained that this was a telephone, the kind they used in the olden days. The boy grew very quiet, with a puzzled look on his face. Finally, he asked, "But how did they get it in their pocket?"

I also am able to draw on the connections and experience that I have built up over the years to continue to work in the community, and this is offering me a wealth of new and challenging opportunities, most, but not all, volunteer. And I don't have to rush out the door in the morning! Recently I was telling a male colleague, who is approaching retirement age, about how much I was enjoying retirement. He was taken aback; the look on his face was confused, even a bit horrified, as he said he couldn't imagine not working. How sad! And how much this tells us about the gap between university and, well, life.

As I reflect back on this zigzag journey, I realize that I got lucky. All those potholes and detours kept me grounded. I'm so glad now that I couldn't take the straight road, which leads directly, and only, to the centre. There, as bell hooks suggests,[9] one sees only the centre, a relatively small reality, and has no idea, really, what goes on outside of that quite elite world. It is those on the margins who understand a much broader reality. hooks was talking about Black women in the feminist movement, and the experience of slaves and domestic servants, but the point is equally relevant in other contexts, including the university.

The principles I have ended up keeping intact were a respect for the democratic process, the importance of participation, and being myself. The struggle continues, however, for me as an individual and for the transformation we seek. We need to model the kind of world we want, not the one we are presented with.

And finally, nurture yourself—continually. Self-care will help keep you grounded, healthy, and whole in the world.

With my warmest best wishes,

Bessa Whitmore

Notes

1. Saul Alinsky, *Reveille for Radicals* (New York: Vintage Books, 1946) and *Rules for Radicals* (New York: Random House, 1971).
2. Bachelor of Social Work as the first professional degree.
3. A Brazilian adult educator, author of *Pedagogy of the Oppressed*, and *Education for Critical Consciousness*.
4. In addition to the coffee and sugar hits that we collectively supplied.

ee, for example, the work of Randy Stoecker (http://www.drs.wisc.edu/stoecker/) or the Canadian Research Institute for the Advancement of Women (CRIAW).

6. Interestingly enough, ivory is found only on the bull elephant, mammoth, and walrus. Only in warthogs, a relatively minor source of ivory, is it found on both male and female animals.

7. Heather Menzies, *No Time: Stress and the Crisis of Modern Life* (Vancouver: Douglas & McIntyre, 2005).

8. Heather Menzies and Janice Newson, "No Time to Think: Academics' Life in the Globally Wired University," *Time and Society* 16, no.1 (March 2007): 13.

9. bell hooks, *Feminist Theory: From Margin to Center*, 2nd ed. (Cambridge: South End Press, 2000).

CHAPTER 22

The University and Its Political Economy:
An Academic Callings Interview

Joel Bakan

Legal Scholar, University of British Columbia

Interview Conducted by Janice Newson

Newson: What kinds of influences have helped to form your ideas about the university?

Bakan: Universities have always been a part of my life. I was an academic brat. My parents were both academics. I was raised in a college town in the U.S. Midwest—East Lansing, Michigan (Michigan State University)—and spent time at Stanford as well, all during the 1960s and early 1970s. My sense of the university was as an intensely political place. My babysitters were members of the SDS (Students for a Democratic Society). My pals and I would play hooky from school and ride our mustang bikes down to student rallies and protests. It was all very exciting.

Newson: So you were aware of [a] lot of the things that were going on in universities in the 1960s. So what kind of vision of the university did you have in your head?

Bakan: I suppose as a young boy I had a nascent sense that the university was a place where people cared passionately about ideas and causes. Students were demonstrating in the streets, my parents were bringing home their intensely animated conversations about their cutting-edge research in experimental psychology—it was all about a passion for ideas, and about questioning the taken-for-granted. As I grew older, this nascent understanding matured into an understanding of the university grounded in political economy—in an understanding of how profoundly the organization of knowledge production shapes the kind of knowledge that is produced. Commercial broadcasting is, for example, one type of organization: Broadcasters sell advertising time for profit. Everything is oriented toward producing an environment conducive to attracting advertising revenue. That imposes limits on the kinds of content you can expect. The university is, ideally, a very different way of organizing the production of knowledge—one that, through public funding, ideals of academic freedom, and boundless inquiry, is supposed to produce a broad range of knowledge and culture that is original, critical, rigorous, questioning, and so on. From quite a young age, this idea of the university was attractive to me. Here was a place, I thought, where I could make a living thinking about the world and engaging critically to try to make it better.

Newson: Given what you have just said, there are probably a lot of other areas that you could have done what you wanted to do.

Bakan: It's true that intellectual work is inherently interdisciplinary, especially when the work you do is critical of mainstream ideas. I was interested, after an undergraduate degree in psychology, in law as a system of norms that governs behaviour in society in a direct and coercive way, not subtly, but through the coercive power of the state, and that also enables coercive action by organizations, like corporations, for example. I suppose the thing about going to law school and becoming a law professor, rather than a sociologist or a political theorist, is that I was able to learn law from the inside, and come to understand it through its own premises. I learned the doctrine and the orthodoxies; I learned the subtle and the difficult-to-put-your-finger-on things about what it means to think like a lawyer, to think through the law, and not just to think about it from some outside position. So I suppose what I have been able to do in my work is to marry that internal knowledge of the legal system with critical theory and social theory that critiques law and its premises from external perspectives. To avoid getting swallowed up by the discipline of law is a challenge. Law is intellectually imperious. Its universalistic pretence can be seductive. I count my blessings to be at UBC where there exists at the law faculty a very fertile and interdisciplinary intellectual community. Not all law faculties are like that.

Newson: Yes, some law faculties are very oriented to that—just the practice and not the grounds or the assumptions on which the practice rests.

Bakan: Exactly, yes. I consider myself very fortunate to have the support of this faculty. I consider myself lucky to be in a position where I can do virtually what I like in terms of ideas. I haven't been somebody who has relied heavily on grant money, and who has crafted an intellectual agenda around the criteria of granting agencies. If there's something I am interested in, if it's consistent with something a grant agency is interested in too, then I'll apply for a grant. Because I don't do empirical work, I am able to get by with a library and various other research tools that come with the job. I have the freedom to pursue my own thoughts and ideas. To me that is the beauty of working in a university—to ask difficult questions that won't be asked anywhere else. They won't get asked anywhere else because of the way knowledge production is organized in those places, so universities create this little enclave where the means of knowledge production are designed to encourage critical thought. That is the value of universities. I don't want to idealize universities in any way, but what I do idealize is the ideal of the university. There is, of course, a gap between that ideal and the reality of the university—a larger or smaller gap depending on where and when you happen to be. Various actors—governments, religious institutions, corporations, and so on—have always wanted to harness the intellectual energy and credibility of the university to their particular agendas. To the extent they are successful, the university becomes less universal, more like a research department. Questions are formed elsewhere and the university is seen just as the place where the answers are discovered or pursued. This is happening today with alliances between universities and for-profit corporations, especially in the sciences, and many people are legitimately worried that the idea of the university as a place to create knowledge freely, not beholden to narrow private interests, and for the good of society as a whole, is threatened. This is a real concern.

Newson: In your book *The Corporation*, you talk a lot about the character of the corporation. Do you see the university as having taken on that kind of character in the way that it functions as an institution?

Bakan: Well, my basic idea with regard to the corporation is that, because of institutional constitutions—their legal mandate to act only in their own self-interest—they function much like psychopathic individuals. The social theorist Max Weber developed an analysis of what happens to institutions when they get too large. His critique was that in such circumstances, individuals within them lose their sense of personal responsibility, and the institutions themselves become irresponsible. In other words, the size of the institution and the creation of bureaucracy become problematic issues that transcend the unique constitution of the institution, so in that sense, one could argue that the differences between a university and a corporation are not that great.

But I don't think that is the case. The differences between universities and corporations are profound. As things currently stand, the university is institutionally structured in accordance with the ideals of the university. Its legal responsibilities and cultural structures still hold to the idea that the university is a place to create knowledge that is in the public interest and for the benefit of the whole society. The corporation, on the other hand, doesn't have that idea. And the extent to which people talk about the university as a corporation serving the interest of society and being for the public good is just talk—good public relations. The university and also government institutions are not at all like a corporation because their function is to serve a broader public interest. But inevitably, certain aspects of university life and university work get tied into the agenda of wealth creation and the interests of corporations through such things as the corporate–university partnerships that have become increasingly prevalent. Ultimately, this contradicts the university's own agenda.

Newson: In terms of the way universities are run, do you see the ideal that we are talking about affecting the way universities are managed?

Bakan: To me, the university is a contradictory institution. It engages different people in different places, and various groupings hold different orientations toward what the university should be and how it should function. Some people want to run the university according to the ideal or principle of free inquiry. Others want to close that down. That tension is always present. How it plays out in different situations and different times is difficult to predict.

However, I think we are shifting in the direction of corporate values. If we look at the course of the last 20 years, there can't be any question about that. It is partly the result of how values have shifted within the university and it is related in some very complicated ways to the broader political-economic situation. More obviously and mechanically, when governments cut back funding for universities, universities went elsewhere—to corporations—to get funding, so how much is this shift the fault of universities, [and] how much is it the fault of government? I know people who berate the CBC for upping the amount of advertising that it airs, but the government has been slashing its budget. How do we deal with these things? And where are we as citizens in this picture? Rather than berating the CBC, maybe we should be berating ourselves. Maybe we should try to elect governments that have a much broader sense of commitment to things like public broadcasting and public-serving universities. But if we allow these things to be underfunded, what do we expect?

I think it comes to a broader political and economic problem. If you asked the president of this university or the dean of my faculty or all of the vice-presidents and the deans of all the faculties what their vision is of the university, or asked them what values they would act on in making their decisions if deans, presidents, and vice-presidents were in charge of where funds would be allocated, I doubt that much more than a small minority, maybe even less, do not hold to the same ideals of university that I hold to. But I think the forces that are affecting the situation are broader than those particular personalities or than the managerial level of the university.

This is not to say that university administrations haven't shifted their approaches to fit in with the ways governments allocate funds. They have adopted more competitive styles in going after grant money, for example, and they direct a lot of their resources toward promoting their own institution as the best bet for government and corporate investments. Universities are involved more in competing with each other to get funding and less involved in collaborating with each other to preserve the ideals of the university. They believe they have to do this in order to survive.

This is the corporate approach and I don't think it's good. It comes out of a commitment to the idea that competition is good, which, in turn, is driven by the ascendancy of market values as the dominant ideological influence right now, but again I am not sure that many people in universities would endorse that belief. Most university administrators would prefer an approach that preserved their institution's autonomy and allowed for more collaboration among autonomous institutions. Most people who choose the university life are at some level, I think, committed to ideals such as the practice of academic freedom and to the idea that universities are unique places that exist for the pursuit of ideas. They are skeptical of government's attempts to influence the agenda of the university.

But the problem is broader than the university. If there isn't a strong commitment to the idea of the university in the broad social order, there isn't a lot for politicians to gain by supporting it. Discussions in the business section of newspapers tell me that business is not so much criticizing particular things that governments do as much as it is criticizing the idea and existence of government itself. In other words, it is challenging the very idea that citizens should have any say over what happens in the economy. This attitude passes on to the university, an institution that exists to serve the public interest and provide a public service. If it is not involved in producing widgets for the marketplace, it is treated as suspect. That, to me, is the fundamental problem.

Newson: As I am listening to you, Joel, I am curious. How is it that someone could label you as a cynic, as you said a few paragraphs back? To me, you sound very optimistic.

Bakan: I am an optimist. I prefer to look at the glass being half full, in spite of the fact that I am a social critic. Some people are confused by this because they think that I am a cynic, but in fact, I am a skeptic, not a cynic. I still believe that we can make ideals of democratic governance and of the university real again. By the same token, I am not going to say that the university has been entirely corrupted. I think some of the ways that it is working have been corrupted and some of the things that it is presently involved in can be corrupting. But I am still sitting here doing the things that people in the university should be doing and there are a lot of other people in this institution and others that are also doing those things. There is a legitimate and healthy debate about what the university should be doing. I would be on one side of that debate and there are other people who would be on another side. But I don't think we have completely lost the ideal. It may have been a little compromised, but it is not lost.

But compounding this problem, in my view, is that many of the approaches adopted by progressive scholars and activists who oppose the ascendancy of market values are counterproductive. For example, I am critical of the idea that the Charter of Rights and Freedoms is a route to progressive politics. I am critical of the notion of corporate social responsibility because I see it as a privatization of progressive politics. In a sense, those who are advocating this notion are leaving it to corporations to, for example, voluntarily look after the environment. As I see it, they have given up on the possibility of democracy. I prefer democratic solutions.

Newson: Do you see a struggle for the university going on?

Bakan: That's a really good question. Yes and no. I guess I don't see a struggle for the university in the sense that many university people have a pragmatic orientation to the way knowledge production is being reorganized. They tend to be unconscious about the relationship between the way the production of knowledge is organized and the kind of knowledge that is produced, yet all of us who do our work of knowledge making in the university should have a very keen understanding of, and be concerned about, it. We should not be pragmatically resigned to the way it is, but I also don't think that it is entirely the responsibility of the people within the university. Nor do I think it is entirely the responsibility of the people within the corporations to try to make the corporation better. A broader political commitment is needed.

We, as academics, could help to cultivate that commitment. There has to be a broader social sense that we are in danger of losing the university as a place to create critical knowledge. For example, the questions that are asked should not be dictated by for-profit companies but rather by concerns about where knowledge should go and what, in a broader sense, the public interest requires. We can argue until the cows come home about what the public interest requires, but that is the argument that has to be had. Many people hold to the theory that the public interest is whatever corporation X is doing because corporations serve their markets, and therefore the public interest becomes whatever the consumer wants. What needs to be understood is that corporations don't have places to think about anything other than their own profit making and achieving their own market objectives. The only way they can ask questions that take into account more than their own profit and advantages—such as, should such and such company be located in such and such country—is in terms of their strategic objectives. To ask strategic questions to maximize their own advantages is their mandate, so it is not that they are bad questions. It is that if they don't think or act in their self-interest, they are acting illegally.

PART 5

Re/generating Publics:
Calls to Collectivity

CHAPTER 23

Exploits in the Undercommons

ALISON HEARN
Communications and Media Scholar,
University of Western Ontario

In my early twenties I had a job playing Papa Smurf at Eaton's. All I could see out of the tiny screen hidden below the nose of my gigantic and sweaty cartoon-character costume were droves of hyper children; some hugged me, some tugged on me, and some just ran away from me in fear. The worst of them would step right up to me, stare directly into my face, and declare sneeringly: "You're not ree-al." Little did I know that being badly paid, disrespected, abused, and rendered invisible wasn't unique to being a Smurf. Life as a part-time instructor in the university system turned out to be scarily similar.

From the very first semester, much of my experience as a working grad student challenged me—the exploitation of students as teaching assistants and research assistants; the strange, unspoken economy of faculty attention and support; the administrative pitting of students against each other for small amounts of funding. And so I began pushing against the parameters of the university, asking questions of the place: What was the nature of this authorizing institution called the university anyway? What was I training myself to do or be? To whom was I responsible or obligated? I finished my master's quickly enough, but kids, a marriage meltdown, and, most significantly, the ridiculous demands and deprivations of part-time teaching held up the completion of my doctorate for 11 years.

I laboured in the wilderness of part-time teaching and limited-term contracts at a variety of universities for all of those 11 years. I started out teaching big undergrad courses at Simon Fraser when I was 29. I got my first tenure-stream gig at Northeastern University in Boston when I was 40. In between I taught at the University of Toronto and at Trent. In those 11 years, I witnessed first-hand the shift of the university from an institution intended to serve the public good while trying to cope with a serious deficit in federal and provincial funding—federal funding for post-secondary education dropped from .5 percent of GDP in 1983 to .19 percent of GDP in 2004[1]—to an institution marked by strategic private-sector partnerships, in the throes of "academic capitalism."

As this volume's editors Janice Newson and Claire Polster, notable American sociologists Sheila Slaughter and Gary Rhoades, and countless others have convincingly argued, the university is now firmly and cozily situated at the intersection of state and market, an enthusiastic participant in the blurring of boundaries between public and private sectors. Universities facilitate the commodification of knowledge and learning, laundering public subsidies into private gains for corporations, which are portrayed as sponsoring research under the guise of the public good. Students are seen as customers being served, even as they are leveraged for fiscal resources. The regulatory ideals of the modern university have become synonymous with the ideals of the free market—resource generation, maximized labour efficiency, and profit.

Along with these huge structural changes, during those 11 years I witnessed a significant shift in the makeup of the labour force in the university, specifically incredible growth in the number of contingent academic workers. In the 1950s and 1960s, faculty members who were hired on part-time and limited-term contracts—non-permanent faculty positions—primarily functioned to maintain the job stability of the tenure-stream faculty in the face of labour market fluctuations. These contingent forms of academic labour increased in the 1970s and into the 1980s as a response to fiscal shortfalls and decreasing government funding. By the 1990s, however, contingent hiring came to be seen as a necessary and ongoing facet of academic staffing in general, a tool to cut costs and increase efficiencies. And so, while tenure-track hiring continued, contingent hiring kept pace with it, arguably outpacing the rate of tenure-track hiring.[2] But, no matter how the general discourses about contingent faculty changed, the material conditions on the ground for the majority of those who held these short-term, unstable positions did not. The pay remained terrible, the support and resources still negligible, the workload impossible, and the respect and recognition non-existent.

In addition, academic labour in Canadian universities has become increasingly segmented. Graduate programs across the country routinely graduate more Ph.D. students than the tenure-stream market can bear. The increased job competition that results from this, however, does not occur between tenure and non-tenure streams but within them, so as the number of non-tenure-stream academic workers increases, so too does the competition for these badly paid and undervalued jobs. As a result, "segmentation (becomes) a strategy of reducing wages and labour standards in the *entire* academic labour market."[3]

At the University of Western Ontario, where I now teach, over 50 percent of undergraduate teaching is performed by contingent academic labour—faculty members on part-time or limited-term contracts. Recent research indicates that the numbers of contingent faculty at other Canadian universities are just as high or higher.[4] In the U.S. today, tenure-stream faculty jobs account for only 25 percent of the instructional workforce in higher education. At the same time, the proportion of faculty salaries in relation to universities' total expenditures have declined significantly, from 31 percent in the late 1970s to only 19 percent in 2004.[5]

This state of affairs is perpetuated by the ideology of so-called scholarly excellence; those most gifted will land the tenure-track jobs, while those who do not are just not good enough. In other words, while statistics show that the number of tenure-stream jobs is shrinking and non-permanent jobs are increasing on the ground, many in the professoriate continue to suggest that a young academic's failure to get hired is strictly his or her own fault. Ironically, in my own experience, faculty on part-time or limited-term contracts often contribute far more than their tenured colleagues to the life of a department or faculty, get better teaching evaluations, and carry on a research agenda for which they are not recognized or paid.

I remember walking the picket line with Trent University's full-time faculty union (TUFA) when they struck in the fall of 1996. It was not a comfortable time since members of CUPE, Trent's part-time teaching union of which I was a member, had been locked out by the university administration. We had decided to support the strike even though historically TUFA had done absolutely nothing for us. In this instance, the executive of TUFA had promised to support us in our push to increase the number of classes a part-timer could teach in exchange for our support of the strike. Predictably, after winning, they reneged on this promise. As my fellow part-timer, David Bateman, and I trudged back and forth through the rain, we spent our time picking out potential husbands from Trent's male faculty. One of the central issues of the strike was spousal hiring and job sharing; at this point it seemed just as likely that one of us would end up marrying into a job rather than acquiring one legitimately.

Sadly, not much has changed since 1996. Today there remains a deafening silence on the part of the tenured and tenure-streamed faculty about the segmentation of academic labour and the fate of contingent academic workers; it seems the professoriate would rather fight for the right to have their spouses hired than fight for fair and principled treatment of their junior colleagues. This might be partly due to what Marc Bousquet has described as the "social engineering of faculty culture" by new styles of administration based on private corporate management techniques such as total quality management. This type of management theory focuses on "the underlying cultural norms that frame daily life" at a university.[6] Administrators become "change agents" seeking, through emphatic leadership, to retool the entire culture of the institution to their interests and to find ways to bind their employees to its new profit-producing values.

In the face of these cultural changes, increased managerialism and bureaucratese, the tenured professoriate aligns itself with the interests of the administration, happily engaging in the commercialization of research. They compete with each other for merit pay, allow the publication of their teaching evaluations in the name of greater accountability (it wasn't until the installation of the new right to privacy laws in Ontario that Western saw fit to remove student evaluations of professors from a public website), send their students' papers off to a private corporation—turnitin.com—to be checked for plagiarism, and install themselves in managerial positions in relation to the contingent academic labourers below them. The complete discursive and practical rejigging of the university into a managerial, corporate culture seems to suit the professoriate, many of whom already see themselves, in neo-liberal terms, as isolated, individualistic, autonomous agents of knowledge. As Bousquet writes: "it has become increasingly difficult to speak of anything resembling 'faculty culture' apart from the competitive, marketized, 'high-performance' habitus designed for them by management."[7] Often, as with the Trent example, faculty unions, threatened by the influx of contingent hirings, work to strengthen tenure protections and behave in a completely self-interested manner. Arguably, faculty unions have "bargained the multi-tier system of academic labour into existence."[8]

When I arrived at my first tenure-stream job at Northeastern University in Boston, I was shocked to learn that rates of undergrad teaching by contingent faculty were as high as 75 percent in my department and across the university. In addition, I soon discovered that the administration at Northeastern was proposing a system whereby a tenured professor could be fired if he or she achieved low merit evaluations for two years in a row. So intense was the goal of achieving fiscal viability that any and all inconvenient vestiges of a traditional university system, such as tenure, were easily tossed aside. After attending a State of the University address by the president where I was asked to applaud the fact that the university had managed to raise tuition significantly *and* keep enrolment stable, I quickly realized I was not in Kansas anymore. I had found ground zero of corporate u.

Ironically, from the moment I arrived, my tenured and tenure-track colleagues began to bombard me with tenure anxiety. I had to keep track of everything I did, from meeting with students, to manning a table at a recruitment event, to taking minutes at a meeting. Every aspect of my job was monetized; I was actually *paid* to go to convocation. Tenure was the Holy Grail; only the highly productive, completely stressed out, insanely focused, and anxiety-ridden few would achieve it. It didn't seem to matter what you had to say, or *if* you had anything to say, papers had to be published and books pumped out. And, meanwhile, down the hall, the part-timers toiled away in the oversubscribed service courses, underpaid, and without a voice in any governance structures. Their position within the overall administration of the university was taken for granted, invisible. What was worse was that my otherwise progressive, tenured colleagues failed to see any problem. I felt as though I was back in grad school, but on the other side of the process; having landed a coveted job, I was being asked to preoccupy myself with the details of career advancement and to ignore the plight of those workers who made my own relatively privileged position possible.

The professionalization of the professoriate within the corporate u depends on a profound institutionalized neglect of what Fred Moten and Stefano Harney have called the "undercommons"—the contingent faculty comprised of graduate students, dropouts, itinerants, and radical thinkers, who refuse the authorizing structures of the place or have been refused by them, upon whom tenured labour depends. Contingent labour is necessary but unwelcome, and its presence produces a reaction on the part of the professoriate that is a kind of disavowal: a registration and repudiation of its threatening difference and a serious ethical failure to do anything about it. The professionalized professoriate represses what it knows about the conditions of its own existence, and helps to create a severely marginalized underclass. In the eyes of many of the professoriate, contingent labour is treated as though it simply isn't "ree-al."

The various layers of moral, cultural, and political failure on the part of the professoriate described above cannot, in the end, be separated from each other; there is no real way to tell which came first, or how and in what way they are implicated in each other's development. To be sure, there are many members of the tenured professoriate who are committed to meaningful collegiality and deplore the current conditions of managerialism in the university, but feel powerless to change it. The degree of response and engagement of faculty unions to the plight of contingent labour is highly variable as well. Given the irrefutable facts on the ground and the growing threats to the tenure system, however, you'd think that faculty unions and the professoriate in general would be working in earnest, shoulder to shoulder, with these contingent workers to address the segmentation and tiering of academic labour. So, while I recognize that many tenured faculty members and their unions are taking incremental steps toward improving the plight of their contingent faculty allies, there remains a very long way to go. Just recently I sat in Senate at Western and watched the majority of its membership vote against a motion to guarantee wage parity for our contingent faculty in the university's strategic plan.

The questions I began asking in grad school about obligation and responsibility in relation to the university are more necessary now than ever. Surely my or anyone else's move onto the tenure track and out of the field of casual and flexible academic labour does not erase or excuse the poor working conditions and disrespect that many part-timers and contract faculty still endure. Employers can capitalize on the divisions among tenured and contingent academic workers; it's our job to counter their divisive tactics and to offer a vision of the university beyond its current corporate managerial confines. As Moten and Harney claim, the undercommons can be seen to embody the productive, unruly excess of the corporate u: the desire to know, to create organic communities, the passion for research and teaching, the impulses of free conjecture and curiosity. In the end, the university should be ours to define, claim, and name. Academic workers of all kinds must express their solidarity with each other, students, and staff, and act now in the name of a *universitas* of thinkers that, in the end, no instrumental logic can contain.

Notes

1. Vicki Smallman, "Academic Labour: The Canadian Context," *Cinema Journal* 45, no. 4 (2006): 108.
2. Harald Bauder, "The Segmentation of Academic Labour: A Canadian Example," *ACME: An International E-Journal for Critical Geographies* 4, no. 2 (2006): 229. While Bauder points out that this trend was first noted in a Statistics Canada study, access to comparable data remains a challenge. The very fact that usable statistics on this issue do not exist speaks to the difficulties of defining the problem of contingent labour as a whole and to the recent proliferation of different kinds of academic work in the corporate university.
3. Ibid., 231.
4. Smallman, "Academic Labour," 110.
5. Bauder, "The Segmentation of Academic Labour," 229.
6. Marc Bousquet, "'We Are Teachers, Hear Us Roar': Contingent Faculty Author an Activist Culture," *Cinema Journal* 45, no. 4 (2006): 99.
7. Ibid., 100.
8. Ibid., 101.

References

Moten, Fred, and Stefano Harney. "The University and the Undercommons: Seven Theses." *Social Text* 22, no. 2 (2004): 101–115.

Newson, Janice, and Claire Polster. "Reclaiming Our Centre: Towards a Robust Defense of Academic Autonomy." *Science Studies* 14, no. 1 (2001): 55–75.

Slaughter, Sheila, and Gary Rhoades. *Academic Capitalism and the New Economy: Markets, State, and Education*. Baltimore and London: Johns Hopkins University Press, 2004.

Academic Freedom, Institutional Autonomy, and the Co-operative University

LEN FINDLAY

English Scholar, University of Saskatchewan

When I arrived at the University of Saskatchewan in 1974 as an assistant professor of English, the calling card that got me the interview and helped get me the job was a doctorate from Oxford in Victorian British Literature, an area in which the department felt it needed to recruit. I thought that in emigrating to Canada with my partner and infant son, as so many other working-class Scots have done, I was leaving the British class system behind me and coming to a true meritocracy or even, given British Trudeaumania at the time, to a *just society*. I was wrong, or at least only half right.

The university I joined, and where I have largely remained, is a popular icon of self-improvement, but it is a positive force marred by three negative forces: colonialism, capitalism, and sexism. As an elite institution, the University of Saskatchewan's dependence on and discreet nourishing of negative forces should not have surprised me. After all, the business of institutions like this is to reproduce elites and control upward mobility. But this was an institution calling itself "the university of the people"[1] as befits a state-owned and supported institution in a province with strong populist traditions. More open in many respects than Oxford, and more responsive to traditions of "the democratic intellect"[2] I encountered as an undergraduate in Aberdeen, the place where I have developed my career nonetheless seems, like too many other Canadian universities, a social as well as academic gatekeeper, its version of the best and the brightest still too often reducible to the best-off and the whitest.

No matter how I try to frame it, the picture offered by my and other Canadian universities is mixed. Here, then, are three versions of that mixed picture designed to critique, challenge, and inspire those embarking on an academic career as well as those feeling homeless or hopelessly compromised within post-secondary institutions.

Mixed Picture One: Academic Colonialism and Academic Freedom

The modelling of the University of Saskatchewan on the universities of Edinburgh and Wisconsin, and on other British and American examples, was not entirely a bad thing. The libertarian and democratic traditions of societies, which provided a large portion of the emigrants to Saskatchewan, are admirable and continue to be forces for good in Canadian law and the other institutions of our parliamentary democracy. But what has not been sufficiently acknowledged, especially at a time when the province of Saskatchewan and its main university have been rebranding themselves in the course of their centenary celebrations, is just how complicit the university was and is with the practices and objectives of colonialism. The denial of this fact, the rewriting and re-whitening of this history,[3] meant that the hard-won protections of academic freedom entrenched in successive university acts,[4] and consolidated by the unionizing of the faculty of the university in 1977, were used to defend exclusionary and oppressive practices in every aspect of university operations from faculty hiring and student recruitment, through curriculum development,[5] distribution of resources and rewards, to institutional self-definition.

A couple of key points are therefore worth emphasizing to those who come calling on the university or who, as alumni and/or potential donors, have the university come calling on them. Academic freedom, like the democracy it is thought to embody and sustain, needs to be regularly demystified as well as strategically affirmed. Academic freedom, like democracy, has a mixed history and sentimental connections with freethinking individualism. Whether actively exercised or held in genteel reserve, academic freedom in former colonies like Canada has to answer for the apparently meritocratic reproduction of White masculinities in the academy. The deep complicity of Canadian universities with colonization has not been matched by their support for the ongoing process of decolonization and redistribution of authority and legitimacy. Indeed, not only are student bodies and faculty complements often tentative or tokenist in their embrace of difference as enrichment rather than contamination, they can also be unabashedly reactionary in their rationalization of past injustice and their understanding of what excellence means, appealing as they frequently do to smugly Eurocentric accounts of the academy's origins and evolution.

It is therefore not surprising to see Peter MacKinnon, a recent chair of the Association of Universities and Colleges of Canada and a much praised university president, arguing in an address to the Judicial Council of Canada that, though there is no doubt about residential schools having been "a tool for the assimilation of First Nations peoples," the Assembly of First Nations may have been wrong in critiquing all sectors of "formal education" in the colonial past and is certainly wrong about the present. For MacKinnon, the charge of assimilation most certainly does not apply in the realm of post-secondary education:

> The University I lead has 2,000 Aboriginal students in part because of the successful partnership arrangements that we built with First Nations communities and with First Nations leadership within the university. A former tribal council chief works in my office; we have an Aboriginal student office, Elder services, and plans are advanced for an Aboriginal centre. And there is no doubt that the curriculum reflects Aboriginal scholarship and perspectives. In these respects, I would argue, the assumption underlying the First Nations Education Plan is outdated. Universities are not a colonizing influence.[6]

The University of Saskatchewan has a better record than many Canadian universities in this matter. And segregation is a no better guarantor than integration of decolonized educational practices. But what President MacKinnon claims differs significantly from my own experience and from what Aboriginal graduate students I have taught and supervised have borne witness to on public occasions at the University of Saskatchewan and elsewhere. However, the system does not welcome faculty critique or award-winning students' accounts of navigating racist and sexist academic spaces. It is interested only in its own version of good news. I have consequently been rebuked as a "reputational deficit," a purveyor of the big lie who takes advantage of academic freedom to deny progress and exaggerate difficulties, thus damaging civil collegiality and besmirching the university's new brand. Dissent is not welcomed by the current leaders and marketers of our institution, especially if it is performed in ways designed to attract media attention and public scrutiny. And three years

214

of service on the Academic Freedom and Tenure Committee of the Canadian Association of University Teachers has demonstrated to me that substantial numbers of senior administrators across Canada now act like thin-skinned patricians while investing hugely in communications and human resources personnel to promote fictions of campus harmony and highly selective versions of academic excellence. In these circumstances, decolonizing universities requires stamina and credibility, passing the test of academic success as well as refusing its complacency and evaluative monopolies. Otherwise, one can and will be written off—or worse—as a mediocre malcontent incapable of excellence and opposed to change.

Mixed Picture Two: Institutional Autonomy and Academic Capitalism

Given that colonization was significantly driven by greed, distinguished by theft and genocide, and dignified by a range of academic alibis, it is no surprise that economic considerations have played a large role in universities and are key to their current neo-colonial practices. Like academic freedom, institutional autonomy is an important but imperfect safeguard of academic integrity. Autonomy is indeed sufficiently imperfect that universities zealously preserve and barter away their independence in virtually the same breath, welcoming critique of all ideologies except the currently dominant one. Endlessly critical of ungenerous governments, universities are remarkably uncritical of corporations, instead modelling themselves in important ways on how they think business does business. Instead of nourishing and protecting an inclusive, historically informed sense of academic value, universities are only too eager to reduce that value to money, and thus reduce students to revenue units and faculty to funding entrepreneurs (rising above a precarious, underpaid rump who do most of the undergraduate, just-in-time teaching). In other words, academic capitalism is so pervasive in our publicly funded and privately abject post-secondary institutions that a system the public takes to be the bastion of reason and free inquiry is dominated by market rationality and market clout. Outsourcing and deskilling abound, while the three Rs have given way to the three Cs: casualization, commodification, and corporatization.

Talk of competitiveness is everywhere on Canadian campuses, but there is little effort to discriminate between appropriate and damaging competition.

Financial power has migrated to the administrative centre, whence patronage is dispensed in a divisive way that buys the silence or vocal support of big beneficiaries while encouraging the marginalization of dissenting individuals and disciplines. Integrated planning obsesses campuses everywhere, leading to homogenization, intellectual species loss, winners and losers at each other's throats, and the radical reshaping of universities to fit the wealth-generating template of the hour. Academic managerialism apes the trends and covets the prestige of the private sector, selling off public space and social legitimacy to corporate and individual donors, naming and renaming campus buildings and programs like a strip mall under rotating ownership, and entering into problematic commercial agreements despite the best efforts of student, staff, and faculty activists to align institutional purchasing with the principles and practices of anti-sweat fair trade. University autonomy turns out too often to be a sham: academic agendas controlled and their public meanings spun by the rich and powerful, including those business leaders so prominent on boards of governors.

Mixed Picture Three: Toward the Co-operative University

Fortunately, not all the news on Canadian campuses is bad. As I have already hinted, there is never domination without resistance, no matter how determined the attempts to reduce collegiality to obedience training and self-censorship. As economic models, language, and goals have gained unrivalled prominence in the furtherance of academic capitalism, so alternative versions and visions of *the* economy can be drawn on to resist neo-liberalism.[7] More particularly, where competitiveness is the mantra and crisis-mongering the mode of operation, co-operation can be the counter. Where private profit is the goal, public dividends can be affirmed as an inclusive, empowering, and dramatically redistributive antidote.

It is not only in a province like Saskatchewan or in a university with a Centre for the Study of Co-operatives that the idea of the co-operative university can be used as a rallying cry against harmful competition. After all, co-operatives are a huge part of the global economy,[8] though you would never think that, given what goes for economic reporting in the mainstream media. Co-operatives are characterized as outmoded, quaint, well meaning, or useful alleviations of some of the most flagrant injustices inflicted in the name of *the* market. But co-operation as theme, values, and practices can offer innovation in a human key, replacing arbitrary hierarchies and fierce careerism with sites of congregation and solidarity, demonstrating that the dominant monoculture can be and must be challenged. The free-market economy may try to own or monopolize the new knowledge economy and its key institutions, but that market's treacherous and damaging freedoms are being effectively countered locally and globally by scholarly and practical proponents of the social economy.[9]

The co-operative university is underway around us (and has been for over a century), and its calling cards are readily available on the Internet under headings like "Mondragón" or "Co-operative College"[10] where one may learn about the effective (though imperfect) alliances between those who pursue economic and social interests for the common good and in response to a quadruple bottom line: economic, social, cultural, and environmental. Historically and currently, education has been crucial to the successes of the co-operative movement in practising democratic governance, anti-racist, anti-sexist, anti-colonial pedagogy and international outreach, and in the valuing of students as much more than revenue units and interrupters of faculty research. At a time when the shift from insatiable growth to smart sustainability is more necessary and more achievable than ever, the shift from the competitive to the co-operative university must begin in earnest, so that the next generation of Canadians, in all their diversity of aptitude and need, can be ethically empowered as well as productively employed, and create a much less mixed, more deservedly admirable and enviable picture of our country at home and across our beleaguered planet. It *can* be done, but only if we work together to make it happen, both inside and outside the reductive value systems of our universities.

Notes

1. Michael Hayden, *Seeking a Balance: The University of Saskatchewan 1907–1982* (Vancouver: University of British Columbia Press, 1983), 11, 16, 295.
2. George Elder Davie, *The Democratic Intellect: Scotland and Her Universities in the Nineteenth Century* (Edinburgh: Edinburgh University Press, 1961).
3. Marie Battiste, Lynne Bell, Isobel Findlay, Len Findlay, and James (Sákéj) Youngblood Henderson, "Thinking Place: Animating the Indigenous Humanities in Education," *Australian Journal of Indigenous Education* 34 (2005): 7–19.
4. Hayden, *Seeking a Balance*.

5. Marie Battiste, "Decolonizing the University: Indigenous Contexts for Academic Freedom," in *Pursuing Academic Freedom: "Free and Fearless,"* ed. Len M. Findlay and Paul Bidwell (Saskatoon: Purich Press, 2001), 190–203.

6. Peter MacKinnon, "Address to Canadian Judicial Council, Tuesday, September 27, 2005," circulated by email but not published. For a glowing summary of MacKinnon's arguments, see Jeffrey Simpson, "The Fatal Flaw of Separate But Equal Native Schooling," *Globe and Mail* (November 25, 2005), A23.

7. Mark Coté, Richard J.F. Day, and Greig de Peuter, eds., *Utopian Pedagogy: Radical Experiments against Neoliberal Globalization* (Toronto: University of Toronto Press, 2007).

8. Brett Fairbairn, Ian MacPherson, and Nora Russell, eds., *Canadian Co-operatives in the Year 2000* (Saskatoon: Centre for the Study of Co-operatives, 2000).

9. Ash Amin, Angus Cameron, and Ray Hudson, *Placing the Social Economy* (London: Routledge, 2002).

10. Co-operative College, http://www.co-op.ac.uk/projects.htm; Mondragón Cooperative Corporation, http://en.wikipedia.org/wiki/Mondrag%C3%B3n_Cooperative_Corporation.

CHAPTER 25

The University Public and Its Enemies

FRANK CUNNINGHAM
Philosopher, University of Toronto

The colleges at my university are mainly concerned with enhancing undergraduate education: facilitating extracurricular life, helping students find financial resources, counselling and tutoring, advocating for student interests, and mounting interdisciplinary programs.[1] My recent stint as principal of one of these (Innis College) thus gave me an overview of the student experience and made me acutely aware of what is generally perceived by students and the public at large as the demise in the quality of undergraduate education in all large public universities in Canada.

I find this perception at odds with changes since I began university teaching over 40 years ago. Recent hires in my discipline are at least as enthusiastic about teaching as my cohort was, and they are also pedagogically innovative and more aware than we were of alternative teaching methods. This may be due to university focus on teaching. While I learned how to teach much as I learned about sex (dubious advice from braggarts, gutter stories from the trenches), universities today prepare manuals, hold workshops, and recognize good teachers with awards.

How is this disparity to be explained? Some administrators maintain that student and public perception is mistaken or is fuelled by posturing student leaders.[2] The main exceptions are administrators with offspring in undergraduate studies. I am sure that they are hearing the same complaints—too often to consider them idiosyncratic—that we and the other colleges hear about: large classes even at senior levels, difficulty getting into courses needed for program requirements, and the unavailability of instructors for consultation. My conclusion is that these things do not result from lack of will but have structural sources.

Some proximate causes became evident to me upon resuming full teaching duties. For many years I taught an introduction to political philosophy to about 30 students. Now it is capped at 200. Moreover, anyone teaching the course faces the pedagogical problem that a large proportion of class members are senior students taking an introductory course due to the relative paucity of undergraduate course offerings. One reason for this is that, like every other department, mine had been reducing its teaching load. Compression has taken place at the undergraduate level, and since hiring has no more than kept pace with retirements, the result could only be a reduction in undergraduate courses. I shall return to the effect of this and other causes after situating university teaching within a certain theoretical framework.

The title of this contribution refers to John Dewey's *The Public and Its Problems*.[3] For Dewey, a public comprises people whose actions affect one another over protracted periods of time and who face common problems that call for collective action. A generic challenge Dewey identified for publics is to recognize themselves as such, and he thought that a democratically organized public was best placed for effective action.[4] Dewey saw education as the most important factor for building a public's awareness of itself and providing citizens with the knowledge and skills required for conjoined problem-solving efforts. In *Democracy and Education* Dewey also recognized that educational institutions are themselves publics, and that crucial to making positive contributions to a broader society is that they approach problems specific to them in co-operative and unified ways.[5]

What problems (or enemies), then, do university publics confront? I shall address two generic ones: walls and funnels. Language, Dewey observed, carries with it an unavoidable tension. By filtering our experiences and focusing our attention, language makes thought and deliberate action possible, but by virtue of these very properties, it also leads us to neglect some aspects of our world and prompts us to think in terms of categories that do not adequately reflect interconnections. This same tension is found at all levels of education. The divisions of subjects, as between sciences and humanities or theoretical and applied courses, separate them in ways that mask interdependencies in the actual world. These are examples of walls. Specialized training is required to meet the needs of a complex society, but specialization also narrows—by funnelling—the educational experiences and acquired skills of students.

Other examples of walls in university education are the sorting of schools or programs into elite and general, the separation of curricular from extracurricular activities, the ivory-tower isolation of the university from its surrounding communities, and disciplinary silos. A main funnel for students is narrow specialization even within a single discipline. Related to this is the concentration obliged by curricular inflexibility, where long menus of pre- and co-requisites within a major subject make it difficult to branch out.

Regarding the origins of walls and funnels, I see two as paramount: underfunding and elitism.[6] The latter refers to a penchant of universities, faculties, and departments to proclaim their superior status within whatever range of other institutions—called rivals on the elitist perspective—the university or discipline places itself. *Mea culpa*. Even in the 1980s, when I chaired the University of Toronto's Philosophy Department and was obliged to produce self-study documents, I found myself crafting them to demonstrate that the department was at least equal to those in the best public universities on the continent and certainly superior to our miserable competitors in Canada. As part of the atmosphere prompting these efforts, much attention is paid to hiring faculty from what are regarded as elite universities (oddly, given the pretences of the self-studies, excluding our own) and encouraging publication in exclusive presses or journals.

Another example of elitism is a penchant to admit students with the highest marks from academic streams in secondary schools. In years past, Innis College was known for carefree and socially engaged students who well knew how to take advantage of the recreational opportunities available in the late 1960s, but with relatively low grade-point averages from high school. By 2000, their entering averages were among the very highest in the faculty (largely due to the construction of a superb residence, which prompted competition among applying students). I confess to lamenting the passing of the earlier generation, but there is no question that the college gained kudos from university administrators for admitting top students.

I retain enough Marxist economic-determinist convictions to suppose that the other source of walls and funnels in public universities—underfunding—is the basis of their elitist aspirations. Universities are in competition with one another for government resources and they increasingly rely on private-sector charity. It serves both purposes to propose oneself as an institution with superior faculties and students. Underfunding also sustains walls and funnels. If one asks, in a class of 100 students, how many are currently holding down jobs, it is rare not to see 70 or 80 hands raised, and student debt load is increasing as tuition and other costs go up. Students therefore cannot experiment with a variety of subjects or take advantage of extracurricular life, and there is pressure to specialize so as to acquire targeted jobs quickly after graduation.

Universities contribute to the vibrant publics that Dewey envisaged by graduating students with broad-based knowledge, interdisciplinary skills, and an ability to integrate theory and practice. Analogous points can be made regarding research. The narrowly focused and closely constrained education of wall- and funnel-infused universities is not conducive to these results. Among the reasons for this is that the nature of such universities as publics is diminished. In Dewey's educational theory, schools that are self-conscious publics will be the best educators.

Walls and funnels in universities impede the ability of their constituencies to see one another as a single public and to address common problems collectively. The lowering of teaching loads for faculty is largely prompted by demanding publication requirements for tenure, promotion, and merit pay. This is also a function of elitism, which fuels the need for universities to prove their high status by reference to the internationally recognized research output of their faculty. As universities compete with one another for star appointees, a further motive to reduce teaching loads is created, namely, to attract and retain faculty who might otherwise be lured to rival institutions. This produces a culture where faculty are more prone to identify just with faculty and senior graduate students working in their areas of research than with all the university communities.

Students are also isolated from one another. When, for reasons of economic exigency, students are holding jobs and many of them are living at home, their opportunities for informal interactions with one another will be diminished. About 1,600 students are enrolled in the University of Toronto through Innis College, yet the students most active in extracurricular activities come from among the fewer than 400 who live in residence. Exacerbating the difficulties of creating university-wide public awareness are the academic specializations students encounter in their studies. This applies as well to faculty. Similar tales of fragmentation can be told regarding the relation of part-time to full-time instructors, administrators to students and faculty, and all of the above to support staff.

One illustration of how common challenges call for collective university action relates to deficiency in writing ability. This poses a special challenge since professors have neither the time nor the mandate to be essay-writing teachers, yet form (composition) and content (formulating and defending substantive opinions) are not easily pried apart. Among the usual solutions is to provide essay-writing clinics, to refer students to manuals on writing, or to mount compulsory courses in composition. In my experience, such measures do not go far enough. One reason is that the problem is not seen as confronting the university as a single, collective public but as specific to students of the humanities and social sciences. However, insofar as one aim of education is to prepare students for post-university careers, writing skills will certainly be advantageous, if not demanded, for graduates of engineering, business, or natural science no less than of law, politics, journalism, and the like. It is also not a problem that admits of satisfactory solution by counting entirely on specialists, such as writing instructors hired to staff writing clinics.

Experiences in the Philosophy Department and at Innis College exemplify this. Some years the department employs graduate students as essay-writing tutors. The service is justly appreciated by undergraduates. But how successful the tutoring is depends upon the skill of the tutor, not as a philosopher but as a writing teacher, and it is beyond the department's expertise or resources to provide training for this purpose. Innis College employs staff who are specialists in teaching writing, but they find that the most successful results require working closely with faculty in specific courses, again something that demands commitment and coordination with departments. Some complain that this problem is not one of the university, but has to do with inadequate training in the secondary schools or with English being a second language for many students. On a Deweyan perspective, this has things backwards. That students come to university with deficiencies regarding writing is a problem calling for a university response.

Among measures to confront the problem are that universities: work in and with the high schools and in communities outside the schools; run summer courses; invite pre-university teachers to interact with university instructors in the universities; involve undergraduate students in high schools; draw upon those students, faculty, and staff from appropriate linguistic backgrounds to mount courses and act as tutors; bring schools of education within universities into closer co-operation with other faculties; encourage research on this problem; and design courses in all disciplines to include non-negligible training in writing. All such measures, and one can think of others, involve university-wide coordination. In short, they require the university to act as the public it potentially is, and this is precisely what walls and funnels inhibit.

A story from my administrative past provides another sort of example. In the academic programs mounted by Innis College, job candidates are required to deliver a guest lecture in an introductory undergraduate course. Having found these interventions very helpful in hiring decisions (much can be learned about both candidates' technical teaching skills and their attitudes toward students), I proposed in a faculty meeting of departmental chairs that it be a policy to require this in all hires.

Though not unaccustomed to having my sage advice rejected, I was taken aback by the strength, indeed vehemence, of the reaction against this proposal. The stated reason for its rejection—that this was an intrusion on departmental autonomy—could not have been the motivating one, since departments accept a multitude of faculty constraints and directives. I concluded that the resistance was due to fear that a stellar researcher might be exposed to students as a poor teacher, so departments wished to escape the resulting bind in making their appointments. Students themselves are not ignorant of the attitude behind this motivation, as many urge the same policy, and there are examples of cases where the practice *is* in place but applicants found wanting as teachers by students are selected nonetheless.

Awareness of such priorities—combined with the programmatic constraints, large classes, and lack of personal contact with their teachers—stand in the way of students thinking of themselves as part of a common community with administrators and faculty. For their part, the latter groups also find it difficult to perceive a common community. In addition to the anonymity of students in large classes, instructors under pressure to publish see teaching obligations as intrusions on their time for writing grant applications and churning out publications. For reasons that sociologists could no doubt explain, there seems to be a correlation between the extent of university underfunding and the growth of administrative bureaucracies with a concomitant tendency for some academics to become full-time and long-term administrators. Such administrators can forget what a normal classroom experience is like.

All these things create community-defeating walls and make collective reaction to common problems difficult. With respect to the writing example, to the extent that undergraduate education is demoted, problems such as writing ability are seen as local to the needs of some students rather than as part of a society-wide problem calling for concerted action to provide more small classes and cross-discipline study to afford all students easy access to appropriate humanities and social science courses (and similarly for humanities and social science students regarding deficiencies in mathematical and scientific literacy). Because such measures infringe upon individual research time and require curriculum restructuring and cross-departmental and faculty co-operation, they demand commitment and a change in orientation on the part of faculty and administration.

Central to the required commitment is concerted attention to the undergraduate experience and in particular the classroom experience. Providing quality education is the one undertaking that is both common to all constituencies in the university and about which experiences can be shared and advice exchanged in a common vocabulary. For the undergraduate experience to be significantly enhanced, the full resources of the university need to be brought to bear on their education, which in turn calls for such things as interaction among faculty from different disciplines and effective communication and mutual learning between faculty and administration and both of them with support staff.

Such interaction is also beneficial for breaking down walls and avoiding narrowing funnels within each constituency. A clear example is interdisciplinary teaching. Instructors who do such teaching discover that if done right, they themselves learn to the betterment of their research as well as their teaching. In my own experience, teaching also benefits research by drawing it out of the seductive comfort of abstraction, which, in the case of philosophy or political theory, can create misleading confidence that one is making sense until obliged to explain it in an interactive classroom setting (rather than just to similarly lost-in-abstraction peers). I do not know whether there is an analogue in the case of empirical studies or the theoretical sciences, but, at the very least, practice in effective teaching must benefit the ability of scholars in these fields to communicate the fruits of their research.

Students are the principal intermediaries between the university and the broader public. They, themselves, are members of this public, and they want their education to prepare them for enhanced engagement within it. To educate students in ways that respond to the problems faced by publics generally, the nature of these problems must be understood within the universities. Education of the educators on this score is the most enlightening when it derives from contact with students, coming as they do from a broad cross-section of society and expressing the aspirations and concerns of their generation. But this potentiality cannot be realized unless students are enthusiastically engaged in classroom environments conducive to eliciting and critically examining their experiences and viewpoints.

Can our universities become full publics? My optimism on this question is based on the principle that what is (or has been) actual must be possible. The colleges at my university have both advocated and sometimes succeeded in creating communities of faculty, students, and staff, making undergraduate teaching a priority, promoting interdisciplinary studies, and maintaining links with constituencies outside the university. In the relatively short period of my college administration, I saw a change in broader university reception to college entreaties, from neglect to endorsement in principle and, to limited extents, in fact. One can, therefore, see a possible trajectory.

Taking a rather longer view, I am also able to compare the university of today with that of earlier epochs. When I began my studies, university elitism was not a response to underfunding but was sincerely endorsed by the talking-book professors (some, to be sure, talking much better than others) whom we confronted in large lecture halls and in courses confined within inflexible curricula. My graduate student and junior faculty years were during the democratic revolutions in the universities, which largely succeeded in transforming them into Deweyan publics. While I have viewed the erosion of this achievement in the intervening years with regret, I am encouraged by the thought that full reversion to the bad old days has so far been averted.

If my earlier hypothesis about structural causes of university walls and funnels is on target, then retrieval of public status for the universities requires successful reversal of underfunding of education generally by provincial and federal governments. This, in turn, requires that the governments come to see themselves as responsible parts of the publics that elect them. I am not entirely pessimistic on this score either, but it is a topic for another inquiry.

Notes

1. At the University of Toronto, undergraduate students in arts and science on the central campus are enrolled through one of seven colleges, which include residences, provide student services, and mount most of the faculty's interdisciplinary programs. I was principal of Innis College (named after the founder of Canadian political economy and communications theory, Harold Innis) from 2000 to 2005.

2. In a recent University of Toronto publication, *Measuring Up* (available at http://www.utoronto.ca/aboutuoft/accountabilityreports.htm), it is granted that, based on its own surveys, benchmark scores for the U of T as "a supportive campus environment" fell from 2004 to 2006, and that "ratings for student-faculty interaction are low." The study and the admissions are to be welcomed, though they are couched in terms of competitive comparisons with Canadian peer institutions rather than in terms of cardinal values embodied in student-experience ideal goals.

3. John Dewey, *The Public and Its Problems* (1927), in *John Dewey: The Later Works, 1925–1953*, series ed. Jo Ann Boydston, vol. 2, 1925–1927, ed. Bridget Walsh (Carbondale: Southern Illinois Press, 1984), 235–371, also available in Denver: Alan Swallow, 1927.

4. I summarize Dewey's theory of democracy in *Theories of Democracy: A Critical Introduction* (London: Routledge, 2002), Chapter 8.

5. John Dewey, *Democracy and Education*, in *John Dewey: The Middle Works*, series ed. Jo Ann Boydston, vol. 9, 1916, ed. Patricia Baysinger and Barbara Levine (Carbondale: Southern Illinois University Press, 1980), also available in electronic form at www.ilt.columbia.edu/publications/dewey.html.

6. I pursue this theme in "The University and Social Justice," *Journal of Academic Ethics* 5 (2007): 153–162.

CHAPTER 26

Reflections on Teaching and Learning

MARGARET-ANN ARMOUR

Chemist and Science Educator, University of Alberta

At the University of Edinburgh, in the late 1950s, I was one of 40 students in the honours chemistry program. Classes were small and the mandatory honours project required close collaboration with a faculty member. I and most of my classmates were in awe of our professors. The question-and-answer sessions that preceded the four-day set of final honours exams at the end of 4th year are etched on my memory as times of open interaction between teachers and students.

These thoughts were in my mind as I reflected on the changes in teaching, learning, and mentorship that I have seen in universities during my career and how they affect the student experience. As is the case for most members of a small, closely knit class, enrolled in a highly challenging program requiring mutual support, 45 years later I am still in contact with several members of that chemistry class. What experience do students of today have in science classes like the ones I was in? What are the critical elements of a meaningful learning environment?

For teaching and learning to be effective, I believe that it is critical to form a relationship between the teacher and the student. Even in the small classes at Edinburgh, this happened only to a minimal extent. The culture was still that of a wide gulf between the professor and the student. At least for me and for some of my student peers, it took great courage to go to the professor's office to ask a question. We were much more likely to try to work out the answer for ourselves, which was sometimes to our advantage. Did a relationship develop between student and professor in those days? There certainly developed a respect for professors who shared their passion for their subject and gave us an insight into the discoveries they had made in their field. Did we know them as people? Probably not. Did we develop the kind of relationship that results in a highly effective teaching and learning environment? Again, probably not, at least not in the classroom. Science was taught at that time as a body of discovered knowledge that we had to learn in our undergraduate courses and then be able to apply. The exciting times of discovery that I remember were the sudden realizations, as I struggled with my lecture notes, that I understood the concepts. I remember laughing with joy at the revelation!

Not only has time affected this teacher–learner interaction within the academy, but I have changed cultures from Scotland to Canada. The formality of student–teacher relationships is less in North America than in the United Kingdom. More opportunity exists to develop the kind of interaction that facilitates engaged learning. However, I have become more and more concerned about how institutional policies are making this interaction more difficult.

If it is critical to effective teaching and learning to develop a meaningful relationship between professor and student, how can this happen in classes that grow larger year by year, with classes of 500 or more becoming common? How can it happen when professors have increasingly heavy administrative tasks and greater expectations of research productivity? How can it happen when the university reward system is geared strongly to research accomplishments and little credit is given for time and effort put into teaching and learning research? Let me try to provide some answers to these questions.

Pedagogical research over many years has shown over and over again that the lecture format, where a body of facts are shared with a large class of students, is an ineffective way of developing interest in and understanding of the material, yet we continue to use the lecture format to share scientific information with large numbers of students. For the small number of students in the classroom who have wanted to be scientists since they were in kindergarten, this way of sharing information is fine. For a large proportion of the students, it amounts to sharing a multitude of what appears to be mostly irrelevant information that they have to learn so that they can pass an exam and continue on to the next course, hopefully something closer to their real interest. Among this large proportion of students are many women, and my own interest in teaching pedagogy was peaked by my engagement in encouraging young women to include careers in the sciences among their possible career choices. Our own experience and that of many others has been that when an intentional effort is made to make undergraduate classroom teaching more relevant to the young women in the room, all students become more engaged. This happens with even small and non-revolutionary changes such as using more relevant examples to illustrate applications of theories, and catching students' interest with application first before launching into a mathematical treatment of theory. These changes do not even move away from the traditional lecture mode of delivery.

In this era of open access to information through the Internet, what a wonderful opportunity we have to move toward the implementation of practices that make for effective learning. At least some classroom time can be used for interaction rather than presentation of a body of knowledge. There can be small group discussions within the classroom—and this is possible, although not easy, even in large classes. Group learning has been practised in many disciplines, but has not tended to be used in lectures in the sciences. The norm has been that individuals must learn on their own; any group learning they do is of their own making. Group learning in the large lecture theatre is made difficult by the physical set-up of the room—so called lecture style with seats that cannot be moved and little space to allow students to move around and engage with one another. Even having seats that swivel would improve the opportunity to have students turn around and discuss in small groups the concept that has been introduced by the instructor.

The use of personal-response devices, or clickers as they are commonly known, is becoming more widespread in science classrooms. These devices allow students to respond during lecture to a multiple-choice question to determine whether they have understood the concept that has just been presented. With appropriate software installed on a computer, the results of the anonymous student responses are displayed graphically on a screen in the classroom, allowing the instructor to decide whether to move on to the next concept or review the previous one. When the questions to which the students respond are carefully chosen, the engagement and interaction of students in the classroom is increased.

These techniques, some simple, some requiring technology, help to make student learning more effective. They support the goal of using time in the classroom to provide the framework and the spark to encourage students to be self-motivated to explore and assimilate the knowledge and to enable understanding of that knowledge. This is easy to write about, but is very hard to make happen. One of the several impediments is that many students are programmed through high school and into university to expect that they will be supplied with the information that they need to know, and it is their task to learn it and apply it when asked to do so in an examination. When an instructor does not fulfill this expectation, students are likely to be unhappy and to give a low evaluation to the instructor. Although, as I have suggested, research-intensive universities pay less attention to teaching than to research accomplishments, not only does a negative teaching evaluation from students lower the morale of the instructor, but in the case of young faculty courageous enough to try such innovations in their teaching, it can negatively influence their tenure decisions.

Innovations such as small group discussions and the use of clickers can improve the learning process even in very large classes, but they have minimal effect on building the instructor–student relationship. Therefore, they are far from implementing an ideal situation. I have a vision of the ideal teaching-learning situation for science students at research-intensive universities, which I hope the new generation of faculty will continue to strive to make more widespread. Science courses, especially at the introductory level where classes are large, have included laboratory experiences and this, rather than in lecture, is where group learning has been practised. With cost and safety concerns limiting laboratory experiences, this group learning activity may become less ubiquitous, yet the laboratory could become a setting where the students discover the satisfaction of taking greater responsibility for their own learning.

It is commonly accepted that students become completely engaged in their discipline when they move into graduate school and become a member of a research group. This is usually the setting where group learning is most highly effective. At its best, it has all of the characteristics of effective teaching and learning: a small team of people with varying levels of knowledge and experience who have intentionally chosen to discover more about a specific area of study; a group in which the members trust and respect one another; a group in which the members value each other's experiences; a group in which there is a commitment to both robust factual knowledge and to intuitive creativity. We know that these teaching-learning conditions lead students to become addicted to learning because they are excited by the joy of understanding. Why, then, have we been so unwilling in our public institutions of higher learning to make sure that these conditions are met as much as possible for our undergraduate students as for our graduate students? What can we do about it?

Experiential learning is what excites students about the sciences. Women in Scholarship, Engineering, Science, and Technology (WISEST) at the University of Alberta has provided this kind of experience to students for almost 25 years. Young women who have completed their second-to-last year of high school spend six weeks during July and August as junior researchers in research laboratories of the University of Alberta. At the end, they present posters of their projects to sponsors, supervisors, parents, and friends. A longitudinal study of the participants in the 1994 program showed us not only that the experience strengthens the commitment of the young women to the sciences and engineering, but it also results in comments such as "This is science; I can do it!" Over six weeks, the students develop a knowledge and understanding of the area in which they are working that is remarkable.

We can translate this kind of experience into the undergraduate classroom. Several universities have developed research opportunity courses that allow students in their second year to spend time in a research lab and get course credit. Not only do programs such as these provide an excellent learning environment, they also allow the development of strong relationships within the communities of learners as well as between teacher and learner. One strength of programs such as the WISEST Summer Research program and the Research Opportunity program courses is that the faculty supervisor becomes a mentor for the student. If they choose to continue their studies at the University of Alberta, students have someone on the faculty whom they know and who knows them. These are the mentors who stimulate their desire to learn and who support them in developing their understanding. They also have met and made friends among the group of students who were in the program with them, and we know that these friendships last for many years.

Programs such as these depend on faculty who are themselves willing to mentor junior researchers, or to have one of the members of their research team mentor them, but faculty members do not always embrace mentoring. I recognize that as faculty members, they are under pressures to be highly productive researchers, and the time and energy it takes to mentor may be perceived as an extra burden. But I suggest that it also means that we are not taking as seriously as we should the fundamental teaching and learning mandate of the university.

Not only is it important for students to have mentors. Faculty members also need to have their own sense of being part of a group of lively and collegial seekers on an intellectual journey. Teaching students is both stimulating and exhausting. Regardless of the method of delivery, teaching involves a giving of oneself and there has to be a place for regeneration. As I look back on my own experience, I recognize with gratitude the communities of people in the academy who were my sources of renewal. Without the support of these communities, my continuation in the academy would have been very difficult. I believe that more than one of these communities is necessary. Sometimes they have to be sought out and sometimes they have to be created if they do not already exist. As a young academic in chemistry, a field with few other women at the time, I was most fortunate that there was an Academic Women's Association at the University of Alberta. This stimulating group of determined and committed women from across all disciplines not only provided a nurturing community, but were acting on a vision to make the university a more equitable and inclusive place, especially for women. Interaction with this group maintained my courage to take risks. All faculty members who are committed to the vitality of the undergraduate teaching and learning function of the university need such interaction. Increasingly, it can be found in communities of academics in Canadian universities who are dedicated to undergraduate education.

But to fully build the relationship with students that is essential to teaching and learning, a faculty member needs to be a respected member of his or her own academic community, a community that is inclusive and one in which people are valued and supported. Such a relationship would be my wish for all. It would reflect a return to the roots of the university where the learned shared their knowledge and understanding with the novice, but without the power differential between the teacher and the student. It would also return us to the very basis of the university, which is not only the discovery of new knowledge, but the sharing of knowledge and understanding from generation to generation.

CHAPTER 27

Offside:
Playing Hockey at the University of Saskatchewan

Glenis Joyce
Adult Educator, and
Liz Quinlan
Sociologist, University of Saskatchewan

Introduction

In January 1999, a student invited a group of us—all community women—to attend a women's Huskies hockey game. A couple of things surprised us: Large numerals, not usually associated with hockey, were visible on the players' equipment bags (they were hand-me-downs from the football team), and very few games were scheduled (chances to play exhibition or conference games were limited). We later learned that the players had no dressing room: Team members were forced to dress in a room shared with several intramural men's hockey teams. The team itself seemed a bit rusty, but played with vigour and determination.

Women had played hockey at the University of Saskatchewan since the early 1900s,[1] and the formal women's hockey program was already into its second year, under the umbrella of the Canadian Interuniversity Sport.[2] So what was going on? Was this an equity issue? Or did it have more to do with funding, with the corporatization of the university, and with a decrease in the university's public service commitments?

That women's hockey game a decade ago triggered a long, arduous quest for equity against a formidable foe. At the time of writing, the quest is finally over, at least in one important respect: A settlement has been reached for a nine-year dispute over women's hockey that found its way to the Saskatchewan Human Rights Commission (SHRC).

But the larger struggle of which our quest was only a part continues. What about outstanding equity issues at the university? What about public awareness of such issues? The journey has at least highlighted a number of factors: the reluctance of one publicly funded university to deliver on equity; the resilience of a community group that took its concern about the state of women's hockey to the Human Rights Commission; and a diverse cast of characters who came to be part of the resulting human rights case.

Scouting: The Players

Women 2000: A community group based in Saskatoon, Saskatchewan whose activism focuses on the hidden dimensions of women's inequality as evidenced by normal institutional policies, procedures, and practices. Some work at the university, others are alumna, and yet others have daughters or sons enrolled in its academic programs. In short, all signatories to the original complaint, and others who form Women 2000, have strong ties and allegiances to the university. It shaped us and we, in turn, attempted over the years to shape its equity landscape.

The University of Saskatchewan (U. of S.): Women make up 57 percent of the student body at this typical, medium-sized university.[3] Although it has a history of providing public education and serving public interests, the U. of S. is currently research-intensive, and becoming more and more entrepreneurially oriented.

The referee in this game of *equity hockey* was the *Saskatchewan Human Rights Commission:* Arm of the provincial judicial system that investigates complaints of discrimination, promotes and approves equity programs, and educates people about human rights law in the province.

Pre-game Warm-up

Gender inequity in sports is hardly new in Canada.[4] As far back as 1970, the *Royal Commission on the Status of Women Report* issued a call to governments to ensure equal opportunities for girls and boys to participate in athletics and sports, and to enact policies that would motivate and encourage them to do so. Subsequently, action proposals were developed in 1974, a Female Athlete Conference was held in 1980, and the Canadian Association for the Advancement of Women and Sport was formed in 1981.

Activity at the national level also inspired feminists at the U. of S., and, in the 1988 Equity Needs of Women Forum, participants reviewed the athletic system.[5] In 1993, *Reinventing Our Legacy: Report of the Presidents Advisory Committee on the Status of Women* was released and three of its recommendations were directed specifically at the athletic programs of the university.[6] A provincial gender and sport workshop was also held at the U. of S. and gender inequities were again highlighted.[7]

Beginning in 1996, the SHRC began a series of discussions about gender inequities in athletic programs with the authors of the *Reinventing Our Legacy* report and various university administrators. In 1999, the U. of S. consistently maintained it was committed to growing women's hockey, and was proud of the fact that the budget for women's hockey had increased in three years from $0 in 1995 to $21,009 in 1998–1999. Why, then, was the women's team budget still less than a third of the men's? Why did the men's—but not the women's—team have a coach who was employed full-time by the university? With such large financial and other inequities, how could the university possibly deliver on its plan for full competitive status for women's hockey by 2002?

Women 2000 met, reviewed the situation of the women's hockey program, and decided to suit up for a contest against an institution that clearly talked one game, but played another. Thinking about the young Saskatchewan women who might someday aspire to wear a Huskie hockey jersey, Women 2000 put on their game faces and hoped the SHRC would prove to be a worthy and courageous referee. The following paragraphs contain highlights, on a period-by-period basis, from their nine-year odyssey.

The Game Begins
Period 1: April 2000 to August 2004

The puck dropped on April 4, 2000, when Women 2000 filed a sex discrimination complaint against the U. of S. under the Saskatchewan Human Rights Code. Women 2000 alleged that the University of Saskatchewan discriminates against women because of their gender. In particular, the women's inter-university hockey program, operated by Huskie Athletics, was being treated as inferior to the men's program. The target of the complaint was not specific individuals but the policies and practices governing Huskie Athletics management, which reflect a larger exclusionary and discriminatory system of norms and values. The complaint specified gender inequities in all of the following: funding allocation, public recognition, access to more competitive events, qualifications and experience of coaches, and team-based fundraising.

The puck was in play for four years—the length of time it took for a human rights tribunal to be appointed to conduct an inquiry into the complaint. In mid-period, we entered into mediation with the university, with a SHRC referee in place. The pace of the game slowed as it became apparent that delay, deflect, and deny were the strategies of the opposing team. Chatter from the university bench focused on how our complaint was unfounded, spurious, and vexatious, how Women 2000 was a group of malcontents with personal axes to grind, and how some mothers even played hockey at the university earlier in the century so surely discrimination was no longer a concern.

Mediation failed, despite the considerable time spent gathering background information, drafting proposals, and presenting a settlement offer to the university. Our offer included equalizing team operating, travel, and recruitment budgets; hiring a full-time coach for the women's team; providing a dedicated dressing room for the women's team; hosting a national conference on university women's hockey; and other measures designed to transform the U. of S. into a national centre of excellence in this sport. The offer was refused and the university would not agree to meet with the SHRC to discuss any further possibility of a settlement.

Women 2000 and the SHRC dealt directly with representatives from university administration during most of period one. However, once the SHRC decided to proceed to a tribunal hearing, the university's legal counsel came off the bench and played for the rest of the game.

The score at the end of the first period: Women 2000—1, and U. of S. administration— zip. The SHRC's appointment of a tribunal had catapulted Women 2000 into the lead.

Following the first period, the dressing room issue came to a head. Women 2000 was concerned about safety and personal dignity under the existing circumstances: The intramural dressing room showers were communal and anything but secure. The university eventually relented and constructed a dedicated dressing room for the women's team in a trailer adjoining Rutherford Arena. In 2003, the university finally admitted that the dressing room issue was problematic, but asserted that the players and coaches were happy and did not complain about their situation. Women 2000 had deliberately avoided involving women players in the complaint process; we didn't want to expose individual players to the subtle forms of retaliation that sometimes accompany a human rights complaint.

It was apparent that the U. of S. team was instituting a new game strategy: Divide and conquer. By appealing to the opinion of individual team members, the university was deliberately setting one group of women against another. Even in the face of these undermining tactics, Women 2000 remained steadfast in its resolve to press for gender equity within Huskie Athletics.

Period 2: September 2004 to May 2006

The second period buzzer sounded when the university's counsel launched a formal application to the tribunal chair to challenge the jurisdiction of the tribunal itself. Various other procedural issues related to the complaint were also raised, including an argument that Women 2000 was not a body with proper standing to file a complaint under the Saskatchewan Human Rights Code. The tribunal chair ruled against the university on this application, but the university was not content to sit in the penalty box.

The university tried a new game strategy when it appealed for help from the Saskatchewan Court of Queen's Bench in July 2005. However, a month later, Mme. Justice Dovell issued her denial. The university didn't stop there, appealing at higher and higher levels, until Mme. Justice Dovell's final judgment with the Saskatchewan Court of Appeal came in March 2006: "The appeal is dismissed."

Late in the period, unexpected help arrived from an off-ice source: An external review of Huskie Athletics, commissioned earlier by the U. of S. administration, released its reviewers' report[8] to the public in the summer of 2006. The report was a stinging indictment, and its 26 recommendations called for drastic changes to all facets of Huskie Athletics. In particular, it condemned the program for underfunding several of the elite sports teams, including women's hockey, and operating them as second-tier sports.

Period 2 was a year of legal manoeuvring. The local media noted various appeals and the reviewers' report, and several articles about the complaint appeared in the news. In the end, the public became more informed about the university's inferior treatment of the Huskie women's hockey team. It also became apparent, though, that the university was willing to spend considerable funds on legal bills to avoid instituting a gender-equitable hockey program.

The score at the end of the second period was Women 2000—5, U. of S. administration—0. Women 2000 had scored four more goals on rulings of the tribunal chair, Court of Queen's Bench, Court of Appeal, and the external review of Huskie Athletics.

Period 3: October 2006 to September 2007

During period 3, Women 2000 dug into the corners. We requested, hunted down, and analyzed information from a variety of sources to assist the SHRC in mounting its case for the tribunal hearing. The SHRC located a number of expert witnesses who would testify on criteria of a demonstrated commitment to an elite women's hockey program, the state of university-level athletics for women in Canada, and the ramifications of systemic discrimination in general. The experts were well known, visible, and national, provincial, or international.

The hearing was scheduled for September 2007. Media interest was running high, but Women 2000 granted only limited interviews. We chose to focus on building a strong case and allowing the facts of our complaint to be subject to full public scrutiny at the tribunal hearing. The start date was one week before a major homecoming event celebrating the U. of S. centennial. Hundreds of alumni, visitors, and luminaries were scheduled to be in town. Women 2000 wondered if the psychological pressure of the impending centennial celebrations would have any impact on the other team. In mid-period, the university's team threw in the towel and asked to settle the complaint.

Discussions continued over the summer of 2007. There were a few skirmishes at centre ice. One involved a potential gag order that would prevent Women 2000 from ever discussing the complaint or its settlement. We valued our right to speak and resisted this vigorously. We also insisted on affirmative action measures for the women's hockey team and, at the end of the period, all agreed to a number of measures that would achieve at least substantive equality between the men's and women's hockey teams in a number of important ways. The university agreed to the following:

- to hire a full-time women's hockey coach with qualifications and duties similar to that of the men's hockey coach
- to put more money into the athletic scholarship program
- to bring several aspects of the women's operating budget into line with the men's team
- to ensure that the women's team would have a proper dressing room in a new arena planned for a future building boom on campus

All players retired from the ice and the game was officially noted as a tie. Whoops of celebration resounded from the Women's 2000 dressing room. We had survived the game, a little bruised and battered perhaps, but convinced that campus women, especially those with a dream to play elite university-level hockey, would prove to be the ultimate victors.

Game Penalties

Throughout the nine years of the complaint process, a number of penalties were incurred against the university for the following:

- consistently defying the SHRC requests for timely, accurate, and comprehensive financial information
- consistently underfunding the women's team
- inequitable allocation of athletic awards
- using money collected from women students to fund men's sports
- saying that women's hockey is an exception
- poorly promoting the women's team
- flaunting equity policies without acting on them

Though the battle was won, many wounds remained. What did it all mean in the end?

Conclusion

Though the U. of S. is a public institution with a long-standing commitment to serving the public, it has seemingly ignored equity initiatives. The university's present agenda of intensive research and entrepreneurial education stands in stark contrast to its historical attitude of social responsibility and public interest. Despite years of struggle that led to a hard-won settlement, the question remains: Where does equity fit within the spectrum of social responsibility and aggressive development? With many current faculty now close to retirement, the question of where equity fits in the tension between the university's quest for research excellence and its unique history will have to be answered by the next generation of scholars.

The university has a unique opportunity to model equitable treatment of groups and individuals. Rather than fulfilling its social responsibility in this way, however, the U. of S. has chosen to maintain the status quo with all of its accompanying structural and systemic gender inequities. Women 2000 repeatedly heard circular, straw-man arguments: It is someone else's fault; it's beyond our control; the budget has gone from zero to $X; the players are happy with the situation; resources are too scarce to redress the current equity imbalances; the teams have different abilities to fundraise; and women's hockey is new.

Here is the true picture: Money collected from women students will now be used to benefit elite women athletes. With a full-time coach and increased funding, the athletes on the women's hockey team will have a real chance to achieve their full potential. The university has an opportunity to move toward its goal of recognized excellence in all of its athletic programs and to meet its stated equity objectives.

Many of these benefits are not measurable, and others may even exceed the capacity of our current, collective imagination. But settlements such as this one shape new aspirations and behaviours, change perceptions about what is possible and appropriate, and create a climate conducive to progressive social change.

A group of women from the community—Women 2000—noticed an inequitable situation developing within the hockey program at the U. of S. We took our experiences as feminists and community activists and resolved to bring about change. This turned into a lengthy battle over a relatively simple issue. The institutional "shoot the messenger, ignore the message" response tested our patience, but we persevered, did our homework, looked to each other for strength, and celebrated our successes.

Changing attitudes and bringing about structural change at an institution such as the U. of S. is clearly not an easy or swift process. Our best advice to other activists about to embark on an equivalent quest comes directly from Nellie McClung: "Never retract, never explain, just get the job done and let them howl."[9]

Acknowledgements

The authors thank Arlene Rey, Rhonda Gough, Bev West, Leslie Belloc-Pinder, Natasha Neuman, Henriette Morelli, and Tracy Marchant for their contributions. We also thank the U. of S. women's hockey team for providing exciting and real on-ice action over the years; their athletic accomplishments in the face of such blatant systemic discrimination are to be commended.

Notes

1. M. Kennedy, *Dogs on Ice: A History of Hockey at University of Saskatchewan* (Regina: Saskatchewan Sports Hall of Fame and Museum, 2006).

2. Canadian Interuniversity Sport (CIS) is the governing body for interuniversity sport in Canada. Accessed April 20, 2009, from www.cisport.ca/e/.

3. *Institutional Analysis*, University of Saskatchewan, 2006. In 2006 there were 11,053 women and 8,428 men enrolled.

4. Anne Innis Dagg and Patricia J. Thompson, *MisEducation: Women and Canadian Universities* (Toronto: Ontario Institute for Studies in Education, 1988). See also Royal Commission on the Status of Women in Canada, *Report of the Royal Commission on the Status of Women in Canada* (Ottawa: Information Canada, 1970), 186–187; Helen Jefferson Lenskyj, *Women, Sport, and Physical Activity: Research and Bibliography* (Ottawa: Government of Canada, Fitness and Amateur Sport, 1988); M. Ann Hall and Dorothy A. Richardson, *Fair Ball: Towards Sex Equality in Canadian Sport* (Ottawa: The Canadian Advisory Council on the Status of Women, 1982). Readers interested in exploring sport history should consult M. Ann Hall, *The Girl and the Game: A History of Women's Sport in Canada* (Peterborough: Broadview Press, 2002).

5. G. Joyce, "Report on a Forum: Equity Needs of Women at the University of Saskatchewan," Equity Needs of Women Forum Report (Saskatoon: University of Saskatchewan, 1988), 9–10. Forum participants used the *Institutional Self-Study Guide for Post-secondary Institutions* produced for the Association of American Colleges Project on the Status of Women and Education in 1981 by Karen Bogart, J. Flagle, M. Marvel, and S.J. Jung.

6. President's Advisory Committee on the Status of Women, *Reinventing Our Legacy: The Status of Women at the University of Saskatchewan* (Saskatoon: University of Saskatchewan, 1993), 179. Recommendations included increased collection of data on gender and sport at the university, the striking of a task group to review the situation and establish a plan to increase the involvement of women at all levels of campus athletics, and that the university host a provincial conference on gender and sport where issues could be raised in a public forum.

7. G. Joyce, "Results of a Workshop on Gender and Sport/Physical Activity in Saskatchewan," Workshop on Gender and Sport Report (Saskatoon: University of Saskatchewan, June 10 and 11, 1994); Janice Harvie, "Workshop Hears Women Lack Sports Programs," *Saskatoon Star-Phoenix* (June 11, 1994), B2.

8. The review called for sweeping changes to the program as "the review team's very general impression of the state of Huskie Athletics is that it is a time bomb on the verge of exploding...." D. Marshall, D. Semotiuk, and K. Shields, "Huskie Athletics Review: Report of the External Reviewers." Accessed April 20, 2009, from www.kinesiology.usask.ca/academics/huskie-athletics-review/.

9. Randi Ruth Warne describes Nellie McClung's statement as a "famous dictum." See Randi Ruth Warne, *Literature as a Pulpit: The Christian Social Activism of Nellie L. McClung* (Waterloo: Wilfred Laurier University Press, 1993).

CHAPTER 28

Making the University Work for Communities

BARBARA NEIS

Sociologist, Memorial University of Newfoundland

I grew up on a family farm in northern Ontario, the middle child of six kids. Five of us went to university; four of the five pursued advanced degrees. We were the lucky generation. Neither of my parents had the opportunity to go to university, and today it is unlikely that so many of my siblings would have been able to go so far because of the high cost of post-secondary education. I often tell my students that when I finished my Ph.D. in 1988, I had $2,100 in student loans. Today many of them have 10 times that by the time they finish their B.A. In those days I don't remember students working during the term— only in the summer—another big change from the past.

I moved to Newfoundland in 1976, where I started my M.A. in sociology at Memorial University. In 1980 I started my Ph.D. at the University of Toronto, also in sociology, and in 1988 I started a tenure-stream job at Memorial. Starting with my M.A., my research has focused primarily on fisheries issues with a heavy concentration on the Newfoundland and Labrador fisheries. Throughout much of my career I have pursued a combination of applied and curiosity-driven academic research, increasingly working with community partners to identify research questions, design research, and develop recommendations for change where appropriate. Over the course of my career, the support for partnered research with industry, government, and community groups has increased. This shift toward partnered research is the central focus of my calling card.

My Ph.D. research looked at the early 1980s crisis in the Newfoundland fisheries. It began with a focus on a plant closure in Burin triggered by the crisis. My research on the organization of a protest line by local women to resist the closure helped me see the importance of gender in understanding resistance, industrial restructuring, and social and economic impacts. While doing this research I met Peter Dunderdale, who spent his summers skippering icebreakers in the Beaufort Sea and his winters teaching dragger mates and skippers. Peter told me about serious injuries on the Newfoundland draggers that were being caused by fishing in sea ice in vessels not designed for these conditions. When I was unable to find anyone at Memorial University working on occupational health onboard draggers interested in investigating this problem, I organized a small group of researchers, named it the Fishery Research Group, and we set out to try to find out what was happening. We applied for research funding and were funded initially by an ecumenical church group, and eventually by Labour Canada to study the social impact of technological change in deep-sea fishing and fish processing with a focus on health and safety and worker-management relations. The result was a 600-page report and many recommendations. The report was broadly rejected by the fish companies, and even the union representing the workers was not particularly supportive. While the union saw the recommendations as unachievable, I felt that this was the first substantive study of its kind in Newfoundland and Labrador, and that it was our job as researchers to recommend not what we thought was doable but what we thought was needed to make workers safe.

The Fishery Research Group report, on which I was the lead author, took a lot of time and was viewed by many of my colleagues as of little academic relevance and, to some degree, as a liability when it came to furthering my academic career. For me, the research we were able to fund through the project, while it may not have been perfect, was needed. I felt then, as I feel now, that, in a democratic society with regulations, it should not have taken a chance encounter between a graduate student and a teacher to prompt systematic investigation of life-threatening conditions. Academically, the research enhanced the information available to me for my Ph.D. thesis and allowed me to concentrate more heavily on theory development in that work. A central theme in the report and in my thesis continues to inform my work today. That theme relates to the need to pay attention to interactions between environment, policy, industry, and society in designing our technologies, policies, and social institutions.

In my opinion, universities are a public resource to which all members of the community should be able to turn in their efforts to protect such public goods as social justice; human, environmental, and community health; and peace and democracy. The Labour Canada study was the first of many research projects I have done over my career, almost all triggered by meetings and experiences in the field. I feel that, as an academic with access to a variety of publicly funded resources, tools, and expertise that are often scarce in rural Newfoundland and Labrador, and in fishery communities around the world, I have an obligation to use that access to study issues of concern to these communities. I have encouraged my students to take the same approach, and am very committed to trying to protect those resources and our ability to access them.

In the early 1990s I co-organized a workshop at Memorial called "The Campus and the Community." The main reason I got involved was my concern about a number of changes that were, I felt, limiting access to universities, researchers, and research funds to a smaller proportion of the Canadian population and channelling research away from key environmental, social justice, and related issues. Escalating tuition fees were making it increasingly difficult for people from poor and working-class backgrounds to go to university; targeted funding programs requiring industrial partners threatened to constrain who could do research and what they could study. I was also concerned about the growing number of units within universities with a mandate to commercialize and patent the results of university research. Through this workshop, I was also hoping to challenge a general lack of concern about these changes in the wider public. I thought one way to ensure universities played the role of a public resource was to encourage women's groups, unions, environmental groups, and others to lay claim to them, insisting that researchers and research funds be put to work in support of their issues. I was also hoping to challenges undercurrents of anti-intellectualism I had observed within many of these groups.

Starting in the late 1990s, a limited number of new programs were introduced by the Social Sciences and Humanities Research Council (SSHRC) and the Canadian Institutes for Health Research (CIHR) to support research designed and carried out in collaboration with community partners. Since that time there has also been a stronger focus on the need to transfer, mobilize, or exchange research results with communities and the wider public in part to help the granting councils justify the expenditure of public funds on research. These new programs include the Community University Research Alliance (CURA) and Knowledge into Society (KIS) programs at SSHRC; and the short-lived sister program to the CURA, Community Alliances for

Health Research (CAHRs), which was part of the transition from the Medical Research Council to the more interdisciplinary CIHR.

My history of community engagement and pursuit of research issues identified through fieldwork and community interactions meant I was well positioned as a researcher to develop successful applications to these new programs. Since 2000, I have been the co-principal investigator on a CIHR-funded CAHR grant on occupational health in marine and coastal work (SafetyNet), principal investigator on a CIHR-funded Knowledge to Action grant, and currently am the principal investigator on a SSHRC-funded CURA project. Good success rates at smaller and regional universities in these programs suggest that they are well suited for these contexts where researchers are often better connected to their communities, and where they often have difficulty competing within standard research programs and programs requiring corporate partnerships.

I believe that community-engaged research can meet essential social needs while also being intellectually interesting and a source of new research questions. However, I remain anxious about the future of Canada's universities and, indeed, of public goods in Canada. Let me explain. I have never seen the applied work I do as a substitute for curiosity-driven research and think that both community-engaged work and curiosity-driven work require public funding, as well as institutional protections for academic freedom and a substantial degree of university autonomy from government and industry.

In reality, even with the programs described above, a very small proportion of overall research funding in Canada goes to community-engaged research in the broad sense of the term—far more goes to targeted research programs that require industrial and/or government partners. University engagement with targeted research and drug testing, and in patenting and marketing research results in partnership with private industry are changing the climate of universities. Research results are less likely to be open access than they were in the past, and the research environment of the university is becoming more private and bureaucratic, more concerned with constraining liability than promoting free, open, and democratic debate and engagement with the wider community. When researchers are encouraged and even rewarded for commercializing the results of their research by, for example, forming a spinoff company they own themselves, as is the case with funding from the multimillion-dollar Canada Foundation for Innovation, a strong financial conflict of interest is introduced into university research. Things can go wrong in any research, but they are particularly likely to go wrong in situations of strong, financial conflict of interest. A poorly tested drug or piece of technology developed at a university and then marketed without sufficient concern for its occupational or other health impacts would threaten the legitimacy, if not the solvency, of that university and the lives of everyone who works there. A linked disaster could fuel criticism of public funding for universities.

In Canadian universities today, there is a very strong emphasis on research grants; all faculty members are expected to apply for grants, and academic success and prestige are more closely tied than in the past to the success of those applications. Like most other sectors of our society, universities are becoming increasingly corporatized and education and research are increasingly commodified. I think the grant-seeking pressures and prestige that come with large grants have, unfortunately, been associated with a devaluing of other kinds of university work, particularly teaching, work that takes a long time to complete, doesn't require large amounts of money to complete, and is not able to claim that it has immediate utility.

Since my time as a graduate student in the 1980s and over the 25 years since I began teaching full-time at Memorial University of Newfoundland, I have thought a lot about knowledge. I have come to see it as a social-ecological product mediated by geography, the biographies of the researchers, the institutional and paradigmatic frameworks within which they work, their research methods, and by relations of power.

The social-ecological character of knowledge is reflected in the gendered and class orientations that graduate students bring to their work. I have supervised a lot of graduate students, many of them Newfoundlanders from working-class backgrounds who have gravitated to me because they wanted their research to make a difference. I think people from poorer and working-class backgrounds and other marginalized groups are less comfortable with curiosity-driven research. One reason for this is, I think, that they and their parents find it hard to understand that it takes an investment of four or five years of work and many thousands of dollars to produce something as intangible as a few hundred pages of text. They are perhaps more likely than the parents of students from wealthier backgrounds to want to know that the fellowships and salaries their children receive for their research will eventually benefit someone. If applied and collaborative research can help make people from working-class backgrounds and those from other marginalized groups comfortable in university and interested in graduate work, I think it can help make universities more inclusive and democratic institutions, better able to help sustain public goods. But this will work only if these students are able to go to university and, more particularly, to graduate school. Tuition increases are keeping working-class and poor kids out of universities, and student debt is eroding their capacity to think and work creatively, to play with ideas unconstrained by working in multiple jobs, and worrying about how they will pay their student loans.

My orientation to knowledge production is reflected in my interest in interdisciplinary research such as work on fishermen's knowledge and science, in working with women's groups and unions, and in participatory approaches to reducing the risk of injury and occupational disease at work. These community collaborations mediate the social-ecological mix associated with my research, including the relationship between that research and wider society. They open up some opportunities for investigation while constraining others; they also introduce the potential for bias and unintended consequences, including benefits and harm. But these challenges are not unique to community collaborative research—they are characteristic of all research. Furthermore, to the degree that community-engaged research is open and transparent and actually manages to give voice to often marginalized groups, I think it is an essential component of democratic societies.

Sometimes I fear that community-engaged or partnered research has played the role of a Trojan horse, muting my own and others' criticism of the corporatization of the university. Subjecting academic research to a strong utilitarian lens can, and I think has, to some degree, opened the door to reductionist science and to the takeover of research councils and universities by political and corporate elites, university administrators, and elite researchers with dwindling ties to the wider community of academics and to non-elite groups. Under the veil of accountability, supported by the claim that academic researchers suffer from "a culture of entitlement," these elites are well positioned to divert even more funds to elite groups and ends.

However, I am not willing to retreat to ivory-tower notions of the university because history tells us yesterday's universities were not actually ivory towers at all. The dichotomy between applied and curiosity-driven research is false: These are really different ends of a continuum. Both have the capacity to inform theory, drive paradigm shifts, and can help change the world in good and bad ways. Where partnered research engages a limited range of interest groups who are also power brokers in the core research area (as with corporate-partnered research), there is a particularly substantial risk of bias and agenda-setting. These risks are especially great in institutional contexts, regions, and subject areas where the partnered research absorbs all of the funding or an entire body of subject specialists, leaving no one to stand outside the research to critically and independently assess its quality, relevance, and potential consequences for wider society.

CHAPTER 29

Recovering the University as a Collective Project

Janice Newson
Sociologist, York University

My calling card has three voices. The first voice was hard to retrieve because little support exists for its expression in contemporary academic life. The second voice journeys toward speechlessness. The third is a voice of recovery—recovery of speech and of vision, and it calls out to others to join in the recovery project(s).

First Voice

I came into the academy as a graduate student in my mid-twenties, swept in by the winds of change that so deeply affected many of my generation during the 1960s and early 1970s. My arrival was part of a movement not often discussed in writings about this time, of people coming out of religious vocations to engage in the social, political, and intellectual struggles that were taking place on university campuses. Not all who came to academic life from this direction were breaking ties with their religious communities. But many, and I include myself as one of them, believed that leaving the dogma-driven enclaves of religious institutions and opening up to the influences of the secular world were not inconsistent with having a spiritual perspective on one's life and hopes for the world. Besides, the university campus was the place for young adults to be, not only to join the campus-based political struggles, but also to engage in intellectual debates about the values and priorities guiding our society. This claim that the university provides young adults with the opportunity to reflect on the world they are a part of and what to do in it was powerfully expressed by Mario Savio, the gifted orator of the Free Speech Movement at the University of California at Berkeley: "The university is the place where people begin seriously to question the conditions of their existence and raise the issue of whether they can be committed to the society they have been born into."[1]

It was hard for students to avoid this questioning even when they were not drawn to it when they first entered university. Whether in a student-organized teach-in, a course lecture, or a particularly lively debate in the senate, discussions focused not only on programs of action, but also on ideas and their relevance to real-world issues. I recall a third-year course given by Lewis Feuer, the renowned sociologist who left the University of California at Berkeley because of his opposition to the student movement, which he criticized as fascist and depicted as an Oedipal rebellion of the sons against the fathers.[2] When he arrived at the University of Toronto, students were waiting for him. His course was held, if I recall correctly, in Convocation Hall and was packed at every lecture, not only with students enrolled in the course, but with anyone who wanted to debate him. And Feuer—brilliant and ever capable of intellectual sparring and defending his views—never disappointed, although he often enraged. After his lectures, the campus was often abuzz about who had taken him on and how he responded.

This was relevant knowledge of a different sort than we hear about in the university today, where relevance is a code word for anything that will help the economy or someone's wealth to grow. The relevance that drew many of my generation into the university was concerned with the kind of social relationships, social institutions, and social orders that will best advance human needs of all kinds. Why wouldn't we want to be there if we cared about the world we were in and the place we occupied in it?

Of course, the entire university was not transformed into a committee-of-the-whole engaged daily in debates about societal transformation. Although interrupted at times by teach-ins and protests, the normal routines of scholarly work, research, and teaching continued. But the university that I entered was, at least for a sustained period, a place where attention both inside and outside lecture halls focused on fundamental questions about our place and purpose in the world, and where a substantial and vocal public comprised of students, faculty members, and people from religious, cultural, and social organizations in the wider community became involved in trying to act on them. Some action took the form of protests, sit-ins, and demonstrations, but for me, the university's most important role was in opening up space for people to engage in wide-ranging intellectual debate and critically reflect on the problems facing the world. Coming from a working-class background and a family that had no knowledge or experience of the university—from a long line of people who did not believe that they were part of making the world, only of finding their way as best they could in a world made by others—it was transforming to observe and participate in these discussions and encouraged me to believe that the struggle I had made to pursue my education in the face of daunting financial and cultural challenges allowed me to have a voice in the course of human affairs.

Many issues of debate had origins in external political and economic institutions, but the way in which university officials responded to campus activism brought the university itself under scrutiny: Its intimate relationship with power elites was questioned and its closed and authoritarian mode of governance challenged. Reform of the institution moved onto the agenda[3] and I was unexpectedly and naively pulled into the centre of it.

Tensions in my department had been building over the leadership style of the chairperson. He had resisted pressures for change, but the writing was on the wall—after all, this was a department of sociology and in the 1960s, sociology was at the forefront of political activism. One week, the chair called a meeting with graduate students to debate a reform-oriented motion that he wanted to see amended, if not defeated. When the motion was presented for debate, I raised my hand. I believe to this day that the chair recognized me first rather than other speakers because he saw me as an innocent—a compliant female student, not one of the (male) activists. With almost no political experience, little knowledge of parliamentary procedures, and no previously thought-through strategy, I moved to call the question. The chair was clearly stunned. Everyone was stunned. People had come to the meeting expecting a confrontation. The chair asked me to repeat my request, which I did. According to the rules of order, he had to put my motion to a vote. It won. The main motion was immediately voted on and also won. The meeting ended about five minutes after it had begun. I walked out of the meeting surrounded by my peers, who were expressing deep admiration for my political acumen. It was my turn to be stunned. Shortly after, two male student leaders asked me to be a candidate for presidency of the newly formed Sociology Graduate Student Association. With their political clout behind me, I won that office easily.

That experience set the course of my career in the academy. I have spent much energy trying to ensure that the university remains a place where free and open debate guides all things academic and grounds them in a collective sense of purpose. For me, this sense of purpose always returns to the possibility—of the university as a space where we focus our minds on in the world, and with the language and intellectual skills of whatever disciplines and perspectives we find ourselves drawn to work within, we critically reflect on the paths we want to pursue as individuals and as members of society to improve the conditions of our existence. The university is not the only place where this kind of critical reflection happens or should be encouraged to happen, but to me, the university symbolizes the value of thoughtful and reasoned reflection and continually calls upon it to infuse the many economic, political, social, and cultural institutions that shape the conditions of our existence.

Second Voice

I found it easy to speak in the First Voice during the early stages of my academic career, but then it became increasingly difficult.

When I began my full-time career in 1971 at Glendon College of York University, I entered into a context of reconstruction. Members of the faculty were intensely involved in institution-building. They attended faculty council meetings and were present in their offices throughout the week, often with their doors open, for students and colleagues to come in to chat. Being present and engaged in the academic community *mattered* and those who absented themselves disenfranchised themselves from having influence on the direction that their departments, their faculties, and the university as a whole were taking. Sharing a sense of common purpose abounded and it resonated with my experience as a graduate student.

However, it was soon clear that what Alvin Gouldner famously referred to as "the long march through the institutions"[4] would not have an easy run, and that nurturing a democratic citizenry, one of the grounds on which policy-makers had justified providing public funding to universities in the postwar period, would not flow from policy rhetoric alone. For one thing, the elitist, closed-club, and authoritarian character of Canadian universities did not disappear overnight. Universities were still "dominated by middle-class, white men in authority"[5] who often used their power and influence to close off new intellectual initiatives and to block the attempts of women and people of colour to gain access.

For another thing, the public funds that had financed university expansion began to dry up. At York, the leading edge of an impending financial retrenchment showed up early in the 1970s when the then president shocked the campus with news of a financial crisis. One hundred faculty members' contracts were to be terminated, including those of some who were tenured, and as the last person hired in my department, I knew my name was on the list. Astute manoeuvring by deans and the leaders of the academic senate led ultimately to the resignation of the president and the cancellation of faculty layoffs, but this experience was a harbinger of events and responses to events that, over the next decade, fundamentally transformed the organizational landscape of universities across the country. Faculty associations became collective bargaining agents to protect their members from arbitrary administrative action and to preserve the role of the faculty in institutional decision making, and administrations grew into management apparatuses that took control of the budget and extended their influence over all, including academic, university activities.

For a time, a sense of common purpose prevailed in efforts to deal with this changing landscape. As a young faculty member, I found myself catapulted into the centre of some of these efforts, as a chair of my department, as a member of the senate, and as a member of the committee that drafted and negotiated my faculty association's first collective agreement. It was still relatively easy, in the difficult debates that ensued over shrinking financial resources, to draw upon the idea and vision of the university as a collective project. To be sure, members of the university community emphasized different aspects of this project and assigned greater weight to their own priorities. Yet still the idea retained currency that in all of these struggles, the university as a whole must be protected as a *distinctive* space committed to knowledge creation and critical reflection, and that its mode of collegial governance must be preserved to allow members to collectively determine their shared destiny.

However, as the budgetary shortfalls of the 1970s gave way to chronic underfunding in the 1980s, commitment to this collective project began to fragment. The university's decision-making centre of gravity shifted from departments, faculty councils, and senates into the expanded and increasingly specialized realms of management. It thus became less relevant and meaningful to participate in collegial bodies. Academic direction emerged through a Byzantine process of plan drafting, largely if not completely controlled by senior administrators who produced documents that collegial bodies were invited to comment upon. The result was a pastiche of fragments rather than a whole. Even worse, it was so hard to track how the pastiche was produced that intervention was almost impossible, and many colleagues began to give up on it. Any semblance of a vibrant intellectual community determining its own destiny was fast disappearing. Colleagues had begun to cut loose from the collective project of the university; they were catching hold instead of one of the fragments and focusing their energies on it.

In the early 1980s, something entered the scene that worsened fragmentation. Public policy began to advance a proposal to solve universities' underfunding problems by partnering with corporations. Alarmed by how quickly this proposal was gaining currency, the late Howard Buchbinder and I decided to write about our concerns.[6] We believed that if colleagues were made aware of it, they would collectively resist this *corporate-serving* agenda because they would see that it would seriously threaten the *public-serving* mission of universities, further fragment the academic community, and undermine its distinctive intellectual purpose.

Other academics—a handful across the country— were also trying to alert their colleagues to the threats posed by this new initiative, but the response from the academic community as a whole was neither strong nor unified. There are many reasons why this was the case, but one that stands out is that most colleagues believed that the effects of this initiative would be marginal at the most. I recall a meeting with colleagues at York where someone said that we were seeing shadows in the bushes, and that only a few researchers in the applied natural sciences would be affected by this new mandate.

Fast-forward to the cacophonous, postered, and fragmented campuses of the mid-1990s. Neither Howard nor I could have imagined how extensively and deeply corporatization would transform the university. Signs of corporate involvement were visible everywhere: buildings renamed after corporate funders, commercial advertisements, student advising services converted to customer relations centres decorated with the business logos of banks and insurance companies, and glossy in-house magazines bragging about the latest partnerships forged with corporate clients. I felt dread whenever I entered the campus. Whatever shocking new element entered the scene—the element that one might think had gone over the line because it was so alien to the intellectual purpose of the university—over and over again was quickly absorbed and its presence made part of the new normal.

I began to envy colleagues who appeared to be able to focus intensely on their research and scholarly work, aided by the new research funds flowing from public coffers. That the campus appeared to become increasingly productive was paradoxical to me. I found myself less and less able to derive meaning from my work either as a scholar or a teacher. The competitive, production-driven, highly individualizing, and isolating campus culture not only failed to inspire me, it also flattened my spirit. Worst of all, talk about the university as a collective project with a distinctive purpose had less and less resonance in the meetings I attended on campus. Other than for departmental meetings, I began to absent myself from campus affairs and descend into speechlessness.

Voice Three

When I returned in 1999 from a sabbatical leave to take up my teaching responsibilities, I was facing something of a crisis of purpose. For several years, I had found it hard to resist the thought that the vision of the university that I had carried forward from my twenties was no longer suited to the changed situation in which the university found itself. That I, and probably others of my generation, would feel this way is not surprising. For one thing, I had been working for almost two decades in a culture that, over time, came to bear little, if any, resemblance to the academic culture that had so deeply shaped my interests and concerns. But there was now another reason: I was that much older, facing the last stretch of my career, and heading down to retirement. So the crisis was not only whether the vision of the university I have held has any relevance for current times, but also whether *I* have any relevance for these times. Coming in for that final stretch, what is there for me to do in this ever-so-fragmented university that seems to have leaped into a future without me on board?

But, thankfully and a little unexpectedly, a sense of renewed purpose began to emerge from the classroom. That may sound odd. Teaching university students these days has become a profound challenge, not the least because they appear to have little interest in things intellectual. Even after spending four years in the university, too many of them have serious deficiencies in reading and writing skills and lack the ability to think in abstract concepts and track whole arguments, yet these students are poised to enter a world that confronts them with huge challenges in politics, economics, our relationship to the natural world, and ideologically based tensions of all kinds. In many ways, they face a situation no different, except perhaps in scope, than the situation generation faced 40 to 50 years ago. To provide a *special* space where they are encouraged to seriously question the conditions of their existence and critically reflect on the kind of societies and communities to which they want to commit themselves is as relevant today as it was then.

It has been a project of recovery for me to regain confidence that the vision that has guided my career is not like a fashion that loses currency as the ephemera of our lives change. I began to invite the students in my courses to help to create space for critical reflection in the classroom, not abstractly but through concrete practices that establish the grounds on which we proceed. I gained inspiration from Hans Georg Gadamer's "Idea of the University."[7] Gadamer calls on us to find the "free space" wherein we are able to create freedom and solitude, the necessary conditions for "living with ideas." And in spite of their intellectual deficits, many students—although not all and not even most—have responded to this invitation.

But it is not enough to try to create the space for "living with ideas" in one classroom or even in many classrooms—to do this is only is to continue to work with fragments. Contemporary universities as wholes need projects of recovery because they face their own crises of purpose. Having gone madly off in so many directions to please so many masters, they have lost touch with their purpose to educate. I am not speaking only of educating the students in their classrooms. Whatever these students' intellectual deficits, they are no greater than the intellectual deficits that pervade much of the public culture. Of what use is it to seed world-transforming technological and scientific innovations, or to invent impressive systems for tracking social, economic, and political processes on a global scale, or to strengthen social and cultural diversity, or even to eliminate various forms of inequality, if the capacities for reasoning and making moral judgments that are needed to guide these undertakings through a deeply fractured world are missing?

In my view, the collective project of the university for these times is the same as it has been for other times: to recover its distinctive educational purpose *for all its endeavours*—research and scholarship, teaching, and service—in order to infuse the values and practices of reasoned judgment and critical reflection into every aspect of society.

Acknowledgements

I want to thank Suzie Young and Susan Weinstein, who helped me to find speech.

Notes

1. Mario Savio, "An End to History," reprinted with permission of Lynne Hollander. Copyright 1998 by Lynne Hollander. Accessed June 23, 2003, from http://www. fsm-a.org/stacks/endhistorysavio.html. Page last changed July 29, 2001.
2. Lewis Feuer, *The Conflict of Generations: The Character and Significance of Student Movements* (New York: Basic Books, 1969).
3. The reform of university decision making during this period was not driven entirely by campus-based political struggles, but by the confluence between these struggles and the growing involvement of the state in publicly funded universities.
4. Alvin Gouldner, *Dialectics of Ideology and Technology* (New York: Seabury Press, 1976), 160.
5. Quoted from Joan Sangster's essay in this volume.
6. Janice Newson and Howard Buchbinder, *The University Means Business: Universities, Corporations, and Academic Work* (Toronto: Garamond Press, 1988).
7. Hans-George Gadamer, "The Idea of the University—Yesterday, Today, and Tomorrow," in *Hans-George Gadamer on Education, Poetry, and History*, ed. D. Misgeld and G. Nicholson (New York: SUNY Press, 1992), 47–59.

About the Authors

JO-ANN ARCHIBALD, from the Sto:lo Nation in southwestern British Columbia, is the Associate Dean for Indigenous Education and Professor in the Faculty of Education at the University of British Columbia. She is the author of *Indigenous Storywork: Educating the Heart, Mind, Body, and Spirit*.

MARGARET-ANN ARMOUR holds degrees from Edinburgh University (B.Sc., M.Sc.) and the University of Alberta (Ph.D. Chemistry), where she is Associate Dean of Science, Diversity. She co-founded WISEST, Women in Scholarship, Engineering, Science and Technology. Awards include a 3M Teaching Fellowship, the Chemical Institute of Canada's Montreal Medal, and the Order of Canada.

JOEL BAKAN is a law professor at the University of British Columbia. A former Rhodes Scholar and Supreme Court of Canada law clerk, Bakan wrote *The Corporation* (2004) and the film based upon the book. Other works include *Just Words* (1997) and numerous journal articles. Bakan, a professional jazz guitarist, lives with his wife Rebecca Jenkins and their two children, Myim and Sadie.

FRANK CUNNINGHAM is Professor Emeritus of Philosophy and Political Science at the University of Toronto, where he retains an appointment in its Cities Centre. He has served as president of the Canadian Philosophical Association and at his university as Chair of the Department of Philosophy and Principal of Innis College.

BRUCE CURTIS teaches in the Department of Sociology and Anthropology at Carleton University, with appointments in the Department of History and the

Institute of Political Economy. With Andrea Doucet he directs the Duncombe Studio for Social and Cultural Analysis, a university research centre.

GEORGE SEFA DEI is Professor in the Department of Sociology and Equity Studies in Education at the University of Toronto. His teaching and research interests are in the areas of anti-racism education, development education, international development, Indigenous knowledges, and anti-colonial thought. Books include *Anti-Racism Education: Theory and Practice* (1996) and *Indigenous Knowledge in Global Contexts* (2000).

LEN FINDLAY is Professor of English and Director of the Humanities Research Unit at the University of Saskatchewan. A Fellow of the Royal Society of Canada, he was the Northrop Frye Professor of Literary Theory at the University of Toronto for 2000–2001. His edition of *The Communist Manifesto* appeared in 2004.

ARTHUR FORER, FRSC, is Professor Emeritus and Senior Scholar at York University. He is an avid bicyclist and plays woodwinds in a variety of local concert orchestras, swing bands, pit orchestras, and in the saxophone quartet A Pack-O-Lips Now. He enjoys research in his lab and in collaboration with an Australian colleague.

BARBARA GODARD, Historica Chair in Canadian Literature and Professor of English, French, Women's Studies, Social and Political Thought, Professor Emerita of York University, writes extensively about Canadian and Quebec cultures, translation, feminist theory, and cultural policy. Recent publications include *Canadian Literature at the Crossroads of Language and Culture* (2008).

PAUL HAMEL is Professor in the Department of Laboratory Medicine and Pathobiology, Faculty of Medicine, and Director of the Health Studies Program, University College, at the University of Toronto. He is also the past president of Science for Peace.

ROBERTA HAMILTON is Professor Emerita and a feminist activist. Publications include *The Liberation of Women: A Study of Patriarchy and Capitalism* (1978),

Setting the Agenda: Jean Royce and the Shaping of Queen's University (2002), and *Gendering the Vertical Mosaic: Feminist Perspectives on Canadian Society* (2nd ed., 2005).

ALISON HEARN is Associate Professor in the Faculty of Information and Media Studies at the University of Western Ontario, where she teaches cultural theory and media studies. With Liora Salter, she is co-author of *Outside the Lines: Issues in Interdisciplinary Research* (McGill-Queens University Press, 1997).

JENNIE HORNOSTY is Professor of Sociology at the University of New Brunswick. She is a recipient of the CAUT's Sarah Shorten Award for outstanding contribution to the promotion of women in Canadian universities. She is a former member-at-large on the CAUT executive; a long-time member of the AUNBT executive, Status of Women and Employment Equity committees; and a member on four negotiating teams. A researcher on family violence in rural communities, she is also a mother, step-mother, and grandmother.

GLENIS JOYCE worked in Women's Studies at the Extension Division, University of Saskatchewan, for over 25 years. Her focus on equity spurred initiatives from the local to the international. She recently completed a Master of Arts in Conflict Analysis and Management at Royal Roads University.

JOHN MCMURTRY, FRSC, is University Professor Emeritus at the University of Guelph. His most recent book is *Value Wars: The Global Market versus the Life Economy* (2002), and he is the author/editor of *Philosophy and World Problems* in The Encyclopedia of Life Support Systems (2009).

JAMIE MAGNUSSON, Associate Professor in the Department of Theory and Policy Studies in Education at the University of Toronto, focuses on globalization, the ideology of science, and equity and social justice–based post-secondary curricula and teaching. Publications include "Universities, Corporations, and Biotechnologies: New Colonialisms of the 21st Century" (2003) and "Canadian Higher Education and Citizenship in the Context of State Restructuring and Globalization" (2000).

BARBARA NEIS is University Research Professor in the Department of Sociology, Memorial University of Newfoundland. She researches gender and occupational health and the social and human health impacts of restructuring in the Newfoundland and Labrador fisheries. Dr. Neis is principal investigator on a SSHRC-funded Community-University Research for Recovery Alliance.

JANICE NEWSON has been engaged throughout her career in efforts to preserve the intellectual and public-serving mandate of the university. She co-authored *The University Means Business* (1988), co-edited *Universities and Globalization* (1998), and has written extensively on the corporate-linked university. She enjoys photography, music, nature, and her friendships with human and animal companions.

CLAIRE POLSTER is Associate Professor in the Department of Sociology and Social Studies at the University of Regina. She has published widely on the transformation of Canadian higher education and its implications for the public interest. She has also been involved in a number of campaigns and organizations aimed at resisting the corporatization of Canada's universities and reclaiming our universities as public-serving institutions.

MARY ELLEN PURKIS, Associate Professor, is Dean of the Faculty of Human & Social Development at the University of Victoria. Her ethnographic research on nursing practice in community-based settings such as home care and specialized settings such as cancer care focuses on the interface between professional practice and the everyday lives of people seeking health care.

ELIZABETH QUINLAN was one of the first graduates of the Interdisciplinary Studies doctoral program in 2004 at the University of Saskatchewan, where she now teaches and researches in the Department of Sociology. In 2009, she was awarded a Teaching Excellence Award. Her research interests include work organization, gender, and health.

NASRIN RAHIMIEH is Maseeh Chair and Director of Samuel Jordan Center for Persian Studies and Culture and Professor of Comparative Literature at

University of California, Irvine. She served as Dean of Humanities at McMaster University (2003–2006) and Associate Dean of Arts at the University of Alberta (1999–2002).

JANICE RISTOCK, Associate Dean (Research) and Professor in Women's and Gender Studies, Faculty of Arts, University of Manitoba, has published widely in the areas of interpersonal violence, LGBTQ studies, and community-based research. She is a happy member of two national interdisciplinary research teams.

KAREN RUDIE has taught in the Department of Electrical and Computer Engineering at Queen's University since 1993. Her postdoctoral, graduate, and undergraduate work has varied between applied mathematics and engineering. She was listed for five years in the *MacLean's Guide to Canadian Universities* ("Popular Profs" list), has won four teaching awards, and was an IEEE Control Systems Society Distinguished Lecturer.

JOAN SANGSTER teaches Women's Studies and History at Trent University. The author of four books, she has written on working-class and women's history, delinquency, the law, and Aboriginal women. Her forthcoming book is *Transforming Labour: Women and Paid Work in Postwar Canada*.

GORDON SHRIMPTON is Professor Emeritus and former Chair of Greek and Roman Studies at the University of Victoria. He was President of the University of Victoria Faculty Association from 1982 to 1984 and President of the Confederation of British Columbia Faculty Associations in 1983–1984 and 1992–1993. Currently he is Speaker of Council for the Canadian Association of University Teachers (CAUT).

DOROTHY SMITH, Professor Emerita of the University of Toronto, is a social theorist, feminist, and activist. She has been honoured nationally and internationally for her transformative approach to creating a sociology that works for people. Books include *The Everyday World as Problematic: a Feminist Sociology* (1987) and recently, *Institutional Ethnography: A Sociology for People* (2005).

JOHN VALLEAU, Professor Emeritus of the Department of Chemistry at the University of Toronto, is a member of the board of directors of Science for Peace. He has been active for many years in a variety of peace and social initiatives.

ANDREW WERNICK, a social theorist, intellectual historian, sociologist of culture, and sometime jazz musician is Professor of Cultural Studies at Trent University. His books include *Promotional Culture* (1991), *Auguste Comte and the Religion of Humanity* (2001), and the co-edited *Shadow of Spirit: Religion and Postmodernism* (1992) and *Images of Aging: Representations of Later Life* (1995).

ELIZABETH (BESSA) WHITMORE is Professor Emerita of the School of Social Work, Carleton University. She is currently working on a SSHRC-funded book on the meaning of success in social justice advocacy work. In her spare time, Bessa tries to change the world as a member of the Raging Grannies.

HOWARD WOODHOUSE is Professor in the Department of Educational Foundations and Co-Director of the Process Philosophy Research Unit at the University of Saskatchewan. His books include *Selling Out: Academic Freedom and the Corporate Market* (2009). He is a member of the editorial boards of *Interchange* and three international journals and a member of the board of trustees of the Association of Process Philosophy of Education. He is also a blues guitarist and singer.